URBAN REPUBLICAN MAYOR

URBAN REPUBLICAN MAYOR

My Story

Greg Ballard

INDIANA UNIVERSITY PRESS

This book is a publication of

Indiana University Press
Office of Scholarly Publishing
Herman B Wells Library 350
1320 East 10th Street
Bloomington, Indiana 47405 USA

iupress.org

Second Printing 2025

Cataloging information is available from the Library of Congress.

ISBN 978-0-253-07318-1 (hardback)
ISBN 978-0-253-07319-8 (paperback)
ISBN 978-0-253-07321-1 (ebook)
ISBN 978-0-253-07320-4 (web PDF)

This book is dedicated to my four chiefs of staff:

Paul Okeson, Chris Cotterill, Ryan Vaughn, and Jason Dudich.

Without them, my efforts would have been in vain. Most citizens of Indianapolis have little notion of just how important these four gentlemen were to the betterment of the city. All were highly competent, dedicated, ethical, and moral in their actions. The city was fortunate to have such people. I can never fully repay their efforts.

CONTENTS

PREFACE

While researching for this book, I was struck by the consistency of my reputation during the earlier stages of my political career. Average Joe, poor speaker, low key, not a typical politician, sincere, honest, hard to get a handle on. A consistent criticism was a lack of vision, although I could not find any other political figure who was asked for their vision quite like I was. It was something for critics to latch onto.

I was not good copy for the press due to my lack of bravado. Being serious and low key play well in Indiana, but for many, I was not vocal enough on important issues. Of course, being a complete unknown at the beginning of my run for mayor, that was part of the strategy. I did not want to make a big mistake on TV that my opponent could use against me. I knew that with my lack of name recognition and my early amateurish reputation, much of it well deserved, a damaging statement on TV would doom my chances. Visual mistakes last much longer than mere verbal mistakes.

I tried to pay little attention to the criticism, kept my head down, furthered my understanding of the issues that were important to the citizens, and improved my presence skills. Once elected, I had a highly effective staff who toned down the criticism by quiet discussions with the press and other influencers in the city.

Within three years, Indiana's highly esteemed governor publicly said I had reached the status of the previous well-respected Indianapolis mayors. When I ran for reelection, the common sentiment was that there were two good candidates running, certainly not the feeling just four years prior when I was looked upon as unknown cannon fodder. In my reelection campaign, as a Republican mayor in a Democratic city, my reputation was one of getting things done and being fiscally sound, and many people supported me who would normally vote Democratic.

By the end of my second term, and thanks to my superior staff, I had won vision awards locally, nationally, and internationally. I was repeatedly asked to run for a third term by both Democrats and Republicans. I had a national reputation on water issues, was known for my national security stances regarding energy, was recognized for being bold and innovative by my fellow mayors, occasionally appeared on national TV shows, and testified before Congress multiple times. When people would comment that I had gotten better at the job, I would jokingly reply, "I think you're supposed to get better in your job." I knew they meant it as a compliment.

Throughout my eight years as mayor, I did what I thought was right, frequently frightening my staff as I sometimes went against Republican norms. I joked with my political team that they never knew what I was going to say or do any particular day as I did not run things by them before announcements, even though I believe my staff kept them informed. I never took a poll to see which way the winds were blowing before I made a decision. I was not a normal politician; I saw things differently. I was a marine who had traveled the world, had been to war, and had come back to my hometown to serve again, and I only wanted what was best for the long-term health of Indianapolis.

I was an urban Republican, moderate in views, practical in governing, but dedicated to doing what I thought was right with little thought to the political consequences, which actually proved to be politically popular. The citizens trusted me even if they did not agree with me because they knew I was acting on their behalf for the right reasons. I was humbled by their trust.

ACKNOWLEDGMENTS

AS ALWAYS, I THANK WINNIE, my wife of forty-one years, who allows me the freedom to live my life as a happy man. She has been by my side for twenty-three years in the Marine Corps and eight years as mayor of Indianapolis, a much different life than she imagined four decades ago. My children provided much-needed insight, as they are more artistic than I and continually reminded me to make the stories and thoughts more personal and not just recite facts.

Lots of wonderful people reviewed either the whole book or designated sections. Professor Ted Frantz of the University of Indianapolis provided in-depth and important feedback early on. My chiefs of staff—Paul Okeson, Chris Cotterill, Ryan Vaughn, and Jason Dudich—corrected me when my memory needed correcting. Joe Loftus, Mark Miles, Robert Vane, Troy Riggs, and Jen Hallowell were gracious enough to take time to read and provide comments as well. My personal editor, Peter Noot, always makes be read better than I deserve.

As I mention throughout the book, my staff was exemplary. They made the city of Indianapolis better in so many ways, and I am still amazed that so many talented people wanted to help their fellow citizens at the municipal government level. It is their accomplishments that mean so much to me.

I thank Indiana University Press for publishing this second book together. I hope they will consider other works in the future.

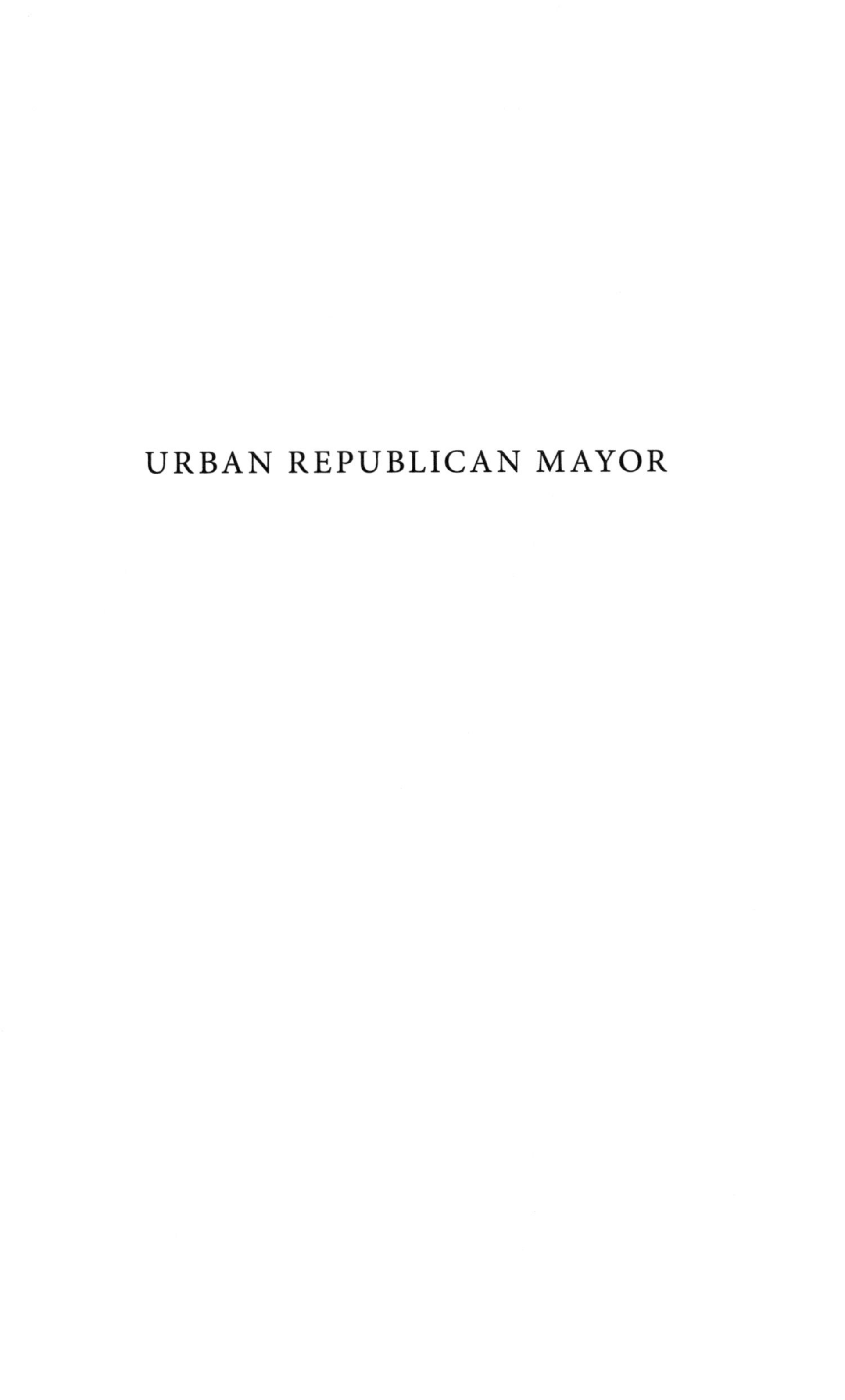

URBAN REPUBLICAN MAYOR

PART I
BACKGROUND

Detractors during my first campaign pointed to my lack of political experience, neglecting to note that I had been in leadership positions since the age of twenty-three, thirty years before I became mayor. However, just a few decades prior, my background of being from modest means and then having a military career was very common for elected officials. Such has the political landscape changed.

I tell people that my election was the classic one-in-a-million shot. I was fortunate that it happened to me. It really is quite the story.

1

AN AMAZING EVENING

By 7:00 p.m. on a frigid November day in 2007, the small auditorium at the Old National Center in downtown Indianapolis was starting to fill up. Just two hours before, the election-night reception for the Marion County Republican Party was to be a more intimate affair for party regulars, to lick their wounds once more as Democrats were expected to win the race for mayor again and to maintain control of the twenty-nine-person city-county council. Most major cities across the United States had long ago turned Democratic, but Indianapolis elected its first Democratic mayor in decades in 1999 and won the council in 2003. The trend was clear: Indianapolis was going to be a Democratic city well into the future.

However, at 6:00 p.m. that day, the polls closed, and the four local television stations all showed that an underfunded political novice, a largely unknown Republican candidate for mayor, was leading the Democratic incumbent. Surely this lead would not hold as more votes came in, but unbeknownst to the public—though certainly known to those tracking the vote counts—most of the uncounted votes were from the southern half of Indianapolis, which is Republican territory.

As word spread throughout the city about the continuing vote count, many of the people who had supported the unknown retired marine drove to the Old National Center hoping to be part of a dramatic story, filling up the auditorium with upbeat chatter as more results came in. The recent former Marion County clerk, Doris Anne Sadler, was in an adjoining room tracking the votes and ensuring that no shenanigans would occur. Having Doris Anne present gave the candidate comfort, as the new Democratic Marion County clerk had numerous mishaps running her first election in the primary the previous May, so the entire Indianapolis political community was watching intently, hoping for a well-run election.

The candidate himself believed he was going to win. Because of a lack of funds, he had no polling data to back up that belief, but during the campaign over one hundred Democrats had come up to him and either whispered in his ear or quietly told him, "I've never voted for a Republican in my life, and I'm going to vote for you." They could not say that in public because of loyalty to their party, but clearly, something was up. There were very strong feelings by many that the city was going in the wrong direction, and for them, party did not matter. Although the Republican candidate was outspent at least twenty to one by his Democratic opponent, here he was leading as the election night wore on.

Sometime after 9:00 p.m., the incumbent mayor called and conceded the race. Word spread like wildfire through the now-packed auditorium. The cheers were deafening. They were at the celebration of what many called "the biggest upset in Indiana political history." Soon thereafter, the media called the race. Now all of Indianapolis knew.

Very few people get to experience the sheer joy and exuberance of winning a major election in the United States. Having the confidence of so many people that you do not even know, but who are now expecting you to shepherd the city toward excellence, is humbling—but also immensely rewarding. Money usually influences elections simply because of the media exposure that it provides, but in this case, money was inconsequential. Most of the political insiders on both sides could not imagine what they had just witnessed, but the beauty of America is that people get to vote.

Many people that I knew or met along the way helped me win. But I also found out after the election that there were many people I did not know about who were out campaigning for me on their own. They were doing it either because they were upset with the direction of the city, or they had met me, or they knew of me from friends and somehow trusted me. They were not organized, nor were they politically connected people, as I had no political friends at all before I started my run for mayor.

The Journey Begins

I was expected to lose by twenty to thirty points. I knew that from the very beginning. The numbers were clear: Indianapolis was a majority-Democratic city. The independents initially were satisfied with the current mayor. However, there is a reason for campaigns.

The journey started when a couple of gentlemen, one a minor Republican officeholder and the other an old newspaper man, asked me to consider running for mayor in late 2006. They told me that no one on the Republican side was stepping up to run. The leading Republican figures in the city, knowing what the numbers were, did not want a loss on their record. They did not want to take on a popular two-term incumbent who was also the president of the National League of Cities, and who many speculated had a bright political future. Bart Peterson was and is a very nice man, and taking him on seemed like political suicide to everyone already in the political arena. However, I was not in the political arena; I had nothing to lose politically. I was cannon fodder.

Even then, I was not the Republicans' first choice. On the advice of the two gentlemen, I called the Marion County chair, Mike Murphy. Mike was about to give up the chairmanship at the upcoming slating in February 2007.[1] At this event, a new Marion County chair and other officeholders for the party would be elected.

I started telling a few people that I was going to run for mayor. Their reactions solidified what a wild, longshot idea this was at the time. I drove with my wonderful wife, Winnie, a Filipina and a naturalized citizen, to nearby Bloomington to tell our children, who were attending Indiana University, that their dad was running for mayor. We took them to dinner at the Colorado Steakhouse, and when I mentioned that I was going to run, both just broke out into laughter. My own kids! I had to convince them that I was serious.

I also asked for a morning meeting at a Panera with Abdul-Hakim Shabazz, a right-leaning local talk show host who had graciously interviewed me about my leadership book a year or so before. He is a humorous but highly intellectual character. When I told him, "I'm going to run for mayor," he immediately shot back, "Of what?" My running for office was clearly not in the mainstream of anyone's thinking.

I left Mike Murphy a message about a week out from slating, and he called me back the day before it was scheduled. I told him that some people had suggested that I run for mayor, and he told me to show up for slating the next day to meet as many folks as I could. I asked him if I should bring anything with me, and he told me to write something about myself and distribute it. That evening, I wrote a one-pager that explained what I wanted to do as mayor. I made seven hundred copies, and early the next morning, one of the gentlemen who had encouraged me to run helped me put a copy of that one-page document on every chair. That was my introduction to the Republican Party.

Most of the people there were kind, but I noticed that the hardcore politicos were largely cold to me. I did not know what to make of that, but it did not bother me too much; after all, this was their turf, not mine. One state officeholder came up to me and taught me how to shake a hand. This was hilarious to me since I was in my fifties and a retired marine officer, but he was serious, as in "I'm the veteran politician; let me show you some things." I also saw that the campaign literature for the incoming party officials mentioned that their goals were to win the council back in the current year, 2007, then win the mayor's race in 2011. This was when I realized that people were asking me to run for an office that party officials expected to lose. At this point, I did not know that Indianapolis was a majority-Democratic city. I did not know anything about the political scene in Indianapolis. I just knew that a couple of guys thought I had the skill set to be a good mayor.

The slating would normally select the preferred mayoral choice along with other offices, but because no leading Republican figure wanted to run for mayor and no one else stood out, the party officials decided not to slate for mayor that day. They did slate the council candidates, and this was eye opening to me. Most of the council candidates were good, serious, and decent people, but some were not. I came to find out that both parties have some real intellectual heavyweights and serious people involved, but most of them do not want to run for office. They do much of the heavy lifting behind the scenes. On some level, I understand this, but our country would be well served if these people did run for office.

"I'm the Guy"

Soon after slating, the new county chairman held a meeting to talk to all those people who had expressed an interest in running for mayor. It was held on a Wednesday evening; as luck would have it, I was teaching at a local college and had a one-hour class at the exact time of the meeting. I asked someone to fill in for me at the chairman's meeting. When I got home from the class, I called him up to ask how the meeting went, and he told me that it was still going on. I asked him if I should come downtown to the meeting, and he recommended I do so. It was only fifteen minutes from my house. When I walked in, it was apparent to me—without a word being said—that from where people were sitting, as well as their demeanors, I was the number-two candidate. I can still read a room pretty well.

The new county chairman, Tom John, told me and the others that he wanted another gentleman at the meeting to be the Republican Party's nominee for mayor, primarily because he could put in his own money. That was something I could not do. I said I understood, and Tom said that he would like me to serve on some committees to discuss policy. I thought that was terrific. I was a nobody in the political game but was now being asked to contribute my thoughts. It sounded great to me.

The city's political schedule mandated that candidates for mayor, in order to have their name on the primary ballot in May, had to register at the county clerk's office by the coming Friday, just two days from our Wednesday-evening meeting. I had already officially entered the race weeks ago, but Tom asked all the attendees at the meeting to withdraw their candidacies as a show of solidarity for his preferred candidate with money. I now suspect this was to ensure there were no surprises in the primary, but I was too naive to think of such things at the time. Being a team player and just happy to help, I said I would withdraw on Friday morning.

The next day, Thursday, the vice chairwoman of the party called me around 2:00 p.m. to ask if I was still going to withdraw from the race, and I told her I would. Two hours later, she called again and asked the same question, and again I said I would withdraw. She then said something like, "We'd really like a guy like you to stay in the race." I was not expecting that; I said I would stay. My instincts kicked in, and I immediately went to the *IndyStar* website and saw local political commentator Matt Tully's column about Tom John's preferred mayoral candidate making some ill-advised and certainly disqualifying remarks. I said to myself, "Holy cow! I'm the guy!"

I did not withdraw on Friday.

I find it fascinating that if Matt Tully had posted his column over the weekend instead of Thursday, no one ever would have heard of me, and I certainly would not have become mayor. If I had withdrawn on Friday as I was asked to do, there was no chance the party would have selected me to run. They would have searched elsewhere, because I was still a political novice seeking a major office—and a complete unknown at this point except to a very few members of the party.

My Slating

Although I was now the preferred candidate of the Republican Party, there was still the matter of slating, which had to be done. The humorous part of the journey was now beginning. Each candidate who wants to be considered for slating must pay a slating fee to the Marion County Republican Party. The amount varies with each office; for mayor, the amount was $9,500. The fee is returned if you lose at slating. At this time, I was teaching and had two kids in college, so I borrowed $10,000 to pay the slating fee. I had to be the poorest individual to win the mayor's race in modern Indianapolis history; it is probably not even close.

The party selected one hundred precinct committee members to vote at the separate slating event to determine the party's preferred candidate for mayor. Only one other gentleman paid the slating fee. He had run for a few offices before but had never won. All the other candidates who wanted to run in the primary and had not withdrawn as was requested at that Wednesday-night meeting decided to skip the slating, probably because of the slating fee. They would still be on the primary ballot, but they would not have the imprimatur of the party.

At the slating, candidates had to be introduced before giving a short speech. Andy Harris was selected to introduce me. I knew him a little by this time; he would serve well in the first few years of my administration before being elected Wayne Township trustee on the west side of Indianapolis.

As I sat on the stage before our speeches, I sat next to the lady who was going to introduce the other gentleman. She leaned over to me and whispered, "Greg, do you know anything about [so-and-so]? I don't know anything about him, and they want me to introduce him." I told her, "No, not at all."

I doubt that I knew five people at this gathering, including her. This was the sort of comic sausage being made on the way to the primary. I was a little taken aback by some of this, but I also knew I was about to be stamped as the preferred Republican candidate for mayor of Indianapolis. I won slating, 96–4. I went on to win the Republican primary with over 70 percent of the vote against four or five other candidates. Now, I really was the guy.

Election Night

The day of the general election in November is fraught with anticipation for most candidates. My small team and I had worked very hard with little money. The vast majority of the city thought I was going to lose badly, but at 6:00 p.m. on election night, that idea was no longer valid. As supporters and party regulars started to fill the auditorium at the Old National Center, the few people who were truly dedicated to the campaign began to believe that victory was possible. Many Republicans who had dismissed my campaign as unwinnable showed up and were now paying close attention. My three brothers, my sister, and much of their families joined us.

My tiny mom, since deceased, was there, cute as ever, and it was funny to see her get a little drunk, insisting that I have the music turned down. I am sure she was thinking about my father, who died in 1999 and had tried to become a state representative decades before only to lose in the primary. None of her five children had done anything remotely political until I decided to run for mayor more than forty years after my father's initial foray into politics.

The party had set aside a small room for me in the Old National Center, and they expected me to stay there throughout the evening. This was a courtesy to me; such niceties on election nights are usually reserved for officeholders or major names. At this point I was neither. But I never went to that room, preferring to stay in the auditorium where my few supporters were. This was the marine in me; I was not going to stay away from those who had helped me. They were with me in that foxhole when times were tough, and I was not going to be separated from them.

The buzz inside the main room continued to build. The expected fifty to seventy people grew to several hundred by 9:00 p.m. The results were holding steady in my favor, and it looked like the Republicans might win the council also. The excitement was palpable. Could this really happen?

Sometime after 9:00 p.m., Mayor Bart Peterson called my campaign manager's phone and asked for me. John Cochran passed the phone to me, and Bart conceded the race. He congratulated me and was kind and gracious, true to who he is. When the people in the auditorium knew the race was trending in my direction, many had started to hang nearby to see what would happen, and when the call came, everybody near me knew what it meant. I had won.

When the call ended and I handed the phone back to John, I immediately noticed that a policeman named Chad Gray was right next to me. A few months back, Chad had thrown me a small fundraiser at his home with a few other cops. I do not think I had seen Chad all night, but I saw him right next to me at that moment, and I knew why he was there. The mayor of Indianapolis always has a small security detail assigned to him, and although I was not yet the mayor, I knew that Chad was not going to let anything happen to me that night. Other than when I went on stage, where he intently watched me and the audience, he never left my side the remainder of the evening until I was in my car heading home. Chad was selected for the security detail and stayed with me for seven and a half years. I still talk with him to this day.

Right after the concession call, I knew that I had to say a few words to the audience, so I sequestered myself to quickly write those few words, focusing on thanking the people who had worked with me despite the long odds. I was so politically naive that I had neither an acceptance speech nor a concession speech written beforehand. I also did not have the phone number for Bart Peterson to concede if necessary. We could have found his phone number somehow, but this helps to explain just how shoestring this operation was. Even the timing of my acceptance speech was part of my naivety. I did not know that I was supposed to wait until my opponent gave his concession speech. People told me afterward that I mishandled it, but frankly, I had no idea of this tradition.

After the call, the communications director for the party started to tell me how and where I was to go to address the now–wildly cheering audience. When he started giving me directions to go around to the side of the stage, walk up the stairs, and wait to the side while I was introduced, I said something like, "The hell with that; I'm going right through the middle of the crowd to the stage." And I did. It was quite the moment, walking through hundreds of people cheering me on.

Unbeknownst to me, the senior Marion County Republican officeholder, Marion County Prosecutor Carl Brizzi, now deceased, took it upon himself to walk on stage to the podium to give a speech. Carl was never one to shy away from the camera, and this was an opportunity for him to talk to the growing television audience tuning in to see the acceptance speech of a long-shot political novice.

The frenzy in the crowd was such that I did not realize that he was up there giving a speech. Unfortunately, he proceeded to trash the arts and culture in the city, along with trails and other sustainability areas, implying that the new city government would not care about these quality-of-life components in Indianapolis. I found out over the next few days that he had done this because organizations that advocated for such issues were adamant that they had to talk to the newly elected mayor, and quickly.

Having lived and traveled in many cities, both in the US and around the world, I had some notion of these issues and how important they were to urban residents. But it was difficult to be mad at Carl, as he was verbalizing how many Republicans feel about such issues.

However, it was the first time I realized that our party had little to no feel for what most citizens in urban areas desired or expected. Republicans gravitate toward fiscal responsibility (other than at the federal level), public-safety/security concerns, and recently some divisive cultural issues. Carl was safely ensconced in the public-safety arena as prosecutor. While fiscal responsibility and public safety are important, those issues alone will not win elections in urban areas unless there are exceptional circumstances. There are many other issues of importance to urban residents, including the arts and sustainability, and I knew that a more centrist approach would be important. Many Republicans in Indianapolis felt the same as Carl, but it was not the sentiment for most residents in Indianapolis nor for other cities across the nation.

When I finally got on stage, my brothers, my sister, and their families were there with me, along with my wife, Winnie; my kids; and my mom. The feeling was overwhelming; it is difficult to describe just how strong this euphoria was, given the long-shot nature of the campaign and my level of political inexperience. However, I was not a youngster in life, having spent twenty-three years in the Marine Corps both in war and peace, been in charge of several units in high-pressure situations, and given many speeches in many different situations. I was composed enough to know that the TV cameras were following my every word and that people were going to comment on what I said.

My short speech was well received as I thanked those who helped and talked about the "ultimate grassroots victory." However, I could have said anything, and the crowd would have cheered wildly. I joked afterward that speeches are much easier to give when the crowd is one hundred percent on your side, cheering your every word.

I stayed around for individual interviews with the media and to thank everyone I could. Winnie and I got home around 1:30 a.m., and I probably fell asleep sometime between 2:00 and 2:30. After the election results had been announced just a few hours before, I had agreed to have all four TV stations come to my house for interviews the next morning, beginning around 6:00 a.m. In retrospect, this was not a good call, simply because of my energy level. And unfortunately, sometime around 4:00 a.m., a high school friend, presumably drunk, started calling my phone. I did not answer any of the three times he called in the half-hour time frame, but he certainly kept me awake heading into the interviews, which were now just an hour or so away. I realized that for election victors, one does not sleep well election night, but the night after that.

It still seems comical to me to remember all those TV trucks parked along our block on the morning after the election. We lived in a diverse, middle-class neighborhood on the northwest side of Indianapolis in a nice roomy house (by Marine standards), but hardly one that shouted "wealthy." I never did ask the neighbors what they thought about that spectacle, but I am sure they thought their world was about to change.

The people had elected a largely unknown "Average Joe" as their mayor. Just who was this guy?

Note

1. Slating no longer exists in Indiana. The gathering of precinct committee members and ward chairs was intended to tell primary voters whom to vote for. Then, only two counties conducted slating, with Marion County, which is Indianapolis, being one of them.

2

UNGUIDED

I DO NOT REMEMBER MY DAD HEALTHY. Rheumatoid arthritis ravaged his body beginning in his thirties. His knees deteriorating, I watched him go from walking slowly with a cane to crutches to a walker to a wheelchair to spending his last few years in bed. His fingers were bent inside at a forty-five-degree angle. He had heart problems. Pain, stress, and prescription drugs were his constant companions. That he still coached me and other kids in baseball and basketball when I was young was amazing, though I did not realize it at the time. He was in and out of Community East Hospital the last two decades of his life. My mom was a saint taking care of him.

Most children think their own childhood is normal; their experience is all they know. Mine was fairly normal for someone growing up in the 1950s and 1960s: a stern if unhealthy father; a loving and accommodating mother; three older brothers and a much younger sister; relatively poor, though I did not know it at the time. My family was not as comfortable as the one seen in *Leave It to Beaver*, but it was also not far off the mark from other families around me. It was not until I had retired from the Marines in 2001, at almost fifty years old and with my father deceased, that my siblings and I realized just how miraculous our upbringing had been. My mom finally started talking to us about the rest of the family, the relatives we did not know about.

I never knew my grandparents. I thought that was normal for families, but of course, it is not. My mom's father died in a work-related accident before I was born, and her mother, apparently a heavy smoker, died of a heart attack either when I was unborn or just an infant. I remember seeing my dad's father one time in my life when I was very young in the early 1960s, and as far as my siblings and I knew, his wife, my grandmother, was dead. That was not true. My paternal grandmother lived until 1982 in a home for the mentally disturbed—an insane asylum, as they used to be called. Neither I nor my brothers and sister knew that. We thought she was dead. Did she deserve to be there? I do not really know. I find it amazing that none of her grandkids knew this until twenty years after she passed.

This was a pattern of our parents, to keep us away from the parts of the family that they did not want us to know about. By most accounts, my paternal grandfather was not a decent man, and that is why our father did not want him around us. We still do not know why our paternal grandmother in that home was kept from us. Our mother told us that our dad had nightmares, remembering his mom being taken away in an ambulance by men in white coats when he was very young. Did my grandmother really have mental-health issues, or was this the action of an angry husband in the 1930s? We still do not know.

After I had retired from the Marines in the early 2000s and returned to Indianapolis, a man walked into my mom's house one day. "Greg, this is your Uncle Joe," she said. It was my mom's brother, who, until that day, my siblings and I did not know existed. As far as we knew, our mom had only two sisters. For some reason, Uncle Joe was kept from our knowledge until that day. Further, I found out only when researching this book that my dad had a sister. I knew he had three brothers, but why this aunt was kept from us I do not know. I know nothing about her.

Both my parents were poor growing up, but I cannot imagine the life that my father knew as a child. At a very young age, he watched as his father had his mother hauled off to that home. Husbands could do that sort of thing to their wives at that time without much fanfare. He then threw my dad out of the house at about the age of sixteen. It was the benevolence of a teacher at his high school in Indianapolis in the 1940s that kept my father going down a largely favorable path and also led to him being hired at Eli Lilly, a pharmaceutical company. Lilly remains a stellar, benevolent company, a major employer in Indianapolis then and now. My father working there for more than thirty years at the lower levels did not make us wealthy, but it did make us more financially secure. The stability was important, although I did not realize it at the time.

Good Men

Later, it was the influence of some good men that he met through fast-pitch softball that changed our family dynamic. Since my father had no role models growing up and certainly had no decent family life that he could emulate, these men, particularly one named Jim McLinn, helped my dad shape his behavior, which gave me and my siblings a chance to succeed. Jim told my father to put his kids in Catholic schools, and we went to Catholic schools through high school. I have come to greatly appreciate this because the public schools I would have attended until the age of twelve, when we moved, were of low quality. I thought that attending a Catholic school was normal, and for some reason, I did not think that our attending these much better schools was out of the ordinary, even though our neighbors did not send their kids to our schools. I also did not realize that my father was working other jobs besides Eli Lilly to pay for that schooling. I was not very observant as a youngster.

Although not all kids attending Catholic schools go on to higher education, it was clear that my siblings and I were expected to go to college, even though my parents never did. In retrospect, it is amazing that our parents thought like this given their upbringing, but this was the influence of my dad's fast-pitch softball friends. No one in that first neighborhood I grew up in went to college. When we moved when I was twelve, I did have many friends who expected to attend college. All five kids in our family earned college degrees, two have law degrees (not including me), and of course, one became the mayor of Indianapolis. If you knew our family when I was young, none of this would have seemed remotely possible.

I continued to learn more about our childhood. I did not attend kindergarten, and I do not think preschool even existed back then. I went to first grade at the age of five. When I was in grade school, everything was easy for me. Other than penmanship, I had top grades in every class. I was in the high ninetieth percentile on all standardized tests through high school. (Such tests then were English, math, and science. I excelled in those areas but later learned that I was not strong in other areas of intelligence. Standardized tests today would probably reflect this.)

Only in the last few years did I find out that the first school I attended, St. Francis de Sales, wanted to advance me from the third grade directly to the fifth grade. My parents said no, and I do not know why, but I was underdeveloped socially and physically. I went to high school at the age of thirteen (standing five feet three and weighing only eighty pounds), and if I had skipped a grade, that would have put me in high school at twelve. Maybe that is why; maybe not. I did wind up getting a full academic ride to Cathedral High School, something that does not occur today at most high schools. I tested third on the entrance exam, and the top four received full scholarships.

That all sounds great, but other than school, I was lacking structure and guidance all through my childhood. Given their background, my parents were amazing in how they raised us, but I (and probably my siblings also) did not have other adults who guided us. I loved doing math homework, but other than that, I cannot recall studying much at all. Yet my grades were great until classes got harder, starting around my senior year in high school. I really did not know how to study because I never had to do much of it.

The same was true in sports. I was a tiny kid but had great hand-eye coordination. If you had asked me at the age of twelve what I was going to be when I grew up, I would have told you a professional baseball player. I was the main pitcher on my Little League team and played shortstop when I did not pitch, batted third in the lineup, and was a Little League All-Star. Soon thereafter, pitchers started throwing curveballs, and suddenly I was a very mediocre ballplayer. No one ever told me to look at the ball as it came out of the pitcher's hand and follow it all the way. I just picked up the ball with my eyes when it was halfway toward the plate, and I was good enough at the Little League level to hit it well. I only learned the proper technique when I started coaching Little League in my forties and bought books on how to coach baseball.

I certainly cannot complain about my life; I know I have been blessed in many ways. That said, I still wonder how my life would have turned out if someone had taken me aside in high school (or even grade school) and said something like, "Greg, if you study hard and do these things, then this path is available to you. You can do these things in life." I am sure to most of the adults around me, it looked like I was working hard because of my performance, but in truth, I was not studying hard or working hard at sports or much of anything.

I am reminded of a quote from Wade Boggs, a Baseball Hall of Famer who rarely struck out. He was challenged by someone commenting on his performance, saying he had natural ability. Boggs retorted to the effect of, "I have natural ability because I hit two thousand balls a day every day when I was growing up." I would have liked to have had someone in my life tell me that sort of thing. That said, I doubt there were many kids at the time who had such guidance. It is far more common today, as it should be.

Attending Catholic schools proved to be the right thing for me, even though, in retrospect, there were some difficulties. In third grade, an announcement came over the speaker system in the school saying that President John Kennedy had been shot. Our teacher, a nun, asked us to pray for the president. Within the next couple of hours came the announcement that the president was dead. "I guess you didn't pray hard enough," our nun scolded us. Tough nun.

Bad Men

I was treated well by nearly everyone, but as we all know now, there were issues with some clergy. Back when priests were considered almost infallible, parents trusted them with their children. This was an unfounded trust. I spent seventh and eighth grades at St. Andrew's. One night, the assistant pastor took me and two other boys on an overnight stay. There were only two beds, and I wound up in the bed with the priest. He asked me to rub him on his upper thigh near his crotch; I did so. I do not remember anything else, as I fell asleep after that. I did not think much of it at the time, but decades later, I found his name on an internet search of priests who were accused of sexual abuse.

Later at Cathedral, a teacher, a Brother of Holy Cross, would ask me about what sort of physical activity my girlfriend and I were engaged in. He explained that it would help him get to know me better. It did not go past that, but I found out decades later that he attempted a more direct approach with one of my brothers a year or two before his talks with me, which resulted in my brother running away from the teacher—and withdrawing mentally from high school from then on.

I do not think either of these incidents affected me the way similar—and much worse—experiences have so sadly affected others. I look back now and am astounded at the audacity of such acts, but I also know that we are all human with basic instincts, and sometimes a person's behavior is below expectations. I still do not think the Catholic Church has come to grips with the basic nature of people, and I wish they would rethink some teachings that go against that basic nature.

In other ways, high school was difficult for me. All through those teen years, I had a cracked, half-missing black front tooth. I had had this since the age of seven when I crashed a friend's new Sting-Ray bicycle, hitting my face on the pavement. Cathedral was an all-male high school downtown, and meeting girls was difficult enough without an ugly front tooth. It profoundly affected me. I rarely smiled and tried to talk while closing my mouth as much as possible. Many thought I was arrogant and not sociable, but in truth I was shy because of the tooth. I believe the level of my introversion comes from this period of my life. It was not until I was twenty years old, well into college, that I asked my dad to get this fixed.

This is related to another issue that bothered me greatly in my teen years and into college. It became obvious to me during this time that we were quite poor. My dad was working hard, but by my teen years, his rheumatoid arthritis was getting much worse, devastating his body. I did not fully appreciate this at the time. All I knew was that I was staying home while my friends were out socializing. My friends, although not rich, had money to go out after ball games and eat at restaurants; they could socialize on a level that I could not. I was envious of those who had money, even resentful. At times, I lashed out at those who could do things that I could not. I was angry. I was angry because I was selfish—ignorant of the sacrifices my parents were making and the stress they endured putting food on the table while providing their five children with a level of education they never experienced when they were children themselves.

Decades later, when I would go by our old houses, I was taken aback by how small our homes were. Four boys and two parents living in that tiny house on Arthington Boulevard on the near northeast side of Indianapolis looks difficult now, but such was the standard for many families at that time. It seemed normal to me.

While I was in grade school and high school, the turbulent sixties did not seem to affect me or our family in any noticeable way. I was oblivious to it all despite getting a stellar education. Then, high schools tended to protect their students rather than engage them with their surroundings and the times. I was coasting, just doing what I was told, not knowing what the future would hold.

In 1972, I attended Indiana University, a wonderful school that I did not come close to utilizing properly. My three older brothers all attended or were attending IU when I enrolled, but, hearkening back to my lacking structure when I was in grade school and high school, I wonder if I would have gone somewhere else if I had applied myself differently. That is doubtful, but I also wonder how my life would have turned out had I taken advantage of the superb instruction and mentoring that was available to me at IU, which I utterly failed to maximize. I did not know how to ask. It remains one of my great regrets. IU remains a great school.

Hanging On

That lack of structure and self-discipline caught up with me in college. More than thirty thousand students attended IU; no one was paying attention to me, and I loved it that way. From the very beginning, attending class was optional in my mind.

Some classes remained easy, but in most of my classes, I paid a heavy cost. Part of my reasoning for not attending many classes was that I had always been able to figure things out when I needed to, but mostly it was because I had enormous freedom for the first time, combined with the fact that I had yet to understand the concept of action and consequence. Previously, there had been no consequences for my lack of study because the results were still good, and everyone around me seemed satisfied. That did not work in college. There were consequences for my laziness, but for some reason, I still did not seem to mind too much. After all, I was at a great university and away from home enjoying life. I got by until I did not. I was more than capable of earning good grades; I just did not care enough to put in the work.

I even had an opportunity to play sports. I was the quarterback for our Delta Tau Delta fraternity football team (even though I was too small to play in high school) and the shortstop for our softball team. I had some skill. In the summers, I stayed in Bloomington to work and have fun, which included playing on a men's slow-pitch softball team. I was still quite skinny, but I could get on base easily with singles; the big boys would drive me in with their power. I played second base on that summer team because we had a state-level shortstop who was remarkable, but I was a very skilled infielder also. One summer, an assistant IU baseball coach was on the team, and he asked why I was not playing baseball for the Hoosiers. I told him I could not hit a curveball. He dropped the subject. I should have asked him to help me learn how to hit a curveball, but again I did not know how to ask for help.

As my college years played out, my dad started providing less support, and I wound up working part time, taking classes part time, and taking out loans. Bloomington became my home. I enjoyed the lifestyle very much, but eventually I would have to grow up. I wound up getting my four-year degree in economics—in six years, plus an additional summer. This from a kid who won an academic full ride to a great high school and was a National Merit Semifinalist.

In that last year at college (1978), Hollywood came to IU in the form of a movie called *Breaking Away*, nominated for an Academy Award for Best Picture. It was a great film about the Little 500, an annual bike race at IU, in which I rode twice. They were looking for former riders to appear in the movie. I considered staying in Bloomington after getting my degree to be in the film, but I thought it was time to move on. I was smart, but I was still undisciplined. The Marines prefer the former—and will not tolerate the latter. My life was about to change forcefully, and all for the better.

3

NEEDED STRUCTURE

As mentioned, many people believed that I did not have the necessary experience to become mayor. I found that an odd comment. Of course, they were thinking that I had no political experience, which was true, but I had learned quickly enough to unseat a two-term incumbent. My experiences once in office were not dissimilar to my marine experiences, except for the continuing political aspect of the job. I told one gentleman who questioned my credentials that I had far more experience than most who entered office. He snickered.

The Marines expanded my horizons. Any marine could tell the story of how his or her time in this organization changed their life. For me, it was the level of responsibility at a young age—leading people; taking care of equipment; travel, which opened my eyes to different cultures and the need to understand each other; the schooling in the later years that provided a strategic way of thinking; and the tragedy of war, which has limitless lessons to ponder.

The Decision

Even though I could have excelled in college, my lack of application had been noticeable, and my grades had reflected that. Floundering at Indiana University with about ninety hours complete, I'd thought about quitting college and joining the military. However, I had not known anything about the military. My dad had spent two years in the Navy, but he never talked to anyone about it, including his kids. At the time, when I'd looked at college graduates, they all seemed to be on a path toward working for a company for forty years, taking two weeks off every year to go to Florida, then retiring and dying. That was the sum total of life. I had known I did not want that.

In retrospect, I think that exploring an alternate path was also about my being the fourth boy born in about a six-year period. To everyone else, I was always someone's little brother; I did not have my own identity. In some way, I knew I had to do something different from my brothers. I could not see the future clearly, but I knew that the "working fifty weeks a year and two weeks in Florida" life was not for me. I needed structure to succeed, but I was not yet self-aware enough to know that. I simply was not motivated in any direction.

At this point, I went into the military recruiters' offices in Bloomington. I did not know there was an officer/enlisted delineation in the services, based largely on college degree/non–college degree. The recruiting office in Bloomington was for enlisted only; all the services used Indianapolis for officer recruitment. I remember specifically that I wanted to talk to the Army, the Navy, and the Air Force, even though I knew little about any of them. I had every intention of avoiding talking to the marine recruiter. Destiny had another idea.

When I entered the building, the Army, Navy, and Air Force recruiters were all busy talking to someone, and the Marine recruiter was in his doorway awaiting his next victim. He came to me and said in a loud, hoarse, and gravelly voice, "Hey, you want to talk about the Marine Corps?"

I was scared to death—certainly too scared to say no to this intimidating figure. I spent two hours with him. He was a former drill instructor named Gunnery Sergeant Paxton, and his love of the Corps was evident. Somewhere in that discussion, I told him that I had completed ninety hours at IU. He told me I should finish the last thirty hours and come in as an officer and then to go to Indianapolis to talk to the officer selection officer (OSO) about my situation. (Fifteen years later, I was the commanding officer of a recruiting station based out of St. Louis, and none of the marine recruiters in my station would have given me that advice. But Gunny Paxton did.)

I went to Indianapolis and talked to the OSO assistant, explaining my situation. He was terrific and recommended that I enroll in the Platoon Leaders Course, where one would go to six weeks of officer training in the summer, come back the final year to finish college, and then complete another six weeks of training upon graduation. The voluminous background checks were completed, and I was "good to go."

Or so we both thought. He assumed I was on a normal path to graduation, taking classes full time, which was clearly not the case after my circuitous route to ninety credit hours at IU. Two weeks before I was to ship out for the first six weeks of training, he asked for my class schedule. I was taking only ten hours of classes that semester as I was working and enjoying life otherwise. However, one had to be a full-time student (at least twelve hours) to qualify for the Platoon Leaders Course. I was out.

I managed to complete the final thirty hours and went back to the OSO office in Indianapolis in the late summer of 1978. I walked into the captain's office and told him that I had graduated, that my background checks were complete, and that I was ready to attend Officer Candidate School—the officer training (actually screening) for those who had already graduated from college. Although he was cordial, I sensed that he thought this was too easy, too neat, and could not be true. However, it was true. They had an opening, and a few weeks later, in the first week of September 1978, I was on my way to Quantico, Virginia, for the ultimate life-changing experience.

When I went to my parents' house to tell my dad that I had joined the Marines, he asked me, "What are you going to do about college?" I told him that I graduated already. He did not believe me. Even after I shipped out, he still did not believe it until my diploma came in the mail. Such was my path at this point—from earning a full academic ride at a prestigious high school to my own father not believing I had gained a four-year college degree after six years.

The day before I shipped out to Officer Candidate School in September 1978, my dad was in the hospital. His hospitalizations were almost routine at this point. When I visited him, he knew I was heading off to something important, something different. He bawled like a baby. Here was this tough, stern man who at times scared me, letting it all come out. I know most of it was pride, but I also sensed some fear for me. I did not know quite what to make of it.

Becoming a Marine Officer

Officer Candidate School is not boot camp. OCS is a screening process. It was made clear to us that the OCS staff did not care whether anyone made it or not; they just wanted to screen for the best potential officers they could find. The difficult training is to ensure that one is capable of leading marines under dire circumstances. There were 200 candidates that began the class, thinking they were physically and mentally prepared, but only 110 made it through—55 percent.

Those who have been through both OCS and boot camp (for enlisted marines) would tell you that OCS is physically more difficult, but that boot camp is mentally more difficult. Boot camp breaks down your mind and then builds it back up to the point where you think you can conquer the world. OCS is designed to ensure you have the clarity and mental toughness to continue leading marines after experiencing physical rigor, fatigue, and other horrible conditions.

The beginning of OCS was weird. Many of us thought that the legendary screaming and harassing that one sees in the movies would take place upon our arrival. That did not happen. We were in an open squad bay with about fifty or sixty other candidates with bunk bed arrangements, just like in the movies, but it was extremely quiet and businesslike as we went through medical exams. Apparently, they wanted to ensure we were in good shape physically and mentally. I do remember that first morning at breakfast, when we took the old silver World War II–style trays and went through a line while food was dumped on the tray. I had never eaten scrambled eggs before, but I did that day. I also had a food that looked sort of like hamburger beef in some sort of gravy; it was the legendary "SOS" (shit on a shingle) that I knew little about but came to love, to the point that it became a staple in our house for decades. But even without the yelling, I was having some doubts at this point, wondering what I had gotten myself into.

All hell broke loose the third or fourth morning. Everything was done in a hurry, physical training, attending classes, eating chow, and at the top of our lungs and the instructors' lungs. Every action was a mistake. Even if you did something correctly, it was still a mistake, and you were loudly told about it. The physicality was overwhelming. By the end of the second week, I sat on my footlocker seriously wondering what I was thinking signing up for this.

Then it started to become a routine. We caught on to what was happening, reacting quickly and smartly. The instructors started teaching and observing how we reacted to leading and being led. Around the third or fourth week, we were let off each weekend. This was to test our maturity level, to see if we would get in trouble in DC or other places, something that automatically disqualified you from being officer material. Some did not make this cut. I stayed in the barracks and studied.

OCS is where I had my first "light-bulb moment" on leadership. Since it is a screening process, candidates are put into different leadership positions to test their ability. There were fire team leaders (in charge of four people), squad leaders (thirteen people), and platoon leaders (about thirty people). The first two weeks I was just a rifleman, following orders as they were given. On the third week, I was named a squad leader. The morning of my first day as a squad leader, we had an early class and then afterward had the usual two minutes (or so it seemed) to stow away our books in the barracks and get prepared for a hike. I was determined to be one of the first candidates ready to march off, and I was. I recall that I was the third or fourth in formation from our thirty-man platoon. I proudly stood at the squad leader's position.

Seconds thereafter, our sergeant instructor, a man we called Barney Fife because of his physical stature, put his nose right next to my chin and said in the meanest, most sarcastic voice imaginable, "Where's your squad?" I looked around, and there was no one there. I understood immediately. I was now not being judged on my performance alone, but on the performance of my unit. To this day, no matter what position I have held, including mayor, I have never forgotten that.

Some who began OCS were a little heavy, and some were pretty skinny. I entered OCS at six feet even and 139 pounds. I think I was the thinnest candidate there. We were told that after ten weeks, those who remained would look alike in physical stature: bigger guys would lose weight, and skinny guys would gain weight. That proved to be true. I left OCS at 165 pounds, and none of it was excess weight. I could do things physically that I would not have believed a few months before, including climbing to dangerous heights with nothing below but the ground.

Something in me clicked; I wanted to finish this course.

After working through some initial land navigation issues (getting somewhere using a map and compass), I graduated from OCS in November 1978, a second lieutenant in the Marines. On that day, I realized that I was on my own. Most other graduates had family there who celebrated with their new marine officer. I was alone primarily because of my dad's health, but I was still sad that I was sharing this moment with no one. After the ceremony, I just wandered around the base by myself, not really knowing what to do. It was an odd feeling, having done something that no one in my family expected or, I suspect, understood. I was on a different path than my friends and siblings.

OCS or equivalent programs for all officers are followed by attendance at The Basic School (TBS). This is a six-month training program designed to give new officers the basics of the Marine Corps: the traditions, how to lead, the different functions of the Corps, where they fit into the national military posture, and so on. It is very thorough and a mix of academics and field training. Just as all marines at boot camp are initially trained as riflemen, all marine officers are trained as infantry rifle platoon leaders; we all have that in common.

We then move on to our specialty. I was lucky that my academics were strong enough to have me finish in the top 10 percent of this six-month class, giving me the honor of being meritoriously augmented, meaning I was now a "regular" officer. Other than those coming from the military academies, officers coming out of TBS typically graduate as "reserve" officers who must petition, based on performance, to join the regular officer corps after a few years on active duty. It is similar to being on probationary status.

TBS is also where you choose your military occupational specialty (MOS). This is where my military naivety hurt me. TBS split the slots for dozens of MOSs into the academic thirds of the class. I was in the top third of this two-hundred-person class, and the staff had no one in the top third academically who wanted to enter the transportation field. Since I was undecided for weeks on what specialty I wanted (not knowing much about any of them), they asked me if I would consider transportation. Despite having minimal mechanical aptitude, I said yes. This was a mistake. My childhood upbringing did not make me mechanically inclined, and although you can lead people knowing little technically, it certainly is not optimal, especially for a young lieutenant in the military at his first duty station trying to find his way. I should have chosen another specialty.

The Fleet

For my first three years in the real Marine Corps, what we call the fleet, I was assigned to an infantry battalion in Camp Pendleton, California, as the motor transport officer. Overall, I was mediocre in the job, but I did not commit any fatal mistakes. However, I wonder if I would have made it into the regular officer corps if I had not been meritoriously augmented at TBS.

During my first year with the Second Battalion, Seventh Marines, First Marine Division, I had a young marine in the final year of his four-year enlistment. During that entire year, he complained loudly and often about how badly he hated the Marines and how he could not wait to get out and go back home to Iowa. This was startling to a new lieutenant, and it made me wonder about motivation, dedication, and so many other aspects of leadership and the Marines in particular.

Then, in the last month of his enlistment, he got a prominent tattoo on his arm of the eagle, globe, and anchor, the emblem of the Marine Corps. I asked him why he would do that as he had badmouthed the Corps nearly every day for a year. I will never forget what he said to me. "Sir, I want everyone back home to know that I was in the Marine Corps." That made me think that I was in the right place at this moment in my life. It was also the moment when I realized that people may complain, but they still can love their environment, their organization—something that was important for a future mayor to understand.

I also knew that my position gave me real-world experience much more quickly than my peers in the civilian world. In my early to midtwenties, in my first real job, I had thirty people reporting to me and a $3 million budget. I was expected to lead this unit on a moment's notice to deploy in the defense of our country. I was not confident that I was up to this task, but I made it through.

We deployed on a routine cycle to Okinawa, Japan, for six months, and we also did exercises in the Philippines; it was my first time ever overseas, and I loved every minute of it. This was less than forty years after the end of World War II, and some of the friction of that war with Japan was still felt. Seeing another culture for the first time had a profound effect on me, particularly impressing on me the importance of countries understanding each other in the pursuit of peace.

This sense of being global, of being part of the larger world that is so necessary to leading a major city in America, began with my first overseas trip in the Marines. It also taught me respect for ethnic differences and the necessity of different cultures understanding each other. On Okinawa, Americans in uniform were the minority, and much of the local population were not happy with our presence. I came to appreciate their position even though working through some issues could be difficult.

A Turning Point

After I had spent three years in this job, in the summer of 1982 all the lieutenants in Camp Pendleton were notified of an opening in Barstow, California. It was for an aide-de-camp position for the new commanding general of the logistics/repair base in the middle of the California desert, where most of the employees were civilian workers. The new commanding general would be coming from Camp Pendleton also.

Aide-de-camp positions usually go to infantry or artillery officers; those military occupational specialties are purposely overpopulated so that those officers can fill the myriad of staff and office positions outside of their MOS as they mature in the Corps. Support MOSs like transportation are usually underpopulated, so those officers are forced to stay in their specialty most, if not all, of their careers. As I was not enthusiastic about staying in my current or similar job, I thought the aide-de-camp position might be something I would enjoy.

The division headquarters, knowing that a general could pick whomever he wanted, was not happy that I applied for the job, and they tried to dissuade me from applying by offering me a transportation position at a larger battalion, something that did not appeal to me at all. I already knew it was the wrong field for me. I also knew the aide-de-camp position was a long shot because the general who selected his new (and for him, his first) aide-de-camp knew the personnel needs of the Corps also.

I do not know why Brigadier General Edmund Looney selected me. I was just happy he did. General Looney was a terrific man and a great boss. He was also a bit of a maverick; he told me that Marine Corps orders are guidelines for common sense; if they do not make sense, then do not follow them. Although I was still wound pretty tight in my demeanor and approach to marine life, this helped to start loosening me up. This guidance was critical to developing my own leadership philosophies. My mayoral staff knew full well when an issue was brought to me that the first question would be "What's the right thing to do?"

I was good in this position, and I stayed with him for two years at that isolated marine base in Barstow. I do not believe I would have stayed in the Corps except for this position. My job was to ensure that he got to the right place at the right time in the right uniform with the right notes. However, there was much more to this job. Instead of worrying daily about my platoon in Camp Pendleton, I was now sitting in briefings with the commandant of the Marine Corps and other high-ranking officers. They talked about subjects I had never thought of, and I started to understand the connection between the lower-level operational units and what Headquarters Marine Corps did to make it all happen.

It was eye opening. I soaked it all in. This was my first time thinking about anything in a big-picture way. Especially considering my modest upbringing, to be able to sit in these briefings helped me tremendously when I became the mayor.

Also of great help to me in that future role was seeing how people treated the general. I am sure he saw himself as a kid from the streets of New York, but everyone treated him differently, with much greater respect and deference. That single star on his collar mattered. Again, I'd never seen this sort of thing before. It was his rank and his position that were the difference, but he seemed to understand that, and it never went to his head. I cannot overstate how much this example helped me when I became the mayor of Indianapolis. I always saw myself as this kid from a modest background, but after the 2007 election, people started treating me in a way I had never experienced before. I understood it because I had seen it more than twenty years before.

Of note, although I talk about her in a later chapter, Winnie and I got married in Barstow, a great decision on my part.

Overseas Again

While in Barstow, I petitioned to change my MOS to logistics, a broader field more in line with my capabilities and interests. It is rare for the Marines to change a support MOS for an officer, but it helped to have a commanding general's endorsement. However, such endorsements do not apply to duty stations. After Barstow, I received orders for an unaccompanied tour to Okinawa for a year. This one-year tour to Okinawa was pretty basic, planning and executing training, although I was able to deploy to both South Korea and the Philippines for exercises along with visiting other countries on vacation. My view of the world was getting wider.

This one year in Okinawa provided another leadership lesson that was critical to being a mayor: asking the right questions. The relationship between a marine and his weapon is sacred. If a weapon is assigned to a marine, that marine cleans it routinely and qualifies with it and is expected to deploy with it immediately if required. If you are not in a real-world situation or on an exercise, that weapon is in an armory with its own precise regulations. For many units, an officer not in the armory chain of command is assigned to check the procedures of that armory as an independent audit. I was assigned such an audit.

It was a monthly, objective audit conducted by captains, which I now was, having been promoted near the end of my tour in Barstow. The audit consisted of counting rifles, pistols, and machine guns that should match the inventory and ensuring that any weapon in the maintenance cycle was also accounted for. I expected that any audit conducted objectively by a different captain every month would result in me finding a well-run armory. What I found was something else.

One missing weapon is a major issue. I found several rifles that were on the armory rolls but were not accounted for in any way. I could not find them, and the armory personnel had no idea where they were. I could not believe it. Off to the side in the armory room, I also found a machine gun with a maintenance tag on it that was not on the rolls, completely unaccounted for. We were in a foreign country, and missing and unaccounted weapons conjure up all sorts of issues that could affect local relations with Japan.

In the mid-1980s, computers were not yet standard. I nervously handwrote a detailed and accurate four-page report. I was not only putting on report a fellow captain in charge of the armory who was my friend but also several captains who in the previous five to six months had signed off on the armory being in tip-top condition. I was so nervous that I asked a very busy lieutenant colonel to read the report before I submitted it. He brusquely took it from me, and I could tell that he did not think he should have to read something about a routine action. Less than an hour later, he came to me and much more calmly asked me, "Is all this true?" I confirmed it, and he said he would take care of it.

This is where "inspect what you expect" became a leadership principle of mine. Several commissioned officers failed at something that was not difficult, with its potential for disaster being great. They did not actually inspect the armory, but they signed off on it. I learned that telling someone to do something does not mean it will get done properly, even in the Marines. One must check on the proper completion of a task. In this case, several officers failed at this.

A corollary to this is something that I have heard many times, and that is people saying, "That's the way we've always done it." Whenever I hear that, my antenna goes up; I am suspicious. If someone says such a thing, that means to me that no one is inspecting that area and that the procedure/operation is either underperforming, costing more money than it should, or, even worse, fraudulent. When I heard this phrase while in office, I always had that area checked out.

Acquisition

My Okinawa stint was followed by a three-year tour to the US Army's Tank-Automotive Command (TACOM) in Warren, Michigan, working on the Marines' Light Armored Vehicle (LAV) program. This is what the Marines call an acquisition tour, working with industry and Department of Defense civilians. The best way to explain it is that a need for equipment is determined by the military services in DC and is put on paper. Those in acquisition perform all the functions to get that piece of equipment from the paper into the hands of those who will use it in the fleet, while also assisting the private manufacturer/contractor who built the equipment.

My primary job was to gather a team of experts and inspect the LAVs when they were delivered from the contractor to the fleet units. I also monitored the retrofits on the vehicles. This was a fun job where I learned much about the manufacturing industry. The vehicle itself was made in Canada, so I frequently visited our northern neighbor. I worked mostly with civilians, including one who was my direct boss, a great guy, and I also had a terrific marine colonel who ran the LAV program at TACOM. Having my MOS changed to logistics provided this opportunity, and I was so thankful I was now in a field where I felt comfortable and could excel.

Learning about contracting and manufacturing helped greatly when I became the mayor. Most marines do not learn these things, but I was lucky enough to learn the importance of getting the contracts right and then following the contracts, and to learn something about manufacturing, since Indiana is a manufacturing-intense state. Both helped when I talked to companies in Indianapolis.

I did this job well and was recommended by my colonel for an accelerated promotion to major. Such a recommendation is rare, and it is even rarer for the accelerated promotion to actually occur. Also, at the end of this tour, I received the Meritorious Service Medal, which in the Marine Corps is usually reserved for majors or higher. I was not promoted ahead of my peers, but I now felt confident that I would be promoted to major when my time came for consideration. Promotion to major ensures that one can remain for at least twenty years, guaranteeing retirement with a pension.

One of the neat parts of this tour was being one of only six or eight marines on an army base while also living on an Air National Guard base. There was lots of good-hearted service rivalry while we were in Michigan, emblematic of the camaraderie that all service members feel in uniform. Also, both our kids were born during this three-year tour.

4

THINGS GET REAL

My subsequent transfer to Camp Lejeune in early 1989 would prove to be my most exciting time in the Corps. In my previous job in Michigan, my travel was extensive, even though we had two newborns at home. I tried to time my check-in so that I would not be deployed soon after I reported. I was still naive.

I should have realized that the unit I was being transferred to, Second Landing Support Battalion (LSB) in Second Force Service Support Group (FSSG), knew I was coming. The day I reported, Second LSB received a requirement from Second FSSG to assign a captain to lead a detachment of marines to Panama for three months. Since I had no position yet, I was the obvious—that is, the targeted—choice. After a six-week training cycle, I would lead a group of thirty marines with logistics specialties to Panama in support of efforts there to counter the growing threat from Manuel Noriega. This effort had been going on for over a year, and my group was to be the latest to fill a three-month tour in Panama.

After ten years in the Corps, both training and filling staff positions, I was now embarking on a real-world mission. The six weeks of preparation before the deployment were important to me not only to get my field skills back up to par but also to get into better physical condition. Exercising in a staff position outside of the fleet is not the same as being ready for the real-world field conditions required of marines. I had not carried a pack in years, so in preparation, on the weekends at home, I hiked in the woods behind my house with a heavy pack to get ready.

During the preparatory training, we were assigned to a unit called Brigade Service Support Group Six, led by a rugged but wonderful infantry colonel. He took us on a hike to test our unit's physical condition, which went well. I added to that by conducting my own evening hike with my unit, which did not go so well. I went at a very fast pace to test them physically and mentally. You find out quickly who can think clearly and rationally when conditions become stressful, and a leader needs to know whom he can count on when times get tough.

The hike was conducted on a humid evening. One of my marines did not put water in his canteens prior to the hike, and he was struggling mightily. Other marines were giving him some of their water, but he still could not keep up. I did not slow down. I made sure he was not going into heat exhaustion, but I was not happy with this situation, and not just because a single marine was having trouble. I was upset because NCOs (noncommissioned officers—corporals and sergeants) are responsible for ensuring that their marines have all their gear ready to go. As a unit, we were going to Panama in a real-world contingency operation, and I had NCOs who failed in a basic, commonly known duty. They did not look out for their fellow marine.

Of course, that is why you train beforehand. The NCOs learned from that situation, and they also realized that their officer-in-charge was not going to tolerate nonsense. I was setting expectations.

The actual deployment went very well. I was pleased with everyone's performance, and my boss in Panama and my boss back at Camp Lejeune were satisfied. I was happy about that because I knew this was my first real test; however, I almost cost my marines a great opportunity in Panama.

One morning, with less than a month before redeployment back to Camp Lejeune, the S-3 (operations officer) of Marine Forces Panama came to me and asked if I wanted my marines to pull some security duty for a few days, guarding an area that an infantry company had been guarding. Although all marines are trained in such duty in boot camp, my marines had not done this sort of thing in some time, as they worked in logistics fields. My marines could have handled the duty well, but we were expected to turn over our equipment in great condition to the next unit that followed us, and I wanted to concentrate on that task. I told the S-3, "Thanks, but I really have to concentrate on the turnover of our equipment."

Within the hour, I knew I had made a mistake. I was still wound a little too tightly at that time. I had taken away an opportunity for my marines to experience something other than their primary jobs and have some excitement doing it. I talked to my small staff, and they also wanted our marines to pull that security duty. I went back to the S-3 and said I reconsidered and wanted my marines to pull that duty. Thankfully, he agreed.

My colonel in Panama had gently warned me that the three- or four-day operation was "a sergeant's post, not yours," implying that I may want to leave this duty to my NCOs. However, I did set up camp the first night off to the side of the security post, as I realized I wanted a different experience also. My marines had been trained in all the proper procedures for the area and had learned enough Spanish to execute the necessary operations. The infantry company commander, a fellow captain, had his troops at that post for two months with no action, but on our first night, we captured two intruders who crossed into the area, even though they proved to be benign. When he came to check on the situation, I could tell he was irritated that my troops, not his, had made the capture. I took great pleasure in this because he had loudly, inappropriately, and wrongly confronted me on a different issue some weeks before. I held my tongue but was smiling inside.

The best outcome for me personally was that I knew I could perform in a real-world scenario. I suspect that there are many in the military who wonder how they will respond the first time they are in a potentially dangerous situation. There were not huge enemy forces approaching us in Panama, but Noriega was testing the US forces from time to time, and there were areas I traveled in that were known as "bad guy country." I strangely felt a sense of calm when traveling in these areas—alert, ready, but calm.

There were also two leadership lessons that really began with this deployment and that were critical in my success as mayor of Indianapolis. The first was to trust your people more than I was doing. When I initially turned down the security duty for my marines, I thought that I was just being faithful to what was expected of me. However, I was clearly not exhibiting full faith in the marines who had performed so well for me in Panama. Could they not pull this extra duty and also prepare the equipment for the turnover to the new unit? Of course they could, but that was not my thought process at that time. As I said, I was wound too tightly.

The other lesson, and one that I believe was critical to the success of our mayoral administration, was to say yes if possible. Most politicians, especially in executive positions, start with no until proven otherwise. It is easier and safer politically to say no. We did not do that. If someone came to us with a good idea for the long-term health of the city, we tried to figure out a way to do it, to say yes. Most would be surprised to understand the goodwill engendered by this approach, even if the eventual answer was no.

This approach also brought in many more good suggestions, as people felt comfortable bringing ideas forward. When the S-3 brought forward the idea of a security detail for my marines, I immediately created an obstacle in my mind. I should have immediately formulated a way to get to yes.

I am so thankful I learned this lesson before I became mayor.

LSB/Saddam Hussein

When I redeployed back to Camp Lejeune, I integrated into Second LSB. Its main function was to conduct beach- and helicopter-support operations, ensuring that equipment and personnel got where they were supposed to go in what are usually chaotic situations. It also had an air-delivery platoon, which built platforms for equipment dropped from airplanes. All members of that platoon were jump qualified, and they were highly motivated marines all the time—a fun group.

I became the company commander of Landing Support Equipment Company (trucks and forklifts), which was a support company to the operational companies of the battalion. I assume I was given this assignment because of my transportation background, and although I performed adequately, I was again uncomfortable. I eventually told the battalion commander that I would be better as a staff officer, which is something most marine officers would never say.

He made me his S-3, the operations officer for the battalion. This is the third-ranking position in a battalion behind the commanding officer and executive officer. This was a major's position. I was still a captain at the time, yet he gave me this assignment even though there were majors in the command who normally would have gotten this position. I had to carefully navigate assigning duties to those who outranked me. I was effective in this position. I also loved being in Second LSB. LSB personnel were known as "red patchers," as they wore red patches on the front of their cover (or hat, to you civilians) and on the side of their trousers at knee level. This was to let everyone else on the beach know who was controlling the flow of people and equipment.

Upon the change of the battalion commanding officer, I remained as the operations officer. Every boss has their personality, quirks, and ways of doing business, and I was used to this sort of thing, so I was happy that the new CO wanted me to stay in the position.

Soon thereafter, in August 1990, Saddam Hussein invaded Kuwait.

It was not initially clear that the marines based out of Camp Lejeune were going to be involved in removing Iraq from Kuwait. This was in the area of responsibility (AOR) of the Camp Pendleton marines in California. As it became clear that a large force from America was required (eventually reaching five hundred thousand from all the services), the Camp Lejeune marines were tasked to deploy in support of Desert Shield/Desert Storm. It is difficult to overstate how much my experience in Panama gave me confidence in planning our unit's ever-changing missions before and during our deployment to the Middle East.

Our new CO was a good guy, but he certainly did not know how to run a meeting. He failed routinely at a well-known military maxim that you should give two-thirds of the available planning time to your subordinate organizations. He would attend meetings with the commanding general of the FSSG and then immediately hold a meeting with his staff, rambling on as things came to his mind. Early in one meeting, he asked me to check with the FSSG staff about something, then continued with his two-hour-plus meeting. As the meeting was finally wrapping up, he asked me if I had checked with the FSSG staff yet, not realizing that we were still in the same meeting where he tasked me to do that checking.

He also had the unfortunate habit of not getting the story quite right from those meetings with the commanding general. I and others caught on to this quickly, and we would always make follow-up phone calls to our counterparts at the FSSG headquarters to get the real scoop. It was funny to me, but I think that some of the other battalion staff were wary of what our life would be like in the desert. Despite his quirks, I felt like our CO had enough common sense and savvy, street smarts if you will, that we would be fine once we deployed to Saudi Arabia.

I cannot recall if the majority of the battalion deployed in late December or early January. I do know that I, the executive officer, and a few other marines deployed in early December as the advance party for the battalion, to get the lay of the land and to prepare our initial positions for the rest of the battalion. Once in Saudi Arabia, my executive officer and I went to receive the initial briefing on the mission for our battalion. We knew that most of our marines would be detached from the battalion and assigned to various units. Their skill sets, particularly helicopter operations, were needed in infantry units, so they were attached mainly to those units. A small number of remaining marines, including the battalion staff, would be assigned additional duties.

This was what we heard we would be doing in the initial briefing: "You will be attached to a unit with one marine infantry division. They will fight their way through the triple concertina wire [that Saddam's units had laid down], fight north toward Kuwait City through eleven Iraqi infantry divisions, and then be prepared to head west to support army units as they also move north."

That got our attention. The XO and I looked at each other, and we could tell what the other was thinking. It was sportscaster Dick Enberg's old saying: "Oh my!"

Plans change, though. Soon after initial processing through Jubail, we moved over one hundred miles straight north to an area called al Mishab, which is not listed on many maps. We were about thirty miles south of the Kuwaiti border and now attached to a temporary unit called General Support Group (GSG) Two. We were also far ahead (north) of most combat units. Our heaviest weapons were machine guns, and we only had a few of those.

Since we were a logistics unit, I was not only the operations officer but also the intelligence officer for the battalion. I had to read the intelligence messages every day to understand what was going on and to see if anything would affect our unit or position. I largely enjoyed this part of my duties, especially being in the know, but it was not always pleasant. Realizing that near-term intelligence can at times be wrong, one report mentioned that Iraqi officers in Kuwait separated mothers from their newborns, placed them in adjoining rooms, cut a rectangle in the bottom of the doors, and forced the mothers to watch their babies starve to death. I cannot confirm whether this report was eventually accurate but, when I read such things, I was more than happy that I was doing my part.

For the first few weeks in al Mishab, we did what red patchers do, mainly helicopter operations. These were normal operations throughout most days, and I cannot recall anything extraordinary occurring those first few weeks. However, what came to be called the "air war" began in mid-January. It was designed to soften up the Iraqi defenses and did so. After taking out the Iraqi air defenses and their command-and-control systems, our air force, navy, and marine aircraft pounded the Iraqi ground forces along with other significant targets.

Our precarious position ahead of most of the combat units started receiving artillery fire. It was a weird experience in that we were connected by communications with a small forward detachment (from which service

I never found out) who could see that the Iraqis were about to shoot at us, and all we could do was wait to see if they hit us. Something like, "Guns up—fire" came over the radio, and we knew that in about a minute, we would hear the shells exploding nearby, targeted for us. I could not help but think, "If you can see this, then for God's sake, call someone to take out that artillery position."

The shelling occurred for about ten days over a two-week period, but eventually that Iraqi unit was taken out by what we were told were marine Harriers (AV-8Bs, called jump jets, that could take off like a helicopter but fly like a jet). We were lucky that the closest artillery shells that exploded were a quarter to a half mile away.

At the end of January and during the air war, the Iraqis began a ground attack, including tanks, through the town of Khafji, about ten miles south of the Kuwaiti border and about fifteen to twenty miles north of our position, which, again, was lightly defended. There were a few combat units north of us, but additional marine units responded and stopped the Iraqi attack in the Khafji area. This battle lasted just a few days.

It did provide for an interesting conversation between my commanding officer and me. Early during the Khafji battle, he had received notice that he might have to pull our unit back, which made perfect sense. Our machine guns could never stop Iraqi tanks, and there were other friendly forces that could move forward quickly to stop the attack. However, he felt a need to talk to me about that and what it would mean. He did not want to be seen as a marine commander who turned tail and ran. I knew what he was talking about and understood how he felt, but I also knew that every senior commander in his chain of command would force him to move south.

It was just common sense. Staying in place in case the Iraqis broke through was suicide; it was tanks versus machine guns, and it was not only his life at stake but also the lives of those marines under his charge who relied on his judgment. History would not judge him harshly at all if we moved south. However, it gives great insight into leaders, particularly military leaders in combat, as to how they want to be remembered.

Soon after Khafji, word came down that the plans for the Allied forces had changed. This is now known as General Schwarzkopf's Left Hook. Our unit was to move about thirty miles west from al Mishab to an area that came to be known as al Kibrit; in actuality, it was just a piece of dirt. General Schwarzkopf, head of all the Allied forces, was a brilliant strategist and a no-nonsense man. He moved all the Arab forces to the east, where we were previously, so they could fight together. He moved the marine, army, and other Western forces out west.

For weeks, large numbers of Arab forces moved east, and Western forces moved west along a path about thirty miles south of the Kuwaiti border. In moving our battalion west, I traversed the thirty-mile east-west swath multiple times, and the dust cloud was enormous, twenty-four hours a day. Unbelievably, Saddam's forces apparently saw none of it; the air war had taken out their "eyes."

Schwarzkopf also very publicly let it be known that there were additional amphibious marine forces in the Persian Gulf off the east coast, and the press reported just that. This held the Iraqi forces to the east, who were now expecting a massive, amphibious Allied effort from the Persian Gulf and from ground Allied forces on the east side of Saudi Arabia moving north. Saddam's forces had no idea that the major thrust was to come from the west, not the east.

Our new mission was to wait for the ground war to clear Kuwait City, where we would then move forward to run its port, bringing forth more personnel and equipment. However, thanks to the air war and the many Iraqi forces who did not want to die and simply surrendered, the ground war was over in one hundred hours. We never moved north from al Kibrit.

Thus began the retrograde of these massive Allied forces down south to Jubail (for the Marines) and Dammam (for the Army), Saudi Arabia. Once we moved south to Jubail, I was put in charge of the huge port there as ships came from all over the world to help with the evacuation of all the equipment back to the States. I became known as "the mayor of Jubail," but it was mostly a nominal position as the Navy did most of the hands-on work coordinating with incoming ships. I just made sure it all worked and tried to maintain cordial relations with the Saudi port personnel.

As happens with any large-scale operation around ports and airfields, infrastructure like roads, curbs, light poles, and the like get damaged. The local Saudi authorities came to me to pay for these damages. I did not have a budget at all, let alone one to pay for any damages. I am sure that other retrograde operations across Saudi Arabia were damaging local infrastructure, but I did not know if US officials were hearing what I was hearing.

After a few weeks of this, the answer came. A message came down from General Schwarzkopf saying something like "America will not charge Saudi Arabia for the airplanes and tanks lost, for the American lives lost, and for saving your country from the Iraqis; and Saudi Arabia will not charge

America for local damage as we exit your country." It was a bit more diplomatic than that, but not by much. I was not asked about paying for damages anymore.

Upon their return to the US, many units encountered a rousing, joyous welcome, beginning in March 1991. The military did the best they could to quickly get home those units that had been there the longest. Since we had deployed in the December/January time frame, we stayed a bit longer. An entirely new temporary unit was put together in the States and deployed to Saudi Arabia a couple of months after the ground war ended to relieve those who had been in the war, so that those who fought the war would not have to stay another year or so just moving equipment back.

I came back in June 1991, six and half months after I deployed. I was on the second-to-the-last plane to depart that carried home those who had fought in the war. Instead of receiving a great joyous welcome, we returned in the middle of the night (2:00 or 3:00 a.m.) to Camp Lejeune, which was fine with me. I just wanted to go home. My wife and kids were there, but I initially could not find them. I still had my keys from home and found our Chrysler minivan before I found my wife and kids.

Once I put my gear in the car, I went back to find them, and a sad moment occurred that I will never forget. My son, just three years old and eleven months younger than my daughter, did not recognize me. Even though it was no one's fault (except Saddam Hussein's), it still hurt. The next day, once he saw that his mother was OK with me, he perked right up.

5

POST-WAR

After the war, I transferred to Marine Aircraft Group (MAG) Twenty-Six at New River, North Carolina. The best part of this was that we did not have to move from our house on base. New River has some air units, and it is literally across the New River from Camp Lejeune. Instead of a ten-minute drive, I now had a twenty-minute drive. We lived about four years in the same house, which is very unusual in the service. The stability for the family was welcome.

Once I checked in, a quota came in for an exercise that needed a major in logistics. This is maddening yet funny at the same time. The exercise was in 29 Palms, California—desert training. I had just returned from the war in the Middle East, but the Marines needed me for desert training. Since I was once again the new guy with no assigned duties, I had to go. Training is always continuous in the Marines, yet I did not want to leave my family once again. But I did.

When I returned to MAG Twenty-Six, I had a wonderful two years, great bosses, and a little bit more low-key work schedule. I deployed to Puerto Rico for a Maritime Prepositioning Forces (MPF) exercise, as I had become an expert in this area.

The MPFs were thirteen ships, part of three naval squadrons, positioned strategically around the world, that stored equipment for marine forces. The idea is that marines could fly quickly to a designated point where the ships would meet them; the marines would take the equipment and then proceed with their mission. This saves an enormous amount of time in fast-moving situations, rather than having to deploy equipment by ship from the marines' home base.

The great lesson I learned at MAG Twenty-Six had nothing to do with anything operational at all, but it was critical to my future development, and the lesson served me well during my time as the mayor. Our commanding officer was a colonel, not my direct boss, and was a stern, sometimes difficult man. He asked me to investigate whether the MAG Twenty-Six marines living in the barracks were getting fair treatment on their maintenance requests. (Barracks maintenance is a civilian function in support of the Marines).

Such requests were frowned upon by the civilians because in the past they had led to some ugly confrontations. The barracks maintenance operation personnel were not required to comply, but they gave the records to me when I assured them that they were for information only. I presented to the CO the records I had cautiously asked for from the civilian head, which indicated that MAG Twenty-Six was indeed being treated fairly. The CO did not see it that way and proceeded to castigate the civilian head. The CO then asked me to go back for more information, but none was forthcoming. There was no way I was getting any more records from barracks maintenance.

What I did afterward was write a memo to the executive officer, a great guy but overworked with a CO like this. I wanted to explain the situation and hoped he could help with the CO. As always, I was careful with my words and wrote a page-and-a-half memo. The next time he came into my office, I presented the memo to him. He looked at it for five seconds and cast it aside. He could not have read more than two sentences, and he clearly was not interested. He asked me about the situation but was not going to read what I thought was a well-written memo.

What I learned from this was that if you want someone to pay attention, put the punch line first and then make the arguments. I had put the well-reasoned arguments up front, leading to the conclusion on what needed to be done. He had neither the time nor the inclination to go through all of that. He was saying to me, "Just tell me what you want." If he cared, then he would want to know why.

When I was the mayor, I was known for saying to people who were talking to me and who were rambling on, "What's the point? Just tell me what you want." I did it nicely but firmly. My thought was, "I'm not a young pup in life. I will understand your request." My staff would prep people who had never talked to me before by telling them, "If he says, 'What's the point?' you've gone on too long."

The lesson for me was that in writing or briefing someone, get to the punch line quickly, then explain. It is easier for everybody and saves an enormous amount of time. By the time I became mayor, that was normal business for me.

A Difficult Tour That Paid Off

While I was at MAG Twenty-Six, I was hoping to be selected for Command and Staff College. It is a midcareer one-year school that also signifies that you are in the top echelon of majors and worthy of additional schooling for future assignments. If you have made major, then you have already proven to be a fine officer, but selection for schooling is another signal of where you stand relative to your peers. The time was right in my career for such a school, but I was not selected. I had already completed the course by correspondence but wanted in-person attendance. Not getting selected made me wonder about my future in the Corps.

I then did something that hardly any majors ever do. I asked to become the commanding officer of a recruiting station. No one joins the Marines to be assigned to recruiting duty. You want to serve your country in a meaningful role, but recruiting duty is not what any marine dreams of initially. Most majors actively avoid such duty—they run away from it if possible—because it is not a natural skill set for gung-ho officers, and if you do not do well as the commanding officer of a recruiting station, then your career is limited. You will remain a major and retire at twenty years.

The irony of this is that the recruiting service usually gets their pick of whom they want. There really are no slackers assigned to recruiting duty at any level. The Corps cannot afford to have anyone other than highly qualified people working in the general populace to bring in more marines. It just does not work. I was apparently in that range among my peers of not quite being selected for school but plenty good enough to be selected for recruiting duty. To the shock of my fellow majors, I actually requested it.

I did this because the new commandant of the Marine Corps, Charles Krulak, had recently mandated that officers who completed a successful tour of recruiting duty would get their choice of duty station or schooling. This was to incentivize the best officers to become more inclined to seek such duty. I was on board. I desperately wanted to go to Command and Staff College in person, and to do so, I was willing to volunteer for the duty that almost all majors dreaded. I wanted to be in an academic setting. I had squandered my time at Indiana University, but my intellectual curiosity was now firing on all cylinders. I was willing to serve on recruiting duty for the chance to go to school afterward.

There were forty-nine recruiting stations commanded by majors or lieutenant colonels, six recruiting districts commanded by colonels, and two recruiting regions commanded by a brigadier general (one star). The generals were also responsible for the boot camps on each side of the country (San Diego, California, and Parris Island, South Carolina).

I was assigned to become the commanding officer of the recruiting station in St. Louis, Missouri. I was in the ninth district based out of Kansas City, which was in the western recruiting region, based in San Diego. My area consisted of the southern two-thirds of Illinois and the eastern third of Missouri, a large area. The CO of a recruiting station is essentially a sales management position with a marine twist. Recruiters went to a six-week recruiting course in San Diego, and the officers went through a two-week Xerox-led sales management training course in Leesburg, Virginia. I had about forty-eight recruiting marines assigned to me along with a small staff, and I was responsible for both the enlisted and officer recruiting in this area. Fortunately, I inherited a great station. My predecessor in St. Louis was stellar, never missing his monthly quota during his three years.

Recruiting is a brutal business in the Corps, even though the marines assigned to it are usually top notch. It was frequently called thirty-six one-month tours. If you make your quota one month, you are a complete hero; if you miss your quota, you are a bum of the lowest quality and are told so. It was a tough business then. We frequently got down to the last couple of days to make our quota, but we almost always made it, and we always made our annual numbers. The very few times we did not make it in the thirty-six months, I refused to pass on some of the venom that I was subjected to. I thought my marines deserved better and, on some level, I thought maybe I could have done something more to help. I wanted them to think positively all the time if possible. It was a tough enough duty.

I was lucky that I inherited a tremendous number of professional recruiters. They kept me on an even keel. Even though marines do not join the Corps to recruit, sometimes some of them get assigned to recruiting duty and love it. If they are also good at it, they can change their military occupational specialty from their original MOS of infantry, artillery, and so on to that of recruiter, which is designated as "8412." I had some great ones.

Six months into my tour, our district commander was fired. He was a good guy, a good boss, but the district was slightly missing their numbers routinely, and the other two districts in the region had to make up the few marines that would ship to boot camp. At the time, in the mid-1990s, the Midwest was a tough area to recruit in. Without going into details, district and station quotas are determined by something called Qualified Military Available (QMA), essentially the number of young people in an area that are eligible to be recruited.

I was completely focused on making my numbers, but some who had been in recruiting much longer than I had suspected strongly that the QMA numbers around the country were not correct. Some districts did exceptionally well while others struggled. However, if the vast majority of officers in recruiting were top notch, then how could one explain the difference in some districts consistently excelling while others consistently struggled over a long period of years?

The new commanding general in San Diego, who had never served on recruiting duty, chose to believe it was strictly a leadership problem in the ninth district in Kansas City. One evening, all the station COs were either on their way or had arrived in Kansas City for a district meeting when we learned the district CO had been fired. It shook me up. All nine station COs worked hard for him; we trusted and respected him. After nearly thirty years, he was now on his way out of the Corps.

It did not take long for the general to realize he had made a mistake, but he could hardly replace the new colonel he had just put in charge. The numbers across the district went down immediately. The replacement CO was much less competent, believing that he was motivating us with his rhetoric when talk was not what was needed. More training and more technical help were needed. It really was something to observe. Although all the station COs were professional and hardworking, the district numbers just never quite matched those of the previous district CO. Chicago, St. Louis, and a few other stations continued to perform well, but the general eventually had to do something, and after a year and a half, the replacement district CO retired.

I do not know how much pressure was put on him, but I did not think the general could allow the district to continuously underperform at the level it was. At the replacement CO's retirement ceremony, he went on for more than half an hour about his thoughts and philosophies. The nine station COs just wanted to get back home and go to work.

The next district CO brought back the technical competence but not the humor of my first district CO. However, he was much easier to deal with than his predecessor because he was all business and little talk. It was a welcome change.

Long after I left recruiting, the QMA numbers were found to be incorrect. Quotas were reassigned. The ninth district suddenly got a lot better at recruiting while some of the other districts that were once stellar producers suddenly got a lot worse. I wonder how many careers were ruined because of those inaccurate QMA numbers combined with the enormous pressure of recruiting.

Besides the monthly challenge of recruiting, I was tested in other ways as the commanding officer. One incident was absolutely vital in shaping how I viewed leadership and in how I approached being the mayor. It involved an 8412 staff noncommissioned officer (staff sergeant and above) who was transferred to me to head a substation where he would lead four recruiters. He had burned some bridges at another station in the Midwest, and I was not thrilled to be getting him, but my district commander in Kansas City wanted him to come to St. Louis. Within the first month, he committed an ethics violation involving a small amount of money. The amount of money did not matter; the principle did.

This put me in a quandary. He was not a junior marine, so he should have known better, but my boss had just sent him to me, and the government had just paid for his entire family to move to the St. Louis area. When faced with a difficult leadership challenge, I would consult with people I trusted. I talked to my district commander, who told me it was my call, and I consulted with a few of my professional recruiters. I finally talked with our recruiter trainer. I asked then–Gunnery Sergeant Karl Mayfield (who later became a chief warrant officer) to come to my office to talk about the situation.

Gunny Mayfield is the type of marine you would want in any tough situation—serious about the mission, but insightfully funny. He was always joking about his lack of education but was one of the smartest and savviest marines I ever met. I knew he would tell me directly what he thought. What he told me changed how I have viewed leadership and life ever since. He looked me directly in the eye and said, "Sir, I don't want to belong to a unit with a guy like him in it."

That got my attention. I realized at that moment that if I did not discipline this marine appropriately, then I would lose the respect and the effort of all those 8412 professional recruiters who were making things happen with honor and integrity. They were proud of belonging to Marine Corps Recruiting Station St. Louis, and they did not wany anyone to tarnish its reputation.

This was my second "light-bulb moment" on leadership: "Everybody wants to be on a good team." It is a way of looking at leadership that I had not thought of before. I kept this thought close at hand when I was the mayor, both in considering the members of my administration—who to this day strongly believe they were part of a great team—but also in believing that the citizens of Indianapolis wanted to be proud of their city. I like to think I helped in that regard also.

I decided to conduct nonjudicial punishment (NJP), Article 15 in the Uniform Code of Military Justice. It is a proceeding used by commanding officers for minor offenses and below a court-martial. I called the district headquarters to get the exact specifications for the NJP. I found him guilty, imposed a minor punishment, and had him transferred.

A few months later, my district CO called to tell me that he had vacated the offense and punishment, essentially wiping away the entire proceeding. When I told him that I had gotten the exact specifications from his staff, he said he did not care. I had done everything correctly and was within my clear authority to act as I did, but that did not matter. I believe the CO did this because he wanted to keep this 8412 in his district and did not want him tainted in any way.

This became another leadership lesson for me: "There is authority, and then there is power." I had the authority to do what I did, but my district CO had the power to do what he did. It was not for me to question other than to find out why, in case I needed to do something differently in the future. Higher commands have different priorities—issues that are important to them. I understand that; there is always a bigger picture. I got back to work.

This was an important lesson for me when I was the mayor. It did not take long to find out that mayors, governors, and some other elected officials have far more power than statutory authority. Many laws are understandably meant to restrict those in office. However, with all sorts of issues and at different levels, what the mayor or governor thinks *matters*, whether there is clear authority or not.

For instance, if a developer wants to build a large project in the city, that developer wants to know what the administration thinks about it, even if the administration has no interest. If the mayor indicates he is not fond of it, that development probably will not go forward. No one has done anything wrong; it is just the way it is. Foundations ask mayors and governors what they think about certain nonprofits. Foundations are sometimes reluctant to give money if a political administration has qualms about a particular nonprofit. That is just the way it is.

Government officials must be judicious about this power. Our administration always tried to get to yes if possible; we did not try to stop much of anything as long as it made sense. However, I certainly got asked what I thought about projects routinely throughout my eight years as mayor. Knowing I had this power, I was always careful with my answers.

Another lesson that I learned in recruiting is that when someone is buying what you are selling (as in joining the Marines), you should ensure that all those individuals who have influence over that buyer are also on board. I constantly reminded my recruiters that even if a young man or woman signs on the dotted line, others like his or her mom, dad, girlfriend, or boyfriend must be on board as well. Otherwise, you may lose that individual, and then all that hard work is down the drain.

As mayor, whenever I was about to make an announcement, my people would call around the city to potential influencers to gauge their reaction before the announcement was made. Even though some of my savvier people already knew this, when I became mayor, I had to find out quickly that it is much easier to move something forward if there is little public opposition. I originally thought that the merit of the idea alone would carry it along, but that is not true. Media love the word "controversy," and they would use that word even if it meant they had found only one person who disagreed with your position. The political opposition will latch on to any "controversy" to thwart a project. However, if the major influencers in the city are on board or silent, then any political opposition will have trouble finding momentum. It is a time saver. Working to blunt opposition that has momentum is much more difficult and time consuming than if you blunt that opposition right up front.

As much as I had studied leadership up to this point in my career, it was the recruiting tour where I started to think of leadership as its own discipline, unrelated to any technical skill set. The leadership required of me during this tour was different from the experiences of a normal military leader and more applicable to my time as mayor. Most military units have the trappings of a base: the CO being in his office, troops in the barracks or conducting organized training, the PX and commissary just a few blocks away, and so on. On recruiting duty, almost everyone is living in a civilian environment and see their fellow marines only at work, so the inherent camaraderie of a military base does not exist.

Some recruiting marines have one-man offices, and they are dozens of miles away from any other marine, including their substation commander. They may see a fellow marine only two or three times a month. That is a different leadership and motivational challenge. I called it raw, naked leadership. Most of these single recruiters worked hard but were lonely, wanting to be with other marines. It was an exceedingly difficult challenge, and I tried hard to visit each of those single posts every month.

I still believe this was the toughest administrative job I ever had, including being the mayor. The hours were overwhelming, and I was not taking care of myself physically or emotionally as well as I should have. The stakes for my future and that of my family were enormous, but I came out on the right side of it. I did miss the assigned quota by very little a few months, but my station was still uniformly recognized as being in the top half of the nation. That was an excellent position to be in as the majors commanding all these stations were already considered to be top-notch officers. I was proud of my marines. Even though I had already been selected for lieutenant colonel, I still chose to attend Command and Staff College, a major's school, instead of choosing a duty station. It was a wise decision.

As soon as our household goods were packed and on their way to Quantico, Virginia, we went straight west for vacation. I badly needed to decompress. It was wonderful being with my wife and kids with no quota to worry about. Traveling through the beautiful states of Colorado and Wyoming helped tremendously. We went on to visit Winnie's family, most of whom are in California. I enjoyed all of it, but I really wanted to get to Quantico. I wanted to learn.

Two Years of Bliss

Military schools are a different environment. They are much more relaxed than regular duty stations. Students are expected to perform, but those attending Command and Staff Colleges and War Colleges are already highly motivated and eager to learn, even though they are in their thirties and forties. I was well past my unmotivated college days and was happy to be in school for a year, excited for classes to begin.

Between the time I departed St. Louis and arrived at Quantico, my number for lieutenant colonel came up. When I reported in, I told the admin office that my name was on the list, so they made me a new ID card on the spot. I was not in uniform; I had a polo shirt on. I always found it funny that my last active ID card picture was in a golf shirt.

Because of my promotion, I was the senior member of the class, the class president. There was not much to this other than introducing the guest speakers, who were usually very high-ranking civilians and military officers—and uniformly interesting—and presiding at the ceremonial "mess night." The class of about two hundred was not just marines. We also had the other services well represented, along with twenty-four foreign officers. (Any foreign officer selected for an American military school has already been designated for future high rank in their respective military). The class was broken up into twelve conference groups; each conference group was led by a lieutenant colonel (mine was air force, a great guy) and a civilian PhD holder. It was a very academic setting. The curriculum was a combination of military theory, national strategy, guest speakers, tabletop exercises and discussion within the conference groups, and some field trips.

I could not get enough of it. Some students acted as if the curriculum was too much, but they knew they were in a good spot. The reading and writing were voluminous, and we had a Berkeley professor who told me his graduate students would balk at the amount of work being assigned to us. I enjoyed it immensely. I read ten additional books that year, something I doubt anyone else did. I also got my master's degree in military science. My thesis was that China's actions today can be explained by a hundred years of embarrassment at the hands of Western powers. It can still be found online if one searches deeply. This was in 1997; about a decade later, some scholarly articles started to appear saying the same thing as my thesis. I do not know what to make of that.

I was selected as a Distinguished Graduate. That was a tough cut, and I am proud of that. I was also selected for a follow-on year of schooling at the School of Advanced Warfighting (SAW) in Quantico. This is the equivalent of the Army's School of Advanced Military Studies (SAMS). We were expected to be superior military planners after this course. Graduates of SAW, like those of SAMS, earned an unofficial title of Jedi Knight.

Graduates of these schools comprise a small group, and I was lucky to be among them.

SAW is a class of just over twenty students, again including some from other US services and foreign militaries. I worried that they would not select me for this school because of my rank, but they did. Again, I was class president, which consisted of passing along the executive director's wishes—not a lot of heavy lifting.

The well-deserved nickname for SAW was "the book-a-day club." There was little class time, but a tremendous amount of reading and writing. The days were mostly our own, but, again, we were expected to perform as elite students, and we did. It was heaven to me.

We traveled to Europe and Egypt to look over battlefields and talk to foreign officers. We were scheduled to go to Israel, but at the last minute, they told us they could not guarantee our security. We understood that.

One highlight for me was accompanying a good friend in the class as we tried to find the area where his dad had parachuted in during the Normandy invasion of World War II. It was emotional for him. The people of Normandy still treat Americans as if we liberated their country just last year. I entirely dismiss anyone who posits that the French do not like Americans.

It is difficult to overstate how much these two years of schooling positively affected me. My ability to think more clearly and more critically and to write more directly have helped me ever since. Understanding the big picture (as in national strategy) was a far cry from my lieutenant days of trying to get a vehicle out of the motor pool. I am so grateful that I was able to spend those two years in Quantico. Volunteering for recruiting duty turned out to be great just for the two years of schooling. But the payoff was about to get even larger.

Graduates of SAW are sought by high-level commands in the Corps, but they are usually looking for infantry, artillery, or air officers for their planning staffs. I was a logistician. By sheer luck, the European Command based in Stuttgart, Germany, a joint command that drew personnel from all the services, needed a plans and exercise marine logistician. I could not believe my luck. Marines rarely get stationed in Europe, and I was being offered a three-year tour. My family was ecstatic. We gladly shipped out in the summer of 1998.

The Final Tour

The European Command and similar organizations like Central Command, the Pacific Command, and others (called combatant commands) are the headquarters that control the operations in their designated areas while the services provide the forces. Most nonmilitary people believe that the services are in charge of the actual fighting, but it is these geographic combatant commands that control the operations in their regions based on guidance from the national authorities.

The European Command was exciting at first, but there was little to no leadership component and certainly no hands-on operations. It was important work, but it was office work. While doing the planning and exercises on paper, I traveled quite a bit and especially loved working with the Navy on their plans and exercises, as their European headquarters were in London. Since most of the work in London was administrative, it was nine to five during the day, and then we were free in the evening. Tough duty.

The work was fine, the people were great, and I was more than happy to be there. It is odd, though, that I remember the nonwork highlights more than the work itself. When the family moved to Stuttgart, the kids were eleven (Greg Jr.) and twelve (Erica)—perfect ages to travel. The base operations always had vacation packages available for long weekends or full weeks, and we took advantage of that. We traveled to London, Paris, Rome, Florence, and so many other great cities. These trips were great learning experiences for my kids, and I am thankful that they learned how to travel at a young age.

I was also the president of the base swim team along with coaching baseball and basketball; we had some wonderful trips from that alone as we traveled throughout Europe for these contests. It was a major thrill to have the swimmers from US bases across Europe swim their championship races in Munich—where Mark Spitz won seven gold medals in seven races and set seven world records at the 1972 Olympics (he was an Indiana University grad).

As the kids were growing up, I really wanted to spend more time with them. I felt this pull between that desire and the Marines' all-in mentality. I followed my gut instinct and decided that Stuttgart was going to be the end of my marine career. Although Winnie wanted me to stay in the Corps,

I feel that high school is important in a child's development, and I wanted to stabilize my kids in high school. If I had stayed in the Corps longer than twenty-three years, I feared that one of my kids would attend three high schools in a four-year period—something I did not want to happen. Some military parents choose otherwise, and I respect that. Military life is a sacrifice, and everyone in the family feels it. The benefits for my kids up to this point had far outweighed any downside, but I feared that would soon change. My selection board for colonel was coming up. I declined to send in the mandatory photograph, and I wrote the board telling them to not select me as I was going to retire.

We decided on Indianapolis because I wanted my kids to call Indy their hometown (and they do), my family was there, I knew the high schools, and I thought my post-marine job opportunities would be good. I had the kids take the entrance exam to Brebeuf Preparatory High School, a rigorous Jesuit high school, a year prior to leaving Stuttgart (Greg took it as a seventh grader), and neither had any difficulty with the exam. On June 22, 2001, we flew home.

I knew I was blessed to have been in so many different fields in my marine career, undergoing daunting leadership challenges in war and in peace. The variety and the intensity of these experiences were critical to any future success I would have, including as mayor of a major city.

When discussing where to live after retirement from the Corps, I told my wife, based on what I knew about terrorism in the world, I did not want to live in New York, Washington DC, Chicago, or Los Angeles. We did consider staying in Europe, but we headed to Indianapolis. It was a good call, as 9/11 happened three months after we returned to the States.

6

CIVILIAN

I WENT TO WORK IN EARLY SEPTEMBER 2001 at a Bayer Diagnostics warehouse and repair facility in Indianapolis. It was easily within my skill set and was a nice job. I was hired as the number-two person in the facility and found out soon after I started that the boss had told the employees he was hiring a retired marine. My nickname even before I started working there was Darth Vader, which I thought was hilarious. It is easier to have that sort of reputation at the start than one as a pushover. I learned in my leadership journey that it is better for a leader to start tough and then ease up rather than to start out being a nice guy and then have to get tough if the unit does not perform to expectations. It is almost impossible to maintain respect if a leader must get noticeably tougher.

On my third or fourth day of work, my boss said he was going to New York on business and that I've "got it." Technically still in the Corps (I was on terminal leave, a combination of the thirty days that the service gives you and my accumulated leave days), I was comfortable with that responsibility after twenty-three years in the Marines.

A couple of days later, an employee came into my office in the morning and said I should turn on the TV. The 9/11 attacks were happening. I watched the TV for half an hour or so and started to assess what to do. Now we all know the intent of those attacks, but that morning, most people in America had no clue what was happening, nor the extent of what was happening. As word spread of the attacks, workers in the facility were starting to panic, with many wanting to go home. My background proved fortunate, as I quickly realized the actions were asymmetric terrorist attacks on high-value targets, and that the terrorists were not coming for our facility.

I called the supervisors together and told them exactly what was happening as I saw it. I then told them to go back to their work units and explain to every person in the facility what was happening and that if anyone wanted to go home, let them. A few people did go home, but most stayed. We had medical supplies to ship out to people that were counting on them, and I thought it was important that we keep working. A few hours later, some workers were getting upset and loud, interrupting everyone else from doing their jobs. I then learned that this was the one unit whose supervisor had not briefed them on what I told all the supervisors hours earlier. This was another example in my career of failing to "inspect what you expect"—one of my own leadership principles. This maxim is especially true when it comes to communicating important information.

After a few years in this role, I was becoming less interested in the job, and it showed in my performance. Feeling like I was on a path to work fifteen or twenty years for this one company before retiring completely, I knew I wanted more than that. Similar to the reasons I joined the Corps—wanting something other than the norm—I went in a completely different direction than most.

I wrote *The Ballard Rules: Small Unit Leadership*, the first book in what was to be a series and, I hoped, a career in talking about and consulting on leadership. In addition to my marine training, I did individual research on leadership books already published. It seemed that leadership books were either general in nature or were targeted to higher-level leadership. Based on my experiences at Bayer and other companies I was observing, it seemed a simpler book was needed to help new and lower-level leaders learn the basics. It was intended primarily for that good employee who is then promoted to a team leader or supervisor position and is now in charge of five or ten people, but to whom no one has explained that this is a different skill set than just being a good employee. I published this book in 2005 and taught it wherever I could. (I republished it in 2016 and included some of my mayoral experiences and how they applied to the original book.)

While I was writing the original book and thereafter, I began teaching (primarily economics) at a local college that was more than one hundred years old but has since closed. I taught a lot of students who were what I called "educationally disadvantaged." Many of them were smart but did not realize it and did not know how to maximize it.

We had grown up poor but had parents who put a roof over our heads and food on the table as best they could. The parents of some of these students were drug addicted. They had boyfriends who beat them up. It always bothered me that there are children born with virtually no chance for success, and I was now teaching some of them. It was heartbreaking at times but also heartwarming for those who started to understand that they could do better than they had ever expected.

Again, I had a reputation as a taskmaster. Students who had me for class would warn my future students about how tough I was and that I marched them to class. It was funny. Any student I taught and who wanted to learn knew what a softie I was and the extra effort I would make to help them learn. Even though I do not drink coffee, I used a Starbucks to meet students who wanted additional help and even gave some tests there for those who had to work during a regularly scheduled test. I loved teaching. It is a time-consuming but extremely rewarding occupation.

Just as I started my leadership business and was enjoying teaching, those two gentlemen that I mentioned earlier pulled me into the mayor's race. I have always told my kids to be open to opportunities, and a big one was coming my way, but my wife needed to approve. She had been with me throughout my most trying times in the Marines. I needed her to be with me once again.

7

WINNIE

On a cold night in early December 1990, I drove my wife and our two small children to the meeting place where I was to board a bus with my fellow marines. Thus began my journey to Saudi Arabia and Desert Shield/Desert Storm, the global effort to oust Saddam Hussein from Kuwait. The headlines throughout the nation were speculating that there would be more than ten thousand US casualties in the first few days once the war began.

The drive was quiet. As I was in charge of the movement of these marines, I had duties to perform upon arrival. Winnie could not stay around for last-minute goodbyes like the families of most of the marines who were leaving with me. I told her that she should take the kids back home. To this day, I still remember the look on her face; it is seared into my memory. She really did not know if she was ever going to see me again. Were our kids in the back seat of that minivan going to grow up without remembering their dad? I have said many times that this was my most difficult day in the Marines. It remains the most emotional day in my life.

Spouses of career marines are a tough bunch. They know what they are getting into: constant moving, school changes for the kids, no career path of their own, their marine being eligible to deploy on a moment's notice. It is not for the faint of heart.

Getting to Know Her

While at Camp Pendleton, California, my first duty station after initial schooling, I opened an account at the Bank of San Clemente. San Clemente, where I lived, is on the north end of Camp Pendleton and about thirty miles from the south end of Camp Pendleton near Oceanside. San Clemente is also famous for being former president Richard Nixon's Western White House or getaway spot, although I never visited there.

I had little money and was living paycheck to paycheck as a second lieutenant, but I found myself wanting to visit the bank more often than my funds merited because of a tiny, pretty Filipina who worked there. I started taking Winnie Sarmiento to lunch or dinner when possible. Just as we started to get to know each other well, in late 1981 my unit deployed to Okinawa for six months. We wrote letters (there was no email then), and when I came back in the late spring of 1982, she picked me up from the base. I have been with her ever since. It helped that I sent two young marines from my unit, who came back a week earlier than I did, to deliver a dozen roses to her at the bank a few days before I flew back.

Winnie is the third-oldest child of eleven children, and when I met her in the early 1980s, she was living with her older sister in base housing, as her sister had married Victor Escobedo, a marine, in the Philippines. Victor then transferred to Camp Pendleton. Unlike my family, who was lower income for most of my childhood, her family in the Philippines was alternately well off and poor depending on the fortunes of a family-owned tailor shop that sold much of their product to the American military.[1]

Winnie's father died in his forties, and the family's fortunes went permanently south. When her older sister married Victor Escobedo, it began a steady transit of the Sarmiento family to America through marriage or other means, and now all of Winnie's siblings are in America, primarily California. Tragically, Victor, a wonderful man, died less than two years after his retirement from the Corps.

After I returned from Okinawa, I was soon transferred to Barstow, a couple of hours away in the middle of the California desert, for the aide-de-camp position, but this did nothing to slow my relationship with Winnie. I came back to San Clemente almost every weekend and any other time I could.

Getting Married

I never proposed to Winnie; instead, we discussed getting married while at a Wendy's in Southern California. Hardly romantic, but it worked for us.

We were married in Barstow at the small base chapel on January 2, 1983. It was a classic military wedding with my commanding officer as the best man and a sword arch for Winnie and me upon departing the church.

When we got married, I was renting a small house on an old cattle ranch turned solar farm in a tiny no-stoplight town called Daggett. We lived there only a few months before moving onto base because Winnie thought we were living in a *Friday the 13th* setting. She was not happy. We would sometimes have cows on our front porch, and there was no one near us. I loved it; she did not.

Most people do not know that Winnie has rheumatoid arthritis. From my father, I knew the potential agony of this disease. It is remarkable that I came to be with Winnie, as I was someone who could understand much of what she was going through. I went to many doctor's appointments with her, and knowing what I did, I recommended that she not do some of the treatments that were recommended, such as gold injections. I do not know everything about the body, but placing inert substances inside it, potentially hampering a future pregnancy, without complete guarantees of success, seems wrong to me. She took one or two gold injections before I intervened, and both she and I are glad she rejected further injections.

A few weeks before our wedding, Winnie's rheumatoid arthritis flared up. For a few days, she could not straighten one of her elbows, and her hands became inflamed. She was scared; so was I. Maybe it was the stress before the wedding that caused the flare-up, but it did calm down, and we proceeded.

She still had flare-ups while we were in Okinawa together, and she got serious about finding the best path forward. After reading a book, she changed her diet, which helped tremendously, and even went to a blind acupuncturist off-base on Okinawa. Since our time on Okinawa, though, her arthritis has largely been in remission.

Winnie became a naturalized citizen in the summer of 1984, while we were stationed in Barstow, prior to going to Okinawa. I had orders for a one-year unaccompanied tour, which meant the military would not pay for the family to join me. (Accompanied tours, where the family moves with the service member, are normally three-year tours and paid for by the government.) Winnie becoming a naturalized citizen was critical because the Marines would not let her go to Okinawa with me unless she was an American citizen. If she were naturalized, she might be able to join me at our expense, but such things were frowned upon, and special signatures were required.

In typical Winnie fashion, she sweet-talked the immigration officer to speed up her naturalization process so she could travel with her marine husband overseas. He helped her to answer the questions, and she received expedited processing. She also sweet-talked the marine officer who had to sign off on her joining me in Okinawa. She can be a bulldog, but with a smile on her face. While in Okinawa, Winnie and I took vacations to Thailand, Singapore, Hong Kong, Malaysia, South Korea, and the Philippines to see her family. These trips further expanded my horizons.

Throughout our marriage, she always made a point of being with me no matter what, with obvious exceptions: deployments for training, some short business trips, Panama, and the Gulf War. We just like being together, although at home we are usually in different rooms. It works for us. I told myself early in the marriage that if we were to break up for any reason, it would be my fault, because she is just too good of a person.

Our two kids, Erica and Greg Jr., were born in Michigan while I was stationed at TACOM. Each was born on the snowiest day of the year, making travel to the hospital difficult. I was lucky to get Winnie to the hospital in time for Greg's birth. We were at the doctor's office for a checkup, and he said I needed to get her to the hospital right away even though she was not having contractions. I had to quickly take Erica (then only eleven months old) back home in a driving snowstorm to drop her off with a babysitter, then take Winnie to the hospital for a forty-five-minute labor. Greg really wanted to be born.

A great military wife, Winnie kept everything going when I deployed. In truth, she did not want me to get out of the Corps. She liked the stability of the military life (I know that sounds odd to most people, but it is actually a very stable existence) and loved living on base. It is fun on base because when you move to a new duty station, there is an almost instant friendship with your neighbors as everyone around you has experienced similar situations. There is true camaraderie.

Before we were married, she was taking some college courses but was not very far along. Getting serious, she began studying for an accounting degree, eventually earning her diploma from Campbell University, a small North Carolina college that had a satellite campus at Camp Lejeune. How she did this while raising our kids with me deployed so often is something I still do not fully comprehend.

She has been the primary caregiver to our children, and they have grown up to be responsible, intelligent adults. I am prouder of this than anything else. Parenting is the most important duty once children are born, and Winnie and I took that role very seriously. We rarely went out on our own, preferring to stay home with our kids. Whenever we moved, we researched school systems as best we could and placed our kids accordingly. When needed, I mandated additional academic work outside of school. Erica and Greg did not like that at the time, but they appreciate it now. Travel supplemented their education.

Running for Mayor

Although reluctant at first, Winnie was right beside me while I was running for mayor. Not understanding all that was going on initially, she caught on quickly. However, it was not until primary night when I gave a short, well-rehearsed speech in front of four TV cameras that she realized, "Oh my God, this is happening."

By the time I decided to run for mayor, she had built up a nice clientele for her bookkeeping business, and she kept that up while I was campaigning. She would attend campaign events with me if she could, but she was also the primary breadwinner at this time. At campaign events, she was very effective, shy but nice, and people were drawn to her.

The most disturbing part of the campaign for Winnie were the Democratic blogs. Blogs were new then and largely unfiltered. (I guess they still are). I mostly did not read them, but Winnie did, and they affected her greatly. It was bad enough that they were saying terrible, untruthful things about me, but then they started attacking our kids, who were in college at the time. It left Winnie crying more than once, wondering why these people would attack our kids. I had to think long and hard about whether to stay in the race, knowing how this was affecting my wife. It was horrible. This sort of campaign activity explains why some wonderful people do not run for office. Fortunately, I had some people on the Republican side who convinced the offenders to knock it off.

After I won in 2007, Winnie had lots of new political friends who urged her to take up a cause as the first lady. They were well meaning, but it was a bit much, especially considering her unfamiliarity with the political system. Confused and a bit afraid, she listened respectfully but did not know what to do. I eventually told her that she could do anything she wanted. "If you want to stay home, then stay home. If you want to work, then work. If you want to be with me, then be with me. It is your life."

Another thing that she was told was to stay in the background; people want to see just the elected official, not the spouse. I guess this was normal for most politicians, but it was not for me or her. I quashed this notion almost immediately. I told my team that Winnie and I were empty nesters, and if Winnie wanted to go with me, then she would go with me. I instituted an unofficial rule: if you want me after 5:00 p.m. or on the weekend, then Winnie will be with me. That's the way it is.

The most amazing thing happened. After about a year, if I went to a public lunch or other event during the day without Winnie, people started asking, "Where's Winnie?" The city had come to expect to see Winnie with me and wanted her to be with me. She became a great asset. I was told frequently that she was the most visible first lady in Indianapolis that anyone could remember, and she became quite beloved by almost everyone, just by being herself. For the first four years, we were out six nights a week, sometimes to multiple events per night, but she was happy to be with me and happy to represent the city. One old-time politico constantly told me that she was my most important vote-getter.

A few months into our administration, Winnie gave up her bookkeeping business to be a more active first lady for the city. She had made a steady income and was quite happy with her small business and her clients, but she gave it up to be with me. Of course, the family also gave up that income over the eight years. Some do not realize the financial sacrifice that many officeholders make. We were not rich, but Winnie wanted to be my partner in this endeavor. It worked out for us and for the city.

After getting more comfortable with me being the mayor, she decided to promote financial fitness in the city. With her training as an accountant, this made sense. She found willing partners, many of whom had been working on this issue for years. She also became good friends with Kate McKnight of the Internal Revenue Service, who provided extremely valuable advice and training. Kate was a treasure.

The financial fitness program consisted of three pillars:

- *Bank On Indy*—Partnering with almost all the banks and credit unions in the city, Bank On Indy emphasized getting the unbanked to use traditional banking systems. With an estimated eighty thousand unbanked in the city, she and her team were able to get 10 percent of them, about eight thousand people, into traditional banking systems the first year.

- *Financial Education*—Much of this work was already being done through community centers, nonprofits, and other organizations. Winnie's program brought more visibility, and more people, to these efforts.
- *Free Tax Preparation*—Winnie's program with the IRS trained twenty or thirty individuals in tax preparation each year, which was then provided free to those earning less than $50,000 a year. These free tax preparation services were provided at senior citizen homes, community centers, parks, the City-County Building, and other places. It was a huge hit. Winnie also got trained every year and provided free tax preparation along with the others. She would always tell me stories about how surprised people were when they learned their taxes were being prepared by the first lady of Indianapolis. To this day, Winnie still does free tax preparation for a few individuals she met through this program.

That Winnie, who was not born in the United States and was unfamiliar with anything political until I got elected, had this much influence to help others in this way was remarkable. It speaks well for her and the city of Indianapolis.

Winnie also began a "Walk with Winnie" series, emphasizing physical fitness through walking. It was fun to see a few dozen women and men walk with my wife as part of this program. This was also part of her being very visible throughout the city of Indianapolis. People loved being with her.

A wonderful benefit to having a wife who is an accountant is that I never do taxes anymore. Ever since she received her degree, I've just signed the tax forms; Winnie does all the work. She also does all the banking and has from the very beginning of our marriage. This is common in military families, as the service member can deploy at any time; the spouse must know everything about the household. I have not seen a paycheck in over three decades, and other than doing some investing, I have no idea about the flow of money in our household. Winnie does it all.

When I decided to not run for office for a third term, Winnie understood and was supportive. Of course, when I made the official announcement at the City Market in late 2014, she stood next to me. Just before I said the words, I looked at her. She was sad, and for a fleeting moment, I thought I might change my mind, but I knew in my heart that it was time for us to move on.

Note

1. The United States and the Philippines have had a long relationship, dating to 1898 when Spain ceded the Philippines to the United States after the Spanish-American War. Despite some violent episodes, the relationship between the two countries has been mostly cordial and close, with America granting Filipino independence soon after World War II in 1946. US Navy and Air Force bases in the postwar area, closed in the 1990s, contributed to the closeness of that relationship.

8

THE CAMPAIGN

Never tell a marine he can't take that hill.

Old marine saying

EARLY IN THE SUMMER OF 2007, the *Indianapolis Monthly* magazine ran an article about the power players in Indianapolis in business, sports, health, politics, etc., and prominently displayed was the incumbent mayor, with the magazine mentioning his potential for higher office. It casually said that he faced "token opposition" in the fall. I was that token opposition.

On primary night, I delivered my well-rehearsed, three- or four-minute statement almost flawlessly. Every TV station had its cameras focused on me; they were just a few feet in front of me, along with print and radio reporters. I had never experienced anything like this before, and I felt self-conscious. Up until this point, there was almost no media coverage of the Republican effort to take back the mayor's office; everyone in the political arena knew for sure that the incumbent would win easily.

The county party wanted a decent candidate who would not embarrass them. But they did not expect to win the mayor's race in 2007. They gave me an office, and I was able to tap into some previous campaign workers who worked full time in other jobs but still wanted to help when possible with press releases and messaging (Lisa Kobe), along with fundraising—no matter how difficult this was (Tara Shaver). However, other than Kyle Walker, then executive director of the Marion County Republican Party, the county apparatus was mostly hands-off for this campaign. Kyle proved to be invaluable not just for his advice but also simply for letting me know that someone from the party would help me. I understood the reluctance from others who did not want to invest in a losing effort, but Kyle was there throughout the entire campaign.

The issues in mayoral elections in most American major cities center on public safety, education, and concerns surrounding taxes and the budget. Sometimes, infrastructure comes into play. For my first election, the property tax issue playing out in Indiana in 2007 affected every mayoral election across the state, even though the people who could and would eventually change the property tax laws (state legislators) were not up for election until 2008. Individual/family and business property tax bills were in complete disarray. People not only had quickly escalating property tax bills but also did not know what their tax bill would be from year to year, causing great havoc in families and businesses. No one could plan an annual budget because no one knew what the Indiana property tax hit would be. This had the great effect (for me) of having the citizens pay more attention than usual to who was in office and what they were doing with tax dollars.

Before I had a campaign manager, Arne Pedersen, a friend and fellow Gulf War veteran, and I put our heads together to come up with a balanced scorecard for the city if I were to win, summarizing the areas we thought were important. The scorecard we produced proved not to be an accurate picture of what became important in running the city, but the effort was worthwhile to get my head more into the game.

We also came up with "The Ballard Rules" for the city, the title being a takeoff of my leadership book. This list held up well and provided insight as to how I would govern. It also told my future staff how I thought about what elected officials should be thinking about.

1. Public safety is Job #1.
2. Local government officials should make financial decisions based on the welfare of the city ten to fifty years out.
3. The education level expected of children reflects the priority of its citizens and government.
4. Community welfare is a direct result of private companies wanting to call Indianapolis home.
5. Citizens are proud of their city, but they live in their neighborhoods.

Little attention was paid to these Ballard Rules. They never caught on across the city, but they were important to me; I feel that I held to them all eight years in office.

By primary night in May, I knew that this was to be a low-budget operation, but frankly I did not realize just how low budget. Along with a shoestring operation comes a low level of organization. It was not chaotic, but it was small time and reactive. My opponent would spend $4 million. Heading into October, a month before the election, I had about $50,000.

My first campaign manager was a serious lady and a seasoned political worker. She had me doing traditional candidate activities, such as dialing for dollars (phone calls to raise money). I was given huge lists of former Republican campaign donors to call, but it did not take long to understand that no one was going to donate to my campaign through phone calls. The lists included some Democrats who had donated to the previous campaign of the governor (Republican Mitch Daniels, a superior intellect and public servant).

One call was to a lawyer who was also the head of the Indiana Democrats' fundraising arm. He was nice enough to me, but when he identified himself as the head of the Democrats' fundraising operation, I said to him, "Well, I guess this call is not going to go my way." He laughed (he is a nice guy) and said I was right. In many cases, both Republicans and Democrats will give to the other party in the name of their business, but then donate personally to the candidate of their party. That's how he came to be on a Republican list.

However, it was also clear that, phone calls or not, most Republicans were not going to donate to my campaign. First, people who donate to campaigns, Republicans or Democrats, do not like to donate their money to a sure loser, which is what I looked like at this time. Second, the incumbent administration had slyly put out the word that if anyone doing business with the city donated to my campaign, they would be cut off from future contracts. (I did not do this to my opponent for my reelection). These two realities ensured that fundraising was going to be a mostly futile effort.

There were exceptions. The late Steve West, head of a philanthropic organization and a former city-county councilor, donated a big sum early to help get me going. When I went back to him to ask for more, he gladly donated the same amount, but I can still see him with his face down and held by his big hands, saying, "Why won't the Republican Party support its candidate for mayor?"

Local legend P. E. MacAllister, founder of MacAllister Machinery and a noted scholar and philanthropist, also chipped in with a nice sum. A local group of Republican women, Women in Neighborhood Service (WINS), donated nicely early on.

Bob Grand, then the local managing partner of a prominent law firm, tried hard to raise money for me and even held a fundraiser at his house. I often joked with Bob that he could make a few phone calls for Governor Daniels and raise enormous sums of money but make dozens of calls on my behalf and not reach $20,000. However, I never forgot his efforts, and he is a good friend to this day.

This was also my baptism in understanding the law firms in the city. When I began running, I had no clue who the law firms were. I'd never needed to know. I was later accused by the local newspaper, the *Indianapolis Star*, of showing favoritism to Bob's firm, Barnes and Thornburg, but the truth is I knew Bob because our kids ran cross-country together in high school. I did not know what he did for a living. It was only much later that I realized just how influential he was, but he also worked his way up from the bottom to get where he is today. He is a wonderful, philanthropic man, doing much more for those less fortunate than most people know.

These fundraising efforts helped to keep the lights on in the campaign, but we were not anywhere close to raising enough money for a serious campaign that would include TV commercials and a mail effort. Dialing for dollars was not working at all. To this day I hate using the phone to ask for anything. We did try to get the press to cover us by using all sorts of angles (known as "earned media"), including a bizarre press conference that wondered if Indianapolis was running out of water. We were never sure that anyone in the press was going to show up, but every effort netted us at least one TV camera.

However, I wondered if getting earned media was helping us or hurting us because of the randomness of the efforts. Some of it was comical. We held a press conference at an abandoned house in a rough neighborhood, and one TV reporter showed up. As soon as I was done with my remarks (two minutes), he looked at me and said, "Greg, we better get out of here; it isn't safe here." We left quickly.

Eventually, I realized that the campaign was not moving us forward and that traditional methods of getting our message out were not going to work. I asked Tom John, the new county party chairman, what I should do. He was good friends with my campaign manager and graciously took it upon himself to tell her that I wanted to move in a different direction. I was still politically naive at this point and hoped this was the correct move.

Tom found John Cochran, a third-generation lawyer who did not have much desire to be a traditional lawyer. We also brought in Kurt Fullbeck, a full-time college student, to help us. Since Kurt could help us only occasionally, I dubbed our group Two and a Half Men, after a TV show I enjoyed watching.

We stopped dialing for dollars. Instead, to get my name known, I just started attending every neighborhood group and business group meeting—any type of group meeting that I could. I was usually not asked to speak since in most cases no one knew who I was. Once I sat quietly through a two-hour land use meeting in the Allisonville area. Afterward, when most people had left, the leaders of the meeting asked me who I was. I told them that I was the Republican candidate for mayor. They seemed pleased to meet me and were nice to me. Although I sensed that they felt that my campaign was a lost cause, I could also tell that they were impressed that I sat through their two-hour meeting that evening just to learn about their issues.

Starting in July or so, I attended some sort of meeting almost every evening (there are about three hundred neighborhood groups in Indianapolis) and also attended some breakfast and lunch meetings. As the citizenry became more and more upset about the property tax issue, I was actually invited to some meetings where I was expected to talk. I had a routine talk about how we could do better, and as long as I was presentable and could put two sentences together coherently, the response was positive. I did not know how much of an effect I was having, but I came to find out that once you attend a neighborhood or business meeting, the citizens pass on to their friends and neighbors that you were there.

Winnie could attest that this method of campaigning was very tiring; almost every night, I was asleep within a half hour of coming home. It was an exhausting endeavor, and although I am introverted, these meetings were much more in line with who I was than picking up a phone and asking strangers for money—which no one was going to give me anyway.

I also attended a lot of fairs and similar events throughout the summer. This is where my introversion was tested. Before this campaign, I cannot ever recall going up to a complete stranger and starting a conversation. This was expected of candidates, yet I could not imagine myself doing it. My first campaign manager told me to get over it and do it.

My first test was at the St. Anthony's fair. With my wife, who stayed by my side for support, I went up to a table at the fair. I was wearing a badge saying that I was a candidate for mayor, and I introduced myself as the Republican candidate. To my utter shock, everyone at that table was very nice and wanted to talk a bit. I continued going around to the other tables, trying to get a read on who would be most receptive, but mostly everyone was friendly and ready to talk. I thought to myself how much of life I had missed by being too shy to go up to talk to people. As a result, to this day I have no fear of going up and talking to people I have never met before. Almost everyone is very receptive. I never knew. I do now.

The most important result of this method of campaigning was that I was hearing firsthand what the citizens thought of their city and what they wanted for themselves and their neighborhoods. It was eye opening. By talking to people individually and attending the various meetings, I could develop these issues in my mind. As I was hearing directly what average citizens thought, patterns started to emerge. The issues I repeatedly heard about were quite similar to what Arne Pedersen and I talked about months before. The Ballard Rules held up well against what I was hearing. but it became clear that some issues were much more top of mind than others.

My campaign messaging, which few people had even heard at this point, changed as the summer moved on. When asked to speak, I mostly repeated what I was hearing in the meetings. I just repeated it with different words.

I also had the fortune to be a routine guest on the Greg Garrison radio show during the campaign. Greg, already famous for his prosecution of boxer Mike Tyson, had a large, mostly conservative morning audience, and his station, WIBC, was the largest in the city and state. I could get the word out to his audience without rebuttal because my opponent would not go on his show. I appeared frequently and went on his show as much as he would have me. Although most of his audience leaned in my direction, it helped me to get better at messaging and more focused in my approach. It was also helpful in convincing Republicans in Indianapolis who might have believed that my campaign was a lost cause to get out and vote. Greg was very helpful, and it is difficult to thank him too much for what he did for me during the campaign. He also, in concert with others, threw me a fundraiser.

Some issues came forward that I had not thought of. The only time that the issue of ex-offenders came up was at a brunch at a Black church. One lady got up to speak for fifteen seconds and said something like "If we really want to do something about crime in the city, we should look at how we treat ex-offenders." I had never heard that before and did not hear it again for the remainder of the campaign. Because no one else brought up this topic, I did not make this part of my message, but I did start to research it, and she was correct. Once in office, I acted on this fifteen-second comment. I believe that we brought more focus and action to this issue than anyone before.

There were other things I wanted to do if I became mayor, such as making Indianapolis a more global city—an urban Republican concept. I knew that American cities had to compete in a global economy, not just with each other. However, this was not something I heard on the campaign trail at the meetings I attended, so I kept this issue and some others to myself. This was just smart campaigning: don't bring up issues that people are not passionate about and don't want to talk about during the campaign. You can address those issues once in office.

Although the campaign messaging was effective, the overall audience remained tiny. We had no mail effort and, at this point, never imagined that I would be able to do commercials on TV. My incumbent opponent dominated the airwaves and the print media beginning in August. I was still an afterthought in the media's eyes and in most of the people's eyes. I kept attending meetings.

The property tax issue grew over the summer of 2007. Although property taxes are primarily a state issue, I started attending many of the rallies protesting the erratic and mostly escalating property tax system. This was the time of the national Tea (Taxed Enough Already) Party getting its legs. In Indianapolis, I attended a protest where people brought their property tax bills, which were collected into a large bag and then dumped into a river. I attended several events that railed against property taxes and started gaining some name recognition. The people were mad and were willing to take it out on anyone in office. (Again, Indiana state elections are held in even-numbered years, so state officeholders were not at risk. But they were paying attention.) This helped me.

A Big Break

Although the campaign had little money, we had decided that our yard signs (if we had money to buy them) would read "Had Enough?" This was not only a nod to the property tax issue but also to an increasing homicide rate in the city. However, it was prescient considering what happened in August 2007.

Despite escalating property tax revenue, the incumbent administration concluded that they needed even more income and proposed to raise income tax levels in the city 65 percent, from 1 percent to 1.65 percent. On top of the property tax fiasco, this was too much for many citizens of Indianapolis.

The fact that the incumbent administration would propose such an increase about three months before an election gives some indication of just how comfortable the incumbent administration felt and how much of an underdog I was. Throughout the summer, people were howling about property tax increases, and now the city was going to raise income taxes 65 percent. It might have been comfortable from the incumbent administration point of view, but to many citizens, it was arrogance. This feeling was compounded by the actions of the Democrat-led city-county council.

The mayor presents the next year's budget to the council each August. As the 65 percent income tax increase proposal became widely known prior to the budget presentation, hundreds of people wanted to attend the budget presentation to make their feelings known. The budget presentation is normally a low-key, uncontroversial event, but in 2007, it was anything but. People lined up early to get in, and it was clear that there would not be enough seats for everyone to attend. I got there very early to watch the presentation and got in, much to my surprise. However, several hundred would not be able to enter the council's chambers.

Just prior to the council meeting, word had spread to the members of the council of the burgeoning attendance numbers. There was tension. The council president then made an unbelievable decision—not just to limit the room to capacity, but actually to lock the doors to the City-County Building. At that time, the front doors to the City-County Building were open twenty-four hours a day, seven days a week, but they were shut for this meeting. It was a very hot, humid, and uncomfortable day, well above 90 degrees, and the hundreds of people who were denied entry to the building were furious.

This became the story. Although the local political media were in the council chambers for the budget presentation, more media began to show up with TV cameras outside of the City-County Building, interviewing those who were denied entry. If people perceived the income tax increase as arrogance, closing the doors to the people's building was absolutely over-the-top, tone-deaf arrogance. All of this helped me tremendously. "Had Enough?" was right.

After this evening, one businessman in the city was so fed up that he made up yard signs on his own and put them on his front porch downtown for people to take. This was also when, on their own, people began knocking on doors across the city on my behalf, telling voters that it was time for a change. (I found this out after the election.) My aunt Catherine kept asking me for business cards (over one thousand, as I recall), which she would hand out to complete strangers, saying, "This is my nephew, and you should vote for him." None of these efforts were coordinated with my campaign or the party. On their own, people just started taking action.

Still, money was not coming in.

The Debates

After the doors of the City-County Building were locked that evening, the tone of the campaign changed. I had no money to conduct polling, but something felt different. The Democrats had money to conduct polling; I found out after the election that this was the period when they realized they were in trouble. The property tax fiasco, the income tax increase, and locking the citizens out of their own building was taking a toll.

Even though people were getting increasingly angry at the incumbent administration, I still had to prove that I was capable of being the mayor of a major city in America. Of some surprise to John Cochran and me, Mayor Peterson agreed to four debates. The last thing that someone leading by thirty points in a campaign wants to do is to give name recognition to his opponent. John and I still believed that we were far behind and wondered why he would agree to giving me four free shots on TV. Perhaps they believed that I could not handle the pressure of live debates, but, as nervous as I was about the prospect, I also realized they had to be done. And I had to perform respectably.

We prepared as best as we could, but there is little to prepare you for a live debate if you have not done one before. I did debate for one year in high school, and that may have helped a bit, but what was more beneficial to me was the use of affirmations that I had begun using a few months earlier.

The college where I was teaching before the campaign brought in an outside consultant for its employees. One of their presentations involved the use of affirmations—in essence, rewiring your brain to think and behave differently. I had never done this before and was not sure I believed in it, but it did work for me. No one knew I was doing this, but I did it routinely from about June and on through the election.

The key is to determine the right affirmations and to say them aloud several times a day. Early in the campaign, knowing that I was expected to lose, I began my affirmations with "I am a respectable candidate for mayor of Indianapolis." I also had a few other lines, like "I speak clearly and distinctly," along with other affirmations that I felt I needed help with. I was trying to work on my weaknesses and build my confidence.

Despite what others were publicly saying about me, I became a respectable candidate for mayor. However, as I grew more confident, I changed that first affirmation. "I am the mayor of Indianapolis," I told myself several times a day. This was a much more direct and confident belief, and I felt that in the last few months of the campaign I *acted* like the mayor of a major city. That said, I still had to learn on the fly many of the skills required to succeed.

The first debate was on Channel 8 with longtime political reporter Jim Shella. Mayor Peterson, Libertarian candidate Fred Peterson, and I were all invited to the debate. It helped that there were three of us instead of two; I was not alone in my inexperience with this forum. What was disconcerting about this debate was that we were to look at Jim when he asked the questions and then turn to a camera to answer the question. I was experienced in talking to audiences but not to a lifeless camera ten feet in front of me. I felt awkward, and I am sure some of that showed on TV. That said, I passed the test. Although most would believe that the incumbent "won" the debate, my job was to look like I could handle the job. I believe I did that.

One big mistake I made was agreeing to do a radio interview live just before the first debate. Many people know that introverts, after being around people, need to recharge. I went to the debate from the interview with little time in between. My energy level was lower than it should have been. I did not make that mistake again, taking three or four hours off before each of the final three debates.

In the other debates, I more than held my own. My opening statement in one of the later debates was bold. I called out the misconduct of one councilor. This misconduct was common knowledge within political circles but was allowed to happen. I said that I was not running against that councilor, but that the mayor knew of this situation. I was shocked that during the entire debate, he did not address my damaging opening statement.

During the debates, I also brought up that the Democrat-led council, in a truly arrogant fashion, passed the budget with seven blank pages. That sounds unbelievable, but it was true. By way of explanation, the council just said that they would fill in those pages as needed. This is how comfortable the Democratic majority in the city was then. I talked about this not just in the debates but everywhere I could.

After two of the debates, I thanked Mayor Peterson for his service to the city. I have always admired those in public service, and I wanted him to know that I was thankful for his service. He thanked me for those comments but never said much of anything else. His reaction made me think that he did not want to be going through the campaign process again. Eight years later, I knew that feeling.

The debates combined were probably a draw, but that meant that the people of Indianapolis saw me as a possible mayor. I held my own in these debates, and it paid off. There were other hurdles, though.

Mayoral candidates in Indianapolis traditionally go before the *Indianapolis Star* editorial board to be questioned. John and I talked about this and agreed that no matter what we did, the editorial board was not going to endorse an unknown, inexperienced (in their eyes) candidate for mayor. We did no preparation for the editorial board. Zero. I went in there and talked about needing to do more on public safety, and that was about it. They asked a few questions, and I gave them the best answers I could, but again, we did not prepare because we knew they would not endorse me. At the end, the editor told me that I really had not given them anything of substance, which was largely true.

They endorsed my opponent as expected, but the *Star* mentioned that I had no leadership experience at all. That sounds devastating, but it proved to be a blessing. If the people of Indianapolis knew anything about me, they knew I was a twenty-three-year marine veteran. The comment about no leadership experience did not sit well with the large veteran community in the area, nor with others. It was a slap in the face. Fortunately, my opponent started to use that phrase in his campaign, including using the *Star* quote in TV commercials. It helped me tremendously, as emails rocketed throughout the veteran community castigating the *Star* for such a quote.

This resulted in even more name recognition for me and hurt my opponent for using the *Star*'s claim against me.

In the last month of the campaign, I could feel that something was happening. The Peterson campaign started attacking me more directly, then much more so the last two weeks of the campaign, further increasing my name recognition. Political insiders know that negative ads from the supposed leading candidate are an indication that the election is close. Maybe the poor poll numbers for the incumbent (from their own polls) started to leak, but there was clearly a much different feel to the campaign. More Democrats whispered in my ear, "I've never voted for a Republican in my life, but I'm going to vote for you." Money started to show up.

One wonderful gentleman that I had never met sent me $10,000. I called him to thank him, and he sent me another $10,000, even though I did not ask for it. I was walking downtown one day in the last month of the campaign, and, out of the blue, a gentleman gave me a check for $2,000. Another near-downtown businessman called me to see if I would visit him. I did that day, and he gave me a check for $2,000, asking for nothing in return. He just wanted a new direction for the city. Lots of checks for ten to fifty dollars started coming in. Things like this were happening frequently in the last few weeks. I had made an impression in the debates, and people who wanted a change in the mayor's office were now willing to invest. It was heady stuff for the campaign run by Two and a Half Men.

I eventually was able to report about $200,000 cash on my campaign reports, but two-thirds of that money came in the last two weeks of the campaign. It came so fast compared to all the previous fundraising efforts of the past six months, and we had to find ways to use that money to further our efforts. We never thought we would be able to do commercials on TV, but now we thought we might be able to buy some ad time.

We filmed our first, then semifamous commercial in the basement of my house. One of the guys in my regular golf foursome is a videographer. I had met some film production types who brought lighting and a teleprompter, and a couple of other film professionals were there to help with presentation. No one was paid; it was all volunteer. I wrote the thirty-second script, including the words "This election should not be about Democrats or Republicans," which made the county party uncomfortable, but as I've mentioned, other than Kyle Walker, the county apparatus was mostly absent during the campaign. On some level, it did not matter what they thought. I had a rendition of the Iwo Jima flag raising in the background to remind people of my marine service. It was low budget but effective, and we got a commercial on the air with five days to go before the election. My opponent had been on TV for months.

Here's what I said:

> I'm Greg Ballard.
> This election should not be about Democrats or Republicans.
> To me, it's about the future of our city.
> Taxes are the highest they've ever been. Seniors and young families are scared of losing their homes, and crime is still on the rise.
> You deserve leadership that is open, honest, and accountable.
> I don't care about the politics.
> I care about this city, and I know you do also.
> So join me in putting Indianapolis back on its path to greatness.
> I ask for your vote on November 6.

While we were quickly planning that first commercial, enough money came in that we could make a "professional" commercial. We did so using pictures from my family, including one that I had someone on the street take, with a cheap camera, of me, Winnie, and the kids in Bloomington while Winnie and I visited Erica and Greg at college. The production company put it all together, and if I recall correctly, this one got on TV with four days to go before the election.

Even though it was very late in the campaign, both commercials were what one would call "introductory" commercials that politicians would normally use early in a campaign. It worked to our advantage. My opponent's voluminous campaign commercials attacking me frequently were shown just before my family-friendly, positive commercials. The contrast could not have been starker. Since no favored candidate goes negative unless it is a tight race, those following the race now knew it was close. Again, we had no poll data to support that, but my opponent did.

The state party, which had been completely absent in the capital city's mayoral race, suddenly found money to help with the get-out-the-vote (GOTV) effort. I do not know if this was because they were getting pummeled publicly by people like loyal Republican Greg Garrison on the radio—or did they now realize that I might win?

Near the end of the race, I told my campaign manager, John Cochran, to not let me make a big mistake on TV. Video can be shown again and again in a devastating manner. I had not given my opponent anything to work with in this regard, and I did not want my inexperience with TV to change that.

Winning

At first during the campaign, I was awkward and inexperienced. I learned quickly, becoming steady in my approach. I kept my errors to a minimum and let the taxpayer revolt play out to its inevitable conclusion. There was power in letting events evolve naturally. I was never flashy; flashy does not win in Indiana. We ran a good campaign with very few resources.

With two weeks to go, I was getting very confident that I was going to win. I doubt that most in the city felt the same way, but four days before the election, I told Joe Loftus, former mayor Steve Goldsmith's deputy mayor, that he would be the first call I would make after the election. He graciously said, "I'd be honored to take that call." I knew he would help me in the transition.

PART II
MAYOR AND BEYOND

The former governor of Indiana Mitch Daniels was fond of saying, "We need elected officials who want to do something, not be something." When I look back on what we accomplished, I am struck by how obvious many of these actions were, but also by the immense challenges involved in tackling the most difficult and complex issues. I felt that we were put into office to do all those things that had been kicked down the road, either for financial or political reasons. I frequently told local audiences that I was the least political mayor they were ever going to have, so they had better take advantage of it while I was in office. I meant it. We faced our challenges head on. I remain proud that our team accomplished so much.

Our paradigm of attracting talent accounted for how nearly all our actions came to fruition. Businesses move to where the talent is. There is true competition between cities and states to attract companies, and you can see that being played out every day in the economic development departments in city and state governments. Cities and states, unlike the federal government, cannot print money to extend payment on debts. Therefore, expanding the tax base within cities and states is paramount if the level of services and social programs is to remain viable, even robust. Police, fire, parks, public works, and a host of other programs must be paid for, and those bills get more expensive every year. Without a continuing expansion of the tax base, services decline.

Democrats complain routinely about companies making profits, but if the social services Democrats demand are to be paid for, companies must make profits and expand their businesses. Otherwise, those companies go out of business, and the government tax base declines. Eventually that means fewer services.

To build a high quality of life in a city, the basics must be strong, and the amenities must be robust. That is what we tried to build in Indianapolis. Many people agreed we were doing just that. Below are just some of the comments about the direction of Indianapolis while I was mayor.

- #1 Next Big Boom Town in the Midwest (*Forbes*, 2011)
- Top Ten City to Start a Business (*Kiplinger*, January 2013)
- #1 City in America for College Graduates (Creditdonkey.com, 2013)
- 4th Best City in USA for High-Tech Industry Job Growth (*Forbes*, 2013)
- Top Convention City in America (*USA Today*, 2014)
- Top Ten Metro for Job Growth (*The Urbanophile*, 2013)
- #1 in Top 10 Best Downtowns (Livability.com, 2014)
- Best US City to See from a Bicycle Seat (Away.com, 2012)
- Top Metro for Exports in 2012 (US Department of Commerce)
- 4th Best Large Metro Area for Home Ownership (Nerdwallet.com, 2014)
- Top 52 Places to See in the World (*New York Times*, 2014), thanks to the Cultural Trail*
- Lucas Oil Stadium—"Best Sports Experience in the World" (Stadium Journey, 2014)*
- Best Airport in North America, routinely awarded annually (Airports Council International)*

* *Started before I was mayor; completed while in office.*

We received such recognition because we believed in the future of our city. Much of what we did was difficult, but our team was determined to tackle everything that we could. We got to yes and figured out how to complete projects that others could not.

The next chapters list some of what we accomplished. Many were high profile, some less so. To this day, I am still amazed at the breadth of accomplishments. My team was amazing.

9

PUTTING THE TEAM TOGETHER

Transition

After that amazing evening on election night, the TV cameras came. Not only did the local TV stations interview me at my house the next morning, but some national media asked to talk to me as well. This was an indication of just how big the upset was, as almost all large cities in America were (and are) led by Democrats. It was a national story. I remember fulfilling all the media requests, but I also knew that I had to rest a bit and then get down to business.

The day after the election was mostly for personal time. After the TV cameras left, I went to get a haircut, and some of the press followed me there. I'm not sure the Nora Barber Shop ever had one of its customers being filmed while getting a haircut. The framed article from the *Indy Star* remained on their wall for years. Outside the barber shop, I ran into a former candidate for the US House who congratulated me profusely. This was a scene that was repeated throughout the day wherever I went.

I made a point of going to my dad's grave to tell him that I had won. Unbelievably, two of my brothers were already at the grave when Winnie and my mother arrived with me. They also wanted to tell Dad what had happened. One of my brothers had on our campaign T-shirt and opened his coat so we could see it as we walked up. The press who were following us around that day took that photo. The family talked among themselves while the press respectfully kept their distance. I very much appreciated their respect around my father's grave.

With a day's rest, John Cochran and I met with Joe Loftus. The meeting was not quite like the final scene from Robert Redford's *The Candidate*, where the underdog but victorious US Senate candidate says to his campaign manager, “What do we do now?” but it was close enough. I was sitting at my desk in the Republican county headquarters, and John and Joe were sitting in chairs in front of me. John was not sure how to proceed, with one of his legs moving up and down nervously. I tried to reassure him that we would just think through this process step by step to put our administration together.

Having never done this sort of thing before, I was not sure how to proceed either, but in my mind, if we had just pulled off this upset election win, then surely we could figure out how to put a team together. In retrospect, it was far more a case of “We don’t know what we don’t know.” We had no idea of the complexities of putting an administration together.

Then the moment happened. After five minutes or so of me and John talking back and forth, Joe Loftus, as only he can do with his low-key demeanor and dry wit, calmly said to both of us, “If I may.” He opened his briefcase and gave us the entire transition plan in detail. You could almost see John’s heartbeat drop to normal. I am sure my demeanor changed also. This was just the first of many silent, brilliant accomplishments that Joe Loftus would pull off.

Soon thereafter on a Saturday, about two hundred of the city’s most brilliant and experienced public servants, lawyers, and businesspeople met at the Barnes and Thornburg offices to go over the transition for this previously unknown, long-shot candidate for mayor. I might have known five of them. It was a humbling experience. They wanted me and the city to succeed, and they were willing to put in the time and effort to get our administration headed in the right direction. I can honestly say that even during my toughest times being the mayor, I never felt alone. That feeling began with this Saturday meeting that made me realize just how deeply all these people felt about the success of Indianapolis.

This group started working with the departments of the outgoing administration as best they could, asking pertinent questions and finding the departments’ strengths and areas where improvement was needed. They ultimately provided me binders stretching over two feet wide of relevant information. It was a textbook transition in many regards, and it is difficult to convey just how professional this process was.

Unfortunately, the outgoing administration would not allow anyone on the twenty-fifth floor except for Bob Grand. The twenty-fifth floor houses the mayor’s office and his closest colleagues such as deputy mayors and economic development. There was going to be no turnover in these areas. Also, for some reason, the incumbent mayor would not meet with me except for one fifteen-minute meeting. I do not know the reason for all the secrecy around the twenty-fifth floor, but it was not the outgoing administration's finest moment. It seemed out of character.

It got worse when I finally entered the twenty-fifth-floor offices on inauguration day. The contents of the office supply cabinet were sprawled out onto the floor as if there was an explosion. The tiny kitchen was trashed with debris and food stains. Ladies from Women in Neighborhood Service (WINS) volunteered to clean it up. It took four women four hours to clean a space that was about ten feet by ten feet. When we arrived on January 1, most offices had no papers in them at all, emblematic of the no-turnover policy on the twenty-fifth floor and ensuring that my senior staff would be starting from scratch.

I asked my staff to not comment publicly on the situation on the twenty-fifth floor, even though my more political-leaning staff wanted me to comment or at least have it leaked to the press. I would not let that happen, and I also informed them that I did not want anyone in our administration blaming anything else on the previous administration.

This thought goes back to my military background, where once you take a position, it is your responsibility alone; there is no looking back to blame your predecessor. So I also was not fond of incoming politicians blaming current conditions on their predecessors. It was a cop-out to me. I wanted our work to speak for itself. I believe we held tightly to this notion, but a few years later, a prominent Republican, trying to make a point about me just going to work without bashing the previous administration, did tell a business audience about the twenty-fifth-floor situation. By then, the press was not paying attention, but I could tell that the comments had an impact on the audience.

Good People

I now have a reputation for attracting great talent, and perhaps it is deserved. However, after I won, I had almost no knowledge of anyone who could fill these very important positions to move the city in the direction I wanted. Many people who voted for me wanted me to "clean house," to get rid of the prominent Democrats and Republicans who worked in or with the previous city government. Because there was minimal Republican support for my campaign and we had just beaten the Democrats (the Republicans also won the council back), these restless folks perceived that I was in a unique position to start fresh with new faces.

It is a nice thought, but competence and experience matters. Also, it was not difficult to quickly ascertain that almost everyone in the Indianapolis political scene cares deeply for the city. They may be political in their approach at times, but most want the best for the city. As far back as Richard Lugar being mayor in the 1960s, there has not been a whiff of corruption from the Indianapolis mayor's office during either Republican or Democratic administrations. There has been some corrupt activity in the city at times over the last few decades, but it has been minimal and at low levels and has usually been caught and dealt with quickly. It did not seem prudent to cast aside everyone who worked in government.

I had been leading people since the age of twenty-three—almost thirty years of varying leadership experiences in war and in peace. I had a good idea of how to motivate people, to set an example, to communicate a vision, to just do the right thing. I now needed talented public servants but did not know where to find them. In the Marine Corps, you get who you get and move forward. When I hired people in the business world, I would put out the job opening through the usual channels, collect résumés, and then interview those I thought might be a good fit. There was not enough time for this. Bob Grand and Joe Loftus from Barnes and Thornburg and Melissa Proffitt from the Ice Miller law firm set about finding talent. I left it to them to find people for me to interview.

They gave me one name for each position. This was certainly not the way hiring is conducted in the business world. However, it worked spectacularly. The quality of the people was extraordinarily high in most cases. I just needed to feel that they would be a good fit and that I could work with them.

I interviewed for about fifteen positions initially, mostly department heads. I told all of them the same thing: "If you're doing this for me or for the party, we are not going to get along. If you're doing this for the long-term health of Indianapolis, then we're going to get along just fine." That was how I felt, and it seemed to connect with them. Of all the people I interviewed, one declined the offer, and one I felt would not be a good fit. We filled those two slots with other people and then moved forward.

I hesitate to mention anyone by name for fear of slighting others through omission, but the level of respect in the city for those who would be working in my new administration was stunning. I took a few brilliant and eager young people (in their thirties) from Governor Mitch Daniels's administration. Michael Huber became my head of enterprise development, and Chris Cotterill became the corporation counsel, the city's chief legal officer. When I interviewed Michael, I told him I wanted him to go out and find the best deals for the city; he looked at me and asked if I really meant to give him carte blanche to move forward on what he thought was best. I said I did. David Sherman, a nationally known water expert, became my public-works director. Olgen Williams, a legendary neighborhood leader, became my deputy mayor for neighborhoods and stayed with me all eight years. Nick Weber became my first deputy mayor for economic development. A few months into our administration, I asked Nick what his true skill set was; he did not mention economic development. Rather he told me that he learned quickly and acted accordingly. That he did. Others proved equally strong in their talent and commitment to the city.

However, when I held a press conference during the transition to announce my public-safety director, everyone in the city really started paying attention. Scott Newman, a Princeton-educated, highly respected former county prosecutor, agreed to take this job. You could almost see all the heads turn in the city, as in "Damn, this new mayor is serious." As good as everyone else was, it was this appointment that gave us a measure of credibility.

Some of these great talents started to leave after two years and others after four years, as is typical for any administration. We usually found more-than-capable replacements, and the most inspiring part of these transitions was that those who left stayed close to the administration. They were just a phone call away and frequently called to offer an idea or to give us a heads-up. I often joked that they did not actually leave the administration—they were just getting paid by someone else. To this day, many of the staff from the two terms keep in touch regularly. They were proud of their affiliation with the Ballard administration and with each other.

As important and talented as all these people were, it was Paul Okeson who was most important in my personal development as a mayor. I knew how to lead people in most situations, but this role was different because of its political nature. Paul was my first chief of staff and instrumental in teaching me my role along with the hard-headed realities and subtle nuances of my position. He gave up a new private-sector job to help me.

Many citizens do not realize that those in appointed offices frequently move between the public and private sector; those that do this are often accused of enriching themselves. However, I found that most do this out of a sense of duty and love of serving the public. Appointed civic positions usually entail twice the workload and half the pay of private-sector jobs, but people love serving in these public roles.

I positioned my chief of staff as the second-in-command. Pretty much everything for my eight years as mayor went through my four chiefs of staff. It was draining both physically and mentally for anyone to fill that role, but Paul also had the unfortunate task of having to teach me about the mayoral facts of life. He was brilliant at it. Always calm, but also direct, he knew the players in the city and the state and told me what I needed to hear. He was patient with me. I appreciated it then and do so today.

I remember one specific instance where I knew I was in good hands. My initial unfamiliarity with the media made for some awkward situations for my staff the first few months. Paul and I had one early conversation about some media situation, and I said something like, "OK, we'll just do this instead." He looked at me and said, "Mayor, that is 100 percent wrong." I had the right chief of staff. Thankfully, most of my staff learned to talk to me directly also. General Colin Powell had a saying that went something like "If we agree all the time, then somebody is redundant." I wanted alternative opinions. That is how the proper solutions are found.

Money

When I won in 2007, the phrase "He doesn't owe anybody anything" was a common refrain. I did not have longtime political allies or donors. A few Republican stalwarts helped during the campaign, none of whom knew me well before I ran for office. Those that did help did not want anything for their efforts except a well-run city. During the campaign, I did have one lady claiming to represent a small Republican contingent come to my office. "If I deliver these votes for you, what do I get?" she asked me directly. I told her, "Good governance." She was not happy, but that is how I felt then and now.

However, an amazing phenomenon occurred right after the election. Unsolicited campaign money just started flowing in at a rapid rate. I assume businesses were doing this now because they had been threatened before the election about donating to my campaign, but that threat was now moot. Some wanted to show support, but some wanted to curry favor. Although more money for my campaign had started showing up the last two weeks of the race, this unsolicited money was extraordinary.

Our small campaign staff was not set up for this rapid influx of money, but the funds just started appearing at the Republican County headquarters. We had no handle on this money whatsoever, and the county party took it in. Our campaign had an agreement about the percentage the party would take for money that was targeted for my campaign; I suspect the party did better the three days after the election than they did all the rest of the year. However, I never did find out the actual division of that money because my mind was on other things, like putting a team together and doing media interviews.

As is common, there was an inauguration ball after the election to raise money. Considering the minimal fundraising that occurred during the campaign, this event was a sight to behold. I finally got to see what real fundraising looked like. This event's nickname was the "Amnesty Ball," which I found hilarious. So many new people I never knew before clamored for tickets. We held the ball at the Indiana Roof, a ballroom on the sixth floor of a beautiful, historic building in downtown Indianapolis. My mom had danced at the Indiana Roof with her high school classmates in the 1940s.

The ballroom is quite large with a balcony above. Not only were all those seats taken but we also had to use an extra room for more people, with a TV feed enabling them to hear the speakers. It was an extraordinary evening, and as I recall, we raised over a million dollars in one night. This was heady stuff for someone who a month before the election did not have $50,000 in his campaign coffers.

I remember talking to two young women who came to me and said, "I'll guess you'll be replacing theirs with yours," meaning I would clear out the people and contracts with the city in favor of my friends. I told them that I would not be operating that way, that I would do what I thought was best for the city. I could tell they did not believe me.

Once we were established in office, my now more robust political team wanted me to get back on the phone and start making fundraising calls. I told them I would not be doing that and to figure out something else. We started doing small dinners for fifteen or twenty people. I would have great chats with the guests during the dinner, then get up to tell them what we were doing in the administration above and beyond what they would read in the press or hear from their colleagues.

These seemed to be very effective, and I loved doing them. I knew who was at the dinners, and many of them became good friends, but I never looked at their checks; someone else collected them, and I usually just asked my team what the total was at the end of the evening. I think my supporters enjoyed these dinners as much as I did. They were intimate, friendly settings, quite different from normal fundraising activities.

I rarely looked at individual donations, and this became a pattern of mine throughout the eight years. I might be alone in the political world in how little I looked at donor lists. I had a good idea of who was donating but not how much. I usually saw total numbers, not individual donations. However, I did know that wealthier people gave in larger quantities, and those that put together events for me were influential in the city. I believe the tremendous financial support I received during reelection was because I was fair and ethical and created a level playing field for everyone. My efforts were directed toward what was best for Indianapolis, not for me and a few others.

Settling Nerves

Many groups and individuals wanted to speak to me almost immediately after the election in 2007. The arts and sustainability folks wanted to talk after Carl Brizzi's comments on election night, and I accommodated them within two weeks of the election. The charter school group wanted to meet with me to see how I felt about the new charter school movement in the city that my predecessor had courageously supported. The mayor of Indianapolis then—and maybe still—was the only mayor in the country who could charter public schools. I not only supported the effort but expanded it while mayor.

The Indianapolis Chamber's board wanted to talk with me, and the four local TV stations wanted to hear from me off camera. I obliged them all, answering their questions, but I also had questions for them. There were dozens of members of the chamber board present, and I asked them if any of them had expected me to win the election. I also asked the same question at the TV stations, all of whom had their reporters, producers, and other employees together when I arrived. Out of these five groups I spoke to, amounting to more than two hundred connected and influential people, I recall only two people who raised their hands, having believed that I might win. I asked all of them a second question: "Do you think there might be some sort of disconnect in the city?" Their silence spoke volumes to me.

Another fascinating phenomenon was happening right after the election, namely speculation about "Who is this guy?" and "How can he possibly think he could be a good mayor?" I have said repeatedly that "most criticism is based on speculation." Look at any news area: politics, sports, finance, arts, etc. Most of the commentary is not on what happened but what might happen. Most of our national news commentary today is opinion pieces rather than actual news. It plays well, especially if said loudly and authoritatively. This was going on soon after my election. Snarky comments like "He'll find out quickly you just can't tell people what to do like in the Marines" and "He's a nobody; his election was a fluke" were common. These came mostly from Democratic politicos, but they were captured in the media. None of the critics knew me or my leadership style, which was largely collaborative and thoughtful, or that I had learned long ago that micromanaging (common among nervous, risk-averse politicians) resulted in much less getting done. Some comments were hurtful, particularly to my wife, but I mostly paid little attention. I just wanted to get to work.

I knew that most in the city were hopeful and wanted me to succeed. I also knew that I had to build up credibility and not make major announcements in the early months. This would not have worked, considering my path to the mayors' office. I had many people around me who were willing to help in concrete ways by working in the administration, by serving on boards and commissions, and in other ways. It was heartwarming to see it start to come together by late December. I cannot thank the transition team enough for what they did, especially considering that most of them had never met me prior to the election.

A side benefit to the election and the subsequent speculation about my leadership was that my leadership book, *The Ballard Rules: Small Unit Leadership*, sold like hotcakes for six months. As I recall, I only made $2.25 per book sold, but several hundred, if not over a thousand, were purchased soon after my election in 2007.

The Beginning

I decided to have a weekly staff meeting at 9:00 a.m. Monday every week, and I kept to this throughout the eight years. It proved to be enormously successful in many ways. It helped me and my staff start the week fresh, with good energy and good ideas. In my leadership book, one of the tenets was "Most meetings should last less than an hour." I felt that I needed to hold true to this thought because staff meetings can get off track quickly if not controlled.

I had about twenty or twenty-five people in the staff meetings, more than would be normal in the Marines or a business setting, but it was the way the city was organized, and we mostly kept to that prior organization. As the first meeting started, the staff, none of them having any idea how I would conduct myself in office, let alone in a meeting, spoke in turn about their areas as they saw them. The meeting finished within an hour. I was pleased. It was easy to tell who knew their area well, who was nervous, who the political veterans were, who wanted to impress me, etc. I was more than satisfied with the staff overall.

The second staff meeting hit the one-hour mark with two people left to brief. I stood up at ten o'clock and said, "This meeting should last less than an hour. I'm done." Then I walked out. I am sure nearly everyone was stunned, but I was not in the room to see it. It was a risky move considering my newness to the political atmosphere, even with my being the mayor, but I never had that problem come up again. They learned that they did not have to impress me, just inform me and the staff what was happening in their respective areas. By the end of my first term, most meetings were about forty-five minutes and, throughout most of the second term, around thirty minutes. The importance of this tactic became clear as the staff blocked off an hour for the meeting, but when it was less than an hour, they stayed, talking to their peers, solving problems, and building the team.

If I recall correctly, it was in the first staff meeting that I asked them to "find me my toll road." This was in reference to Governor Daniels's deal to lease a portion of a toll road in northern Indiana for about $4 billion. It was a stunningly effective deal that provided an enormous amount of money for infrastructure needs in Indiana for years to come. Knowing that the city budget was going to be tight in the short term, I asked my team to find a similar deal that would result in cash in the city coffers for infrastructure. They eventually found it, and I was not surprised that most of the staff got off to a fast start and started improving things in many areas almost immediately. Some were low-hanging fruit, some were longtime problems that needed to be addressed, but my incredible staff tackled them directly, looking out for the long-term health of Indianapolis. I was blessed to have so many great people around me.

10

THE PHILOSOPHY

GOVERNING IN AN EXECUTIVE POSITION is a practical endeavor, not an exercise in political ideology. Legislators do not need to be practical. They can and do vote for bills they do not believe in, knowing their vote will have little practical effect on the citizenry, thus allowing them to maintain status in their caucus and giving them flexibility in their rhetoric for future campaigns. Executives such as mayors and governors have no such luxury. They make decisions every day, and the consequences are on them; they cannot hide in a legislative body somewhere.

Those governing in executive positions who attempt to maintain ideological purity for future campaigns for different offices have difficulty with the day-to-day decision-making from which they cannot escape. Practical reality can intrude on ideological purity. My life experiences told me that it is better to gather all the information you can and then do what you believe is correct, no matter what others may say. Whether a government executive leans left or right, if there is a moral compass that guides him or her, then the citizenry, including those that may disagree with a decision, will understand. I had several conversations with citizens who asked me why I did something, such as building a bike culture, but once I explained it, they understood even if they disagreed. They respected me for being honest with them. Our administration consisted of straight shooters, kind and compassionate, but not afraid to act decisively. We had a "bias for action," and everyone knew it.

The Right Thing to Do

The longer I am out of office, the more I realize just how different our governing model was. As I have said, when I interviewed people for jobs in the administration, I always told them that they must be doing the work for the long-term health of the city of Indianapolis. If they were coming to work to promote me or the Republican Party, then we would probably have some trouble along the way. I never asked anyone's political persuasion, and though I am confident that at the beginning of my first term, I hired only Republicans, we did keep two directors on who were Democrats. Later during my eight years in office, I hired at least one Democrat (who was and still is a superstar in Indianapolis and Indiana). I knew that he was a Democrat because he felt a need to tell me, even though I had not asked the question. Since I never asked the political party of anyone, I do not know if I hired additional Democrats.

As mentioned, I also did not make decisions based on a potential next office, something that I see frequently in officeholders of both parties. That sort of governing, especially in an executive position such as mayor or governor, is anathema to me. Some may not have liked a particular action or policy of mine, but most felt that I was doing what I thought was right. The people of Indianapolis, after a couple of years of my being in office, realized I was governing this way and liked it. They trusted our administration.

I never took a poll to determine a position or advance a policy. Taking polls on issues is very common in the political arena, but I felt I had a good sense of what was right for the city and what the people generally felt about an issue. Much of this was because of the Mayor's Night Out. The primary staff and I would visit an area of the city and take questions from the audience. It was very effective in letting us know what people were concerned about and in assuring people that our administration was listening to those concerns. We held Mayor's Night Out every month the first four years and every other month the second four years. I knew what citizens were thinking because my staff and I heard it directly. I imagine my political staff had some sense of where folks stood on various issues, but I frequently joked with my political staff that they never knew what I might say or do the next morning—I never ran my ideas past them. Instead, I worked with my administrative staff and trusted that we had a good idea of people's views.

We also started with yes. If there was a good idea on the table, we did not worry about the political implications; we wanted to see if the idea was feasible. Did it make sense? Most officeholders start with no. It is easier; some weak explanation is often brought forth to explain the lack of action. We were just the opposite. If we believed an idea was in the long-term interests of Indianapolis, then we tried our best to make it happen. Those from outside the administration very much appreciated this approach.

Also, ideas did not have to come just from me or those closest to me. We were open to ideas no matter the source. We vetted all the ideas, of course, but it was not important that they originated from my office. This is one reason we were able to address so many ideas simultaneously. Later chapters will show just how powerful being open to ideas, no matter the source, can be.

My staff also knew that my main question on any issue would be "What's the right thing to do?" We never began any issue from a political point of view. It was far more important to me to get the best outcome and then message appropriately. I was not good at the messaging part the first year or so in office, but we still did what was right. After a while, when I got smarter at the communications part, we did what was right and then ensured the message was right also. We did adjust timing and the messaging occasionally, but we never changed what we thought was right just for political purposes. This is so different from almost every other political officeholder. I also think it attracted good people who wanted to work in our administration. As I have said frequently, when people did leave us, their replacements were more than capable, and those that left seemed to want to stay engaged. It provided great depth for the team.

Some issues were popular almost immediately, such as our infrastructure program, Rebuild Indy, or the citywide robotics competition that just exploded and morphed into the largest statewide VEX Robotics program in the nation. There were other issues that took more persuasion, such as positioning the city to be more global by doubling the number of sister cities and actually visiting them to spread the word about Indianapolis, or the bike culture that was finally unleashed in Indianapolis with our administration.

Many people in cities want their mayor to simply stay home and run the city, but that ignores the reality of a global economy. I said many times that people (and businesses) around the world know New York and Los Angeles, but they do not know Kansas City, Nashville, or Atlanta. Except for the largest one-day sporting event in the world, the Indianapolis 500, almost nothing is known about Indy around the world. So if this is a global economy, how do we get businesses in other countries to look at our city? You must visit them and tell them.

My visiting the global technology company Infosys campus in Hyderabad, India, began a relationship that eventually resulted in a three-thousand-job promise and a national headquarters for Infosys on the west side of Indianapolis. There are other benefits to sister city programs, particularly the personal relationships, but if done correctly, a strong sister city program should benefit the city economically.

The expansion of the bike culture became important to Indianapolis, but if I had taken a poll before embarking on putting down bike lanes and more trails along with sponsoring bike events, I am confident the poll would have told me to not do it. However, I thought it important to do so for one major reason: the attraction of talent.

The Key Paradigm: Attracting Talent

It does not take a long time as mayor to realize where the digital and the legacy economies are headed. This is why joining organizations like the US Conference of Mayors or the National League of Cities is so important. They have access to academics, historians, futurists, CEOs, and the like who routinely speak to mayors. Any mayor who does not join at least one of these groups is doing a disservice to his city. Any mayor paying attention quickly realizes that talent and capital are more mobile than ever and that cities like Indianapolis are not just in competition with other cities like Kansas City or Atlanta, but also Auckland, New Zealand, and Stockholm, Sweden. The key is attracting talent.

A dramatic example of this changed the course of another city. What is amazing about this story is that it was told at the annual summer meeting of the US Conference of Mayors in Indianapolis in 2016, as Mick Cornett, then mayor of Oklahoma City, a Republican city in a Republican state, ascended to become the president of the US Conference of Mayors. In his inaugural speech, Mick, a wonderful guy, spoke in front of hundreds of mayors about the moment when Oklahoma City realized it had to change the perception and the reality of the city.

In the 1990s, an airline was looking at multiple cities to build a maintenance facility for its larger airplanes. Oklahoma City, wanting to up its profile nationally and bring jobs to its city, chose to bid aggressively for the facility, to the point of raising local taxes to provide incentives. I had never heard of such a thing and find it remarkable that they did this.

Oklahoma City had by far the most incentive-laden package, including tax incentives, and the city felt confident that it would win the bid. When the airline scheduled the announcement of the winner, the Oklahoma City media attended the press conference, in another city, expecting good news. When the airline made the announcement, the winner was Indianapolis. All of Oklahoma City was crushed. How could this have happened?

The then-mayor of Oklahoma City wanted to know why they did not receive the bid for the maintenance facility, but the airline would not tell them, which is standard. From Oklahoma City's perspective, the city did everything possible to help the airline financially. But after repeated urgings from the mayor, the airline finally told him why his city did not receive the bid.

The airline told him that they had sent several middle managers with their families to Oklahoma City for a long weekend to evaluate the city. Those families then told the leaders of the airline that they could not imagine living in Oklahoma City. The amenities were minimal, and there was little culture and few activities for their families. The quality of life was poor. The airline knew it would be unable to find enough good workers for the facility. This decision by the airline made the mayor and others realize that Oklahoma City would have trouble attracting talent for any future businesses because of the low quality of life in Oklahoma City then.

This was devastating to the city leaders, but they acted. Realizing that the quality of life in a city is not just about lower taxes, Oklahoma City—with the citizens' approval—increased taxes temporarily to address shortcomings. They looked at several cities, including Indianapolis to see what we had done.

Indianapolis is well known for the Indianapolis Motor Speedway, nicknamed the Brickyard. If you go to Oklahoma City right now, you'll see they have an area called Bricktown. They have a canal through their downtown, just like Indy. They have public art, and the downtown is vibrant and clean. For those who think sports do not make a difference, Mick would tell you that Oklahoma City getting an NBA team positioned its city differently in the eyes of the nation. It is now a wonderful city to visit and to live in. It was the quality-of-life issues that needed to be addressed in order for more people to move to the city, thus increasing its tax base.

Almost every decision we made, from public safety to infrastructure to robotics to bike culture, was based on doing one thing: attracting talent to the city. Unfortunately, too many in the Republican Party believe that taxes are the dominant factor in attracting talent, but this is just not true. Young talent prefers an upgraded quality of life more than lower taxes. I like lower taxes also, but the trick is to find the right mix of taxes and quality of life to attract talent.

That talent is more mobile than ever, choosing where they want to live based on a perceived quality of life. This is unlike folks in my generation, who accepted the best job offer no matter the quality of life of the city. Creating the kind of city where talent wants to reside is important today. This includes a vibrant arts-and-culture community, a sense of environmental sustainability, a sports scene, mobility options (like mass transit and a walking and bicycle culture, in addition to cars), and a global sense of itself.

This is important because businesses move to where the talent resides. No business today, with the plethora of data available, is going to move to an area where it cannot hire a talented workforce. This is quickly obvious to mayors who make economic incentive decisions.

Every mayor should be focused on expanding the city's tax base, which means focusing on the quality-of-life issues. If talent and businesses do not consider residing in your city, then the tax base erodes, which means basic public services (like police and fire) decline, let alone the city's investments in parks, sports, bike trails, the arts, etc., which talent insists upon.

One of the difficulties in attracting talent and businesses in Indiana is that its cities are reliant on income tax and property tax. Income tax in Indiana is based on where you live, not where you work. That means a great company may choose Indianapolis, but many of their employees may choose to live in the great suburbs surrounding the city. I kept bringing up to the local realtors that they should show off Indianapolis, but for high-income earners, the realtors usually went straight north of Indianapolis to the wealthy suburbs. I wanted Indianapolis to have that income tax and property tax because we brought the company to Indianapolis, but far too many times, that new income tax and property tax went to another city.

That said, we were successful in bringing some great businesses to Indianapolis because the city continued its journey, begun in the 1970s, to have an ever-improving quality of life. Kronos expanding to Indianapolis is a great example.

Based in Boston, workforce management company Kronos, now UKG after a merger, wanted to expand to another city east of the Mississippi River and began investigating cities quietly so that their employees in Boston would not get upset. (These were to be new jobs, but I understand their employees' anxiety). Indianapolis was not on their original list of cities, but someone convinced the company to visit. They did, and Indy made the final ten cities, then the final four, and then the final two. The name of the company was still unknown to the city, other than it was an IT firm. With the final two cities, they insisted on talking to the mayor. I went and talked to them, not knowing who they were, assuring them that they would be happy in Indianapolis.

They chose Indy. I had the opportunity to talk with the local Kronos leader and asked why they had chosen Indianapolis. He told me that with the final cities in competition for the expansion, they talked to college students studying IT. In Indianapolis, they talked to students at IUPUI (Indiana University–Purdue University, Indianapolis). The students told Kronos two things: (1) we can do what you want us to do, and (2) we want to stay in Indianapolis. That is why Indianapolis was chosen for the Kronos expansion: the local emerging talent liked our city.

I want tax rates to be low, but the focus should not be on lowering or increasing taxes per se but using tax dollars wisely to increase the overall tax base, which in today's environment means attracting talent through a higher quality of life in the city. This is a different paradigm than forty or fifty years ago.

Showing Up

Based on my experiences as an aide-de-camp in the Marine Corps, I already knew what it meant for the top leader to show up. My staff was great in filling in for me when needed, but I also knew the signal it sent when the sitting mayor showed up at an event. Presence matters.

Even though I was the mayor, I still felt about myself as I always did. But I also knew that people were going to perceive and treat me differently because of my position. I stayed grounded and true to myself as best I could, but I also had a sense of what people wanted in their mayor. A major part of what they wanted was to *see* their mayor. I did this in two ways: scheduling and being there in times of stress.

The volume of scheduling requests was overwhelming. As I recall, seventy-five to one hundred requests came in per week. Obviously, I could not attend all the events requested. Initially, the staff who had worked in political offices before wanted to screen the requests for political purposes; this was common practice. They did not want me to go to any event that did not help me politically. They did not want me to even see some requests in case I wanted to go to those events. I understand they were trying to protect me, especially as I was a novice to the political world, but I insisted that I see every request. I felt that I had to get a sense of what to attend or not attend. I also felt that seeing every request would give me some sense of what people were supporting in Indianapolis. The mayor showing up at a charity event or some other good cause added weight to the event. I understood that.

After a few tough months of finding our way on scheduling, my executive assistant, my scheduler, my primary communications representative, and I got these meetings down to about an hour. I saw every request and tried to attend as many events as possible, as long as it did not interfere with the policy aspect of our administration. If I could not go, I asked a member of the staff to go if feasible. If I remember correctly, we had a representative show up at more than 80 percent of the requests, which I find remarkable. This also made our administration popular and kept our ears to the ground in the process.

To have me show up for an event, the request had to be submitted at least six weeks in advance, and preferably two months in advance. That still sounds odd to me, but such is the nature of being the mayor of a large city. There were some exceptions. When a councilor wanted to talk, we usually made room for him or her within two days. The Democrats loved to say that I would not talk to them, but actually we moved the schedule around very quickly whenever a Democratic councilor requested to meet. Other exceptions would be dignitaries from Washington and from foreign countries.

It became obvious quickly that I did scheduling differently from my predecessors and other officeholders. I attended some annual events where they told me they had sent invitations for ten or twenty years, but no one had ever come. For those types of events, I tried to go every year because they were for great causes. I am still asked to some of these charities to this day, and I go if I can. I also attended family reunions for people I did not know. I attended small business openings, not just the large ones that drew the media. I attended lots of sustainability events, as this was an emphasis of mine. I attended a great number of arts events, and I became known as the mayor who supported the arts with my attendance more than any previous mayor. I particularly loved going to dance events. This was a far cry from my election-night reputation. I attended a Chinese business group meeting at midnight (still in a tuxedo from a previous event), as that was when they routinely met to talk about issues. One Saturday I attended fifteen different events. We were all in.

I had a well-deserved reputation for showing up and staying. Most officeholders come to an event to pick up an award, or say a few words and then leave while the event is still going on. Winnie and I usually stayed to the end, particularly for evening events. Sometimes there were other events to get to, but if not, we enjoyed the conversations with the people doing good work in the city. People really appreciated that we stayed to talk.

The other way that we manifested showing up was during times of tragedy or stress. Again, this is a lesson from my marine days, when the leader had to be present to demonstrate awareness of what was happening and to calm people. Especially in government, it is important to let the citizens know that the administration is aware of and working on the issue. This not only calms people but also prevents the spreading of wild rumors. I also took care to never drink to excess during my eight years in office. Emergencies can happen at any time, and a clear-thinking mayor should be expected by the citizens.

One night in 2012, while I was at a band event at Lucas Oil Stadium (where the Indianapolis Colts play), my security guard received an alert about an explosion in the Richmond Hill neighborhood on the south side. I was still in a tuxedo, again, from a previous event. I headed straight to the neighborhood, arriving, I believe, about thirty minutes after the explosion. Already there were rumors that a small plane had hit a house and caused the explosion.

Everyone within a few miles of the explosion heard it. The devastation was tragic, yet the scene was amazing by the time I got there. Despite the late hour, already a school had opened its doors, nurses had shown up without prompting, sheriff's deputies were on hand organizing the people who were now coming in from their homes, and police had already cordoned off the neighborhood. This is the beauty of Indianapolis. People react swiftly and appropriately in a time of tragedy.

However, the people still wanted to know what happened and whether the city was aware of and working on the issue. It is best in such cases not to delegate this responsibility if possible; people want to hear from the mayor.

By the time I got there, I was aware of the rumor about the plane. I proceeded to immediately walk the neighborhood in my tuxedo with the police by my side. It was a tragic scene, and it seemed that there had to have been injuries or deaths associated with the blast. One home was completely destroyed, and the one next door also had tremendous damage. Other homes nearby had severe damage. Even homes a block or two away had some damage, such as garage doors blown off.

There was no plane to be found. This explosion clearly began in one of the two most damaged homes, though no one yet knew what had occurred. What I remember most about that night was the severity of the damaged homes, the people coming to the school looking for help, and the spontaneous positive reaction of the people on the south side of Indianapolis.

I held a press conference immediately after I toured the neighborhood, at approximately 11:00 p.m., which I believe helped the situation. The people now knew that a plane was not involved and that there were organized activities on site to help. Over the next few days, supplies started showing up in large quantities. Indianapolis is an amazing city.

Within a day or so, the police strongly suspected what had occurred but publicly acted as if they were still investigating to find out the cause. People speculated about a gas leak. It was gas related, but it was purposeful: a homeowner and accomplices leaked gas to collect insurance money when it caught fire; they did not expect to blow up the neighborhood.

Tragically, a young couple next door died. The fire department was magnificent as usual, but they could not reach the couple in time to save them—though it was close. I went to see the fire crew a week or so later; they still had heavy hearts because they could not save the couple. It weighed on them. I went to the couple's funeral service.

The city worked with the homeowners in the neighborhood over the next few months to help them recover, including working with insurance companies to ensure the homeowners could recoup their physical losses. This is the sort of activity that can be cumbersome in a bureaucratic setting, and I was afraid those affected homeowners would at some point become angry with the progress. Just the opposite happened. As a group, they were so happy that the city stayed with them through it all that the neighborhood hosted a dinner for the city workers who stood by their side. It is easy to cast aspersions on government workers, but with over thirty years in government, I found that the vast majority care deeply about their work and the people they serve.

The explosion's perpetrators, a woman and two men, will be in jail for a long time.

Another nighttime tragedy occurred at the State Fairgrounds the year before in 2011. A country music group was about to perform at an outdoor venue when a straight-line wind of enormous velocity struck down the stage, killing several people and injuring many others. Coincidentally, I was again at Lucas Oil Stadium for a band event and headed straight to the fairgrounds after my security guard alerted me. I believe I was there within twenty to twenty-five minutes of the incident, and despite the developing tragedy, what I found was amazing. A triage site had been set up almost immediately with both doctors and nurses, who were in abundance, as this had occurred during the state fair. Ambulances started rolling in soon after I got there. Although this was on state property, the fairgrounds are physically located in Indianapolis, so I stayed to help as necessary to calm things down. I was the only political figure there.

The fair leadership and I kept the information flowing as well as possible, but there was little we could do. The doctors and nurses performed magnificently. Finally, at around 1:30 a.m., the fair director and I, along with others on the fair board, thought we should hold a press conference to update everyone. After some discussion, it was agreed that I should kick off the press conference followed by the wonderful executive director of the fair, Cindy Hoye. It may not have been my jurisdiction, but again, I believe my presence helped by letting everyone know that the government was aware and working on the issue.

Another incident occurred on a frigid early morning in winter. Most cities now understand how important their downtowns are, but Indianapolis was ahead of most other cities by two decades. Our downtown was frequently rated in the top three in the nation because of Monument Circle in the center of downtown and its vibrancy and easy mobility, even during the winter months. Our canal area is a highly walkable but mostly residential area, while other canals around the country are mostly commercial.

I tended to wake up early while mayor. I would turn on the news at four or five in the morning to see if anything had happened overnight. If there was not a major story about Indianapolis within ten minutes, I would then turn the TV off and go back to sleep for a few more minutes, or I would get ready for the gym, where I went around 6:00 a.m. two to three times a week.

On this particular morning, for some reason, I woke up between 3:00 and 4:00 a.m. and turned on the TV. The local stations were covering a fire on the canal, and it looked bad. A homeless man had begun the fire in a residential construction site along our downtown canal. I was worried not just about the construction site but also the hundreds of homeowners who were already living on the canal. I quickly texted my morning security person, and he picked me up by 4:30. By then I was in a suit and tie and overcoat, ready to go to work. I went straight to the fire.

The fire department took me as close as they safely could, then brought me back inside to an incident trailer they had set up. During the briefing, they told me that the fire was already under control, even though it looked like it was raging at the time and not yet under control. They explained to me in detail how the fire was burning and that it was not moving toward current residents. They told me how the fire would play out.

At 6:00 a.m., when many people were waking up and watching their first news of the day, I was doing a live interview with a local TV station, explaining how our fire department had the fire under control. I could tell that the reporter (who was a terrific journalist) was surprised that I said that, because the fire was still going full bore, but I had confidence in the fire department.

I went home to eat breakfast and turned on that same station. As the fire burned in the background, the reporter was now explaining how she did not think the mayor had been correct. It was a funny moment to me, but the fire indeed played out just as the fire department had explained it would.

I got a lot of comments about that interview; people could not believe that I was doing a live interview at 6:00 a.m. on a fire downtown, while they were just waking up. The perception that I seemed to be everywhere was enhanced. I believe it made people feel secure that their government was on top of things. In truth, I was lucky that I woke up earlier than normal that day. However, I did think it was important for me to show up to help people through the incident.

There were other incidents where it was difficult for the citizens and me, including the city losing three cops to violence in my eight years in office. It is hard to explain just how painful those losses were. The city came together during those tragedies.

Every mayor should be physically present when tragedy is occurring or has occurred. This is mandatory—politics be damned. There were several other tough moments throughout my two terms, but I did not avoid showing up or worry that the incident might affect me politically. To me it is unforgivable when a mayor is absent during or after a tragedy in their city.

I was far from perfect as a mayor, but when tragedy occurred, I did my best to respond appropriately. I showed up.

11

INFRASTRUCTURE

During public discussion on whether the city should build a new hospital, a Republican state representative told me that she thought it was OK as long as there "aren't any babbling brooks" inside. Although she was a competent elected official, that was a weird comment, but one similar to how many members of my party feel about such things.

"It is OK to put up a building as long as it is gray, minimally functional, and ugly" seems to be the sentiment. That may be an exaggeration, but not by much. Anything that went against the notion of higher costs on the front end was verboten. Of course, such decisions lead to lower tax revenue on the back end because people do not want to live in communities that are ugly. They will move somewhere else and take their income tax and property tax with them.

Buildings matter. When any city is highlighted nationally on TV, as with sporting events, the broadcasts always show the prominent, beautiful structures of that city. Likewise, the basic infrastructure of a city matters. Decent streets, nice sidewalks with curb cuts for people with disabilities, alleys that are functional, and sewers that work are part of the quality of life that matters to citizens. In addition to having architecturally significant buildings, the nuts and bolts of infrastructure need to work.

Similarly, I was perplexed when I took office by the common feeling that there is only one solution to fix a government problem. "Sewers need fixing? OK, let's do it." It is just accepted there is only one way to do it. "Need a new building? Let's build it and move on." Then praise is heaped on those in government for taking action—any action.

Infrastructure matters in a city. But *how* you do something also matters. Just building or fixing something without proper thought is common in government because the taxpayers will fund it, and in truth, there is little scrutiny to such decisions. This sort of thinking went against all that I knew. I was looking for what was best for the city and for value for the taxpayer dollar.

While we had infrastructure challenges ahead of us that we wanted to tackle, when I became the mayor, the country was heading into the Great Recession. The economy was slowing down, and revenues to governments at all levels were heading south. People were losing jobs, and small businesses were in danger of closing. It was a tough environment for years for business, government, and nonprofits. Building out infrastructure seemed a nonstarter to some, but we were determined to keep the city growing, to keep people employed, and to keep businesses operating.

The Biggest Engineering and Environmental Project in Indianapolis History

Near the end of my first term, I was jokingly complaining to Rafael Sanchez, a well-respected and funny local TV reporter, that no one in the city covered our high-stakes negotiations and subsequent success with the Environmental Protection Agency, increasing the effectiveness of our federally mandated sewer improvements while dramatically lowering the cost.

He said, "Mayor, no one cares about infrastructure. It's not sexy stuff." He was right. Probably as a favor to me, he did a short story on our success. No one else covered it at all.

I inherited a $1.8 billion sewer upgrade, mandated by the Environmental Protection Agency. This was because the city was dumping more than seven billion gallons of raw sewage into the waterways every year. Of course, rates were going to go up.

Initially, I did not think much about it; this federal mandate seemed set in stone. I had more pressing issues and achievable goals with which to deal. However, I had also hired David Sherman, a former water company founder and one of the acknowledged water experts in the country, to be my public-works director. He knew the technical, financial, regulatory, and legal frameworks of almost everything related to public works, but he was particularly adept at water issues. I did not know the extent of his vast expertise in this field as I took office, but if there was ever a cost-saving hire by a city anywhere in the country, it was David Sherman agreeing to become the public-works director in Indianapolis.

Through my association with the US Conference of Mayors (USCM), I came to find out that the EPA had begun cracking down on cities across the nation for their aging sewers. At this time, we had a Democrat in the White House, and I am sure the EPA felt justified and supported in its actions. However, the USCM is composed primarily of Democratic mayors, and it was obvious that those mayors were disgusted by their treatment from the EPA.

It got to the point that the Ohio Democratic mayors drafted federal legislation to rein in the EPA's treatment of mayors and asked their congressional representatives to push the legislation forward. It included words like "Stop treating mayors like criminals." The Water Council of the USCM was the most attended session in the biannual meetings because of the EPA's actions, and most discussion in the Water Council centered on the treatment of cities by the EPA.

More than seven hundred cities were involved. Mayors knew their sewers had to be upgraded, but the manner in which the EPA was approaching the issue was onerous. For example, when meeting with city representatives on these issues, the EPA would bring members of the Justice Department with them. This was an intimidation tactic.

The EPA also had a policy that 2 percent of a city's median household income was the dollar amount that must be spent on sewer upgrades. In other words, the quality of the sewer improvement was not the primary consideration—the dollars spent by a city was. This was simple arrogance. The EPA will deny this fact to this day, but it came out in a court battle with another Midwestern mayor and was made known forcefully and loudly at a Water Council meeting of the USCM. (More on that meeting below.)

Federal agencies are full of well-meaning people, but some cross the line over to naked activism no matter the cost. In this case, the federal level of the EPA was a bit activist but would listen to reason. However, some of the regional offices of the EPA were overly activist. The EPA office in Chicago was over the top in this way, and every mayor in the Midwest knew it.

Sometime early in my administration, David came to me to say that he could look at reengineering the federally mandated sewer upgrade at less cost. This was going to be a ratepayers' savings, not a taxpayers' savings, but it did not matter to me. It was the right thing to do.

David put together a team to reengineer our $1.8 billion project. Value engineering is the term frequently used to describe a project that would be more effective at less cost. The team came up with an innovative plan that used both gray (traditional underground piping) and green (natural water retention methods like bioswales and other plantings) infrastructure. The highlight of this was a seven-mile pipe (part of a twenty-mile system) that was 250 feet below ground and 18 feet in diameter. We called it the Deep Rock Tunnel, and it was dramatic in scope.

By everyone's account, this plan was, as I frequently said to different groups, "bigger, faster, cheaper, and greener."

But we had a problem. It was $740 million cheaper. It was cheaper because David and his team reengineered the project, such as rejecting a $290 million secondary treatment process that was approved and designed and replacing it with a more effective $54 million project. Such actions caused havoc with the contractors and the EPA; they were already moving in one direction but had to adjust to our new approach.

The EPA regional office in Chicago fought back. They wanted us to spend the $1.8 billion, not $1 billion. Everyone, including the EPA, concurred that our new value-engineered plan was superior, but it did not matter: spend the agreed-upon amount of money. It did not matter that rates would have to increase even more, hurting the poor especially; just spend the money.

We said no.

This is where the value of someone like David Sherman matters. He not only brilliantly reengineered the technical elements of the plan, but based on his experience, he also knew we had a strong legal argument to present. It seems gutsy, maybe insane, for a city to take on the EPA and the Justice Department, but David knew we were right on the merits of the case. I trusted him, and we went forward with taking the EPA to court.

After a year of wrangling and strong-arming, the EPA realized they would not prevail in a court of law and agreed with us. We became the first city in the nation to successfully renegotiate a federally mandated consent decree on sewers. The EPA put out a press release more quickly than we did, essentially saying, "See, cities, we're easy to work with. You can negotiate with us just like Indianapolis did." We had saved the ratepayers at least $800 million, though we claimed only $740 million at the time. It was huge news around the nation for those who followed such things. The innovation in the reengineering of the project was the cover story on two national trade periodicals, *Public Works* and *Engineering News-Record*.

One little-known aspect of this effort was David's continuing insistence on listening to technical experts for guidance and not the administrators.

Another was his insistence on hiring women- and minority-owned subcontractors, a practice that began when he founded his own company decades before. For years afterward, some of these company owners would thank me for the work they acquired from the city, but in truth it was David Sherman and his team that made that happen.

As a result of our successful renegotiation with the EPA, I was asked to become a cochair of the Water Council of the US Conference of Mayors. I was reluctant at first because I felt we won the case because of David, plus I am hardly a technical expert in water. However, the USCM provides staff representatives who are technical experts. David and others convinced me that I should accept, and I eventually did.

When my other cochair left office, I became the sole chair for quite a while. As such, I was the USCM's representative on water issues and attended several national meetings along with the National League of Cities and the National Association of Counties to talk with the EPA on water issues. I also held Water Council meetings for the USCM around the country a couple of times a year. Because the Water Council was so prominent in the USCM, my status among mayors across the nation changed. Indianapolis was becoming known for innovation, but no one in Indianapolis knew. Infrastructure is not sexy.

A Heated Meeting

At one Water Council meeting, representatives of the EPA attended along with members of the Council of Environmental Quality (CEQ). The CEQ are the actual advisors to the president on environmental issues. As such, the EPA is always concerned about how the CEQ briefs the president. Although the EPA would occasionally send someone to the Water Council meetings, the CEQ never attended; it was not their job. However, they came along with the EPA on this meeting. I can only assume the EPA invited them so that they could show off their improving relationships with the mayors.

The Water Council always had a large room because of the number of attendees, but for this meeting, it was now standing room only. I was the sole chair at the time and ran the meeting. The 2 percent MHI requirement (referring to the percentage of a community's median household income going to pay for water and/or wastewater services) came up. The EPA denied this was a requirement.

The aforementioned mayor of a Midwestern city, part of that standing-room-only crowd, went off. He came to the forefront near the tables, pointing his finger at the EPA representatives, yelling, "You lie! You're liars! I was in the court when your representatives testified that it was a requirement. You lie!"

He just kept going at the top of his lungs, absolutely furious at the EPA. I leaned over to my primary staff expert from the USCM and whispered, "Should I let this go on?" It was funny to me but also very awkward. I let it go on until he was finished. I knew of this mayor's struggles with the EPA, the Justice Department, and a local judge who was less than receptive toward that city's sewer issues. That mayor had had enough. I will never forget that moment.

The EPA eventually did try to work with cities and varying organizations to mitigate their original stubbornness on the median household income requirement. It helped that the USCM staff had put together some data that was very in depth, detailing the rate increases in localized areas, particularly in California, of how much poor households would have to pay out of their income if the city they lived in followed the 2 percent MHI requirement. In some areas, the sewer rates in these poorer neighborhoods would have taken more than 30 percent of a household's income if the EPA's mandate was enforced. When the EPA saw this in print in a book that the USCM had put together, they backed off, and quickly. The USCM agreed not to make this data public, and the EPA agreed to work with cities more closely.

It was sad that it came to this. But a federal agency should never mandate a dollar amount to be spent by cities versus telling each city what needed to be done and letting the city figure out how to do it. Most cities' budgets are very tight; these sewer improvements cost real dollars, and real people were being affected. The EPA was oblivious to this for far too long.

A Transfer of Assets

The transfer of the water and wastewater assets to Citizens Energy was the largest financial transaction in the history of Indianapolis. As mentioned, at one of my first staff meetings, I tasked a few of my new staff to "Find me my toll road," a reference to Governor Mitch Daniels's leasing of the Indiana toll road for seventy-five years in the northern part of the state to an Australian-Spanish consortium for nearly $4 billion. The toll road ran from Chicago to the Ohio Turnpike. Mitch told the citizens that the money would be spent on improving Indiana's infrastructure, and it was.

The infrastructure in Indianapolis was also in poor shape, and to be fair, it is difficult to keep in good condition with the annual tax revenue. I was hoping to find some sort of cash influx that could provide decades worth of infrastructure improvement to the city.

My team took my request to heart and put out something called a Request for Expression of Interest (REI). Governments at all levels put out Requests for Proposals (RFP) or Requests for Information (RFI). However, my team was not sure if there would be any interest on what they had come up with as my "toll road," which was a sale of the city-owned water and wastewater assets. They made up the term REI from whole cloth.

Mayors and other city leaders across the country routinely buy and sell such assets to "extract value." It is usually a short-term way to generate cash for the government entity. Of course, politics frequently come into play with such maneuvers, as mayors and others try to find extra cash for projects.

Our REI received quite a few expressions of interest, mainly from private water companies. However, keeping in mind what was best for the long-term health of Indianapolis, we chose to pursue selling these assets to Citizens Energy, a local public charitable trust. Citizens was formed in 1887 by the city leaders at the time (including Eli Lilly and Benjamin Harrison) to operate a natural gas company for the benefit of the citizens and the community. It was designed "to protect the gas company assets from takeover by monopolies like Standard Oil and from political patronage."

Citizens is run like a business but does not make a profit, and as long as it fulfills its mission, it cannot be sold. They have an impeccable reputation in the city for competence and integrity. Every city should have an entity like Citizens. Ironically, Citizens had wanted control of these water assets since the 1930s, but the city would not do so. Now they had a mayor who was asking them to buy the assets.

Chris Cotterill, a brilliant lawyer and my first corporation counsel (head of the city's Legal Department) who was now operating as my second chief of staff, was the lead city negotiator. We also hired Nate Feltman, another excellent lawyer. Together, Chris and Nate worked so that the city and Citizens could come to a mutually agreeable number while haggling over numerous details. I do not think Citizens expected the city to drive such a hard bargain, but we did.

The reengineering project added value to our side. Although I was not involved in the day-to-day negotiations, I know there were some contentious moments when my team wondered whether Citizens would walk away. We wanted fair value and every dime we could get to help with the infrastructure in the city.

The city and Citizens came to an agreement of $1.9 billion. As there was about a billion and a half of debt with these assets, the city netted $425 million cash. We put $80 million into a Fiscal Stability Fund, which we created as financial reserves for the city since the normal reserves seemed inadequate to us. (When the Democrats won back the council in 2011, they tried to use this money for various projects, but we were able to fend off most of those requests; there was still $78 million in that account when I left office.)

The remaining cash, about $345 million, was designated for infrastructure improvement. David Sherman, still our public-works director, leveraged that money with additional state and federal funds into over half a billion dollars for infrastructure. The city normally spent about $25 million to $30 million annually for infrastructure, so this money was significant. Rebuild Indy was born.

After the deal had been reached with Citizens, there were still several hurdles to jump. The council had to approve. To help the councilors with their constituents, Citizens CEO Carey Lykins and I conducted a few town halls around the city. This was also in line with our philosophy of listening to the citizens' concerns. This helped to soothe most of the nerves in the city. I believe we did four sessions, and although there were lots of questions, most people were happy. I was used to such forums; Carey was not. There was one session where political opposition tried to make it hard for Carey and me, particularly attacking Carey, but we stuck to our guns, and people were satisfied.

My communications team thought we should emphasize the cost savings that would occur from the consolidation of assets, mostly back-office functions. Although this was a valid point, it was also very Republican. I thought it would sound like the same old GOP pablum. Politics in utilities have plagued cities around the country for decades. I believed that the main point was that we would be taking politics out of water and wastewater forever. I repeated this over and over at the town halls and every other chance I got. It played well because I believed it. And it has proven to be true.

That said, the money was significant. As I recall, we said that there would be $40 million in savings by the third year. Soon after the first year, Carey told me that Citizens had already saved $60 million. We did not feel a need to trumpet this publicly, but it was good to know that the ratepayers got a good deal.

In addition to a council vote, other boards had to vote on this deal—and one board actually had to vote itself out of existence. That was difficult to pull off, as people like serving on boards and commissions. We believed we had a one-vote margin on this one board, but to ensure success, we had one of our staff accompany a wavering board member throughout the day of the vote so that no one else would get to him and convince him to change his vote.

Even though Republicans had a narrow majority of the council at this time, we were not quite sure the council would vote for the deal. A couple of Republican councilors always threatened to vote against us on some issues, wanting to ensure that our administration was paying attention to them. However, one Democratic councilor, who was grateful for my efforts in acknowledging the victims of crime, had promised me he would cast a vote for our administration one time when I needed it. I called that favor in on this vote. He was true to his word.

We signed the papers in August 2011, just three months before reelection. To some, this may seem like a contentious issue before an election, but again, people pay little attention to infrastructure. Plus, we had held several town halls, and those who wanted to comment had already done so. It was a great deal for the citizens of Indianapolis.

Rebuild Indy

Rebuild Indy was the moniker we gave to the infrastructure improvements in Indianapolis that were possible because of the more than half a billion dollars available from the sale of the water and wastewater assets to Citizens and the state and federal money that we were able to secure as matching funds. The numbers on Rebuild Indy are staggering, but the impact on the neighborhoods along with other positive effects was more gratifying.

We listened to input from councilors, from the Mayor's Action Center, from Mayor's Night Outs, and from routine neighborhood meetings. We then took action. This kept so many people employed during the Great Recession. Businesses were grateful.

To give a sense of the magnitude of Rebuild Indy, the city normally fixes one or two bridges per year. With Rebuild Indy, we fixed fifty-six bridges in a two-year period. We paved over one thousand lane miles of roads. Almost five hundred thousand feet of sidewalks and curbs were built. Longtime flooding issues were addressed—David Sherman was remarkably effective in figuring out how to prevent flooding when others could not. We solved drainage issues for 2,800 homes and businesses. Whenever a hard rain would fall, the first neighborhood that the TV cameras went to was Frog Hollow. No more. We demolished more than two thousand abandoned homes that were blights on the neighborhoods and crime magnets. We built about six thousand ADA-compliant ramps to help people with disabilities.

What I heard most about was alleys. In some of the poorer sections of the city, alleys had been neglected for years. We paved over fourteen miles of alleys, and the citizens of those neighborhoods were very appreciative and told us so. Rebuild Indy provided those much-needed jobs during the Great Recession, but the city also became much more attractive and welcoming in the neighborhoods—all without a tax increase. President Obama's stimulus package in 2008 added some money, for which we were thankful, but that money flowed through the state, and by the time it reached Indianapolis, a few more roads were repaved, but it did not add significantly to the overall magnitude of Rebuild Indy.

Two specific projects stand out. When we repaved Burdsal Parkway in the Riverside area, the neighborhood could not believe it. Burdsal, designed as an east-west connecting road, was originally built in 1915. At that time, it was a beautiful, prominent road in the city. A century later, the neighborhood is not as prominent as it once was and is now a lower-income area. However, the Riverside neighborhood is a proud one, full of wonderful people. Unfortunately, sometimes these areas get neglected amid conflicting priorities. With the Rebuild Indy money, we were intentional on using much of the money to improve such areas. Burdsal Parkway was one example of this, and it sent a strong signal that we cared about all areas of the city.

Another highlight was David Sherman finding a way to put a combination sidewalk/path along a busy northwest thoroughfare, Michigan Road, that at times had walkers on or near the road. I even saw a wheelchair on that dangerous road. For years, even before our administration, no one could figure out how to build a safe walkway for pedestrians without flooding the nearby neighborhoods. We were able to do this with Rebuild Indy money and David's expertise—a huge win for the area. This is what listening and innovation can do for citizens.

As mentioned, Rebuild Indy's effect on the construction and engineering companies in Indianapolis was important during the Great Recession, a period of severely reduced economic activity in the country that began in 2008. In many places around the country, workers in construction had been laid off. Rebuild Indy kept both blue-collar and white-collar jobs in these industries at work and saved several companies from closing. We frequently heard from these companies about how appreciative they were of our efforts.

Connectivity

When our team discussed the plans for Rebuild Indy, I told them that we could not just redo what has already been done, even if it was on a grander scale. I said that we had to leave something behind also, something memorable. To me, this was the notion of connectivity.

It is difficult to describe the reactions when a Republican talks to other Republicans about connectivity. This is not our strength, not one of our go-to moves. Blank stares were easy to spot, along with some inquisitiveness. Connectivity was still a new term to most when I started using it in 2010 or so. However, I understood it and realized its importance in attracting talent into our city and state. Attracting talent means attracting business, which means expanding the tax base, a term Republicans are more comfortable with, even if they have trouble connecting these particular dots.

Connecting multiple modes of transportation works, and it's something that young talent expects. When I was stationed in Stuttgart, Germany, I would frequently fly to the United States or to other European cities. When I returned to the Stuttgart airport, I would go down a floor to catch the train to a station near my home. My wife would pick me up from there, but I could have taken a bus right next to the base from that train station if I had wanted to. A plane, a train, a bus, all connected, could deliver me from anywhere in the world to the base where I was living. In America, our modes of transportation frequently compete. Most of the world learned a long time ago that connecting them is more efficient and productive for their citizens.

So too within a city. Connecting our mass transit assets, our bicycling assets, and our trails and sidewalks made perfect sense to me. It was a new concept to others. Of course, part of the problem was almost all our potential connective public assets were lacking, almost nonexistent.

We, along with most mature cities across America, were dependent on the car as the primary mode of transportation. I understood that, but I also understood that to increase our quality of life, to attract talent into the city, we needed to become a much more connected, multimodal city. The streets were for everyone, not just those with cars. Thankfully, we found many partners to help us and to advocate for us.

Mass Transit—Indy Connect

A lady in the Devington area on the northeast side of town, where I lived from the age of twelve until I went to college, told me her story, which capsulized all that was wrong with our horrible mass transit system. She was on hourly wages. She was referred to a doctor on the northwest side of the city, very near to where I lived as mayor. It took her three buses to get to the doctor and three more to get back home. It took her all day to complete the mission, and she missed out on all her wages for the day. If I or almost anyone I knew had such an appointment, we would at most take two hours to go the doctor's office and back and not lose a penny from our salary.

When I was campaigning in 2007, I heard my opponent mention at a Rotary presentation that he would "not touch mass transit." I understood what he was saying. Mass transit was almost a forbidden subject to talk about in our city, and it was certainly a politically sensitive topic in the middle of a campaign. However, just a few years before, I had used those multiple modes of transportation all over Europe and had in my mind that Indianapolis could do more with respect to mass transit.

The sensitivity of the term "mass transit" did not bother me, although it was not a campaign issue in 2007. Once in office, I believed part of my charge was to tackle issues that had been kicked down the road for one reason or another. In Indianapolis, the mass transit was so bad that we were usually ranked either ninety-ninth or one hundredth of the largest one hundred cities in the nation. If someone missed their bus to go to work, it would be an hour or two before another bus would come. For lower-income folks on hourly wages, this was devastating.

Transportation is a major expense for the poor. If the mass transit system cannot get them back and forth to work, then they must buy a rundown used car. While most new cars now get thirty or forty miles per gallon, run all the time, and have scheduled maintenance at the owner's convenience, a poor person's car gets ten miles per gallon and breaks down monthly, resulting in many more maintenance dollars than newer cars.

Republicans love to tell stories of Americans who have been poor but then found success. However, if our party cares about economic mobility, then the need to address this situation is very clear. The poor stay poor because their necessary expenses cannot be covered by their wages. In some cities, transportation is a major part of a working person's income. Mass transit done correctly becomes a minor expense for citizens and allows poorer people to get to work and to move up the economic ladder. Good mass transit is also something that young talent, and therefore businesses, are looking for.

The catalyst for moving on mass transit was a meeting about six months into my term as mayor. I attended a meeting of the Central Indiana Regional Transportation Authority (CIRTA). Tasked with enhancing transit in the region with few dollars available, members of CIRTA are appointed by the regional municipalities and some by the governor. It can be dominated by Indianapolis, but my representatives worked hard to be fair. The purpose of this meeting I was attending was to have the members of CIRTA come to a consensus on what the first rail line would be in the future of mass transit in the region. (Indy had only buses but was planning for rail.) I usually did not attend these meetings, but my CIRTA representatives wanted me to add weight to this decision.

CIRTA had concluded that the first rail line would be a diesel train from the northeast corridor of Indianapolis to downtown. To many, this looked obvious, as the commute from northeast Indy to downtown was normally packed with very slowly moving cars, for miles on end, every working day. No other plans for better mass transit were yet formulated. Since this meeting was thoroughly prepared and was a little bit of a show with the media present, I did not object to the proposal. However, the overwhelming thought in my mind was, "They've been working on this for fifteen or twenty years, and this is it?"

I went back to my office pondering what to do. I talked to some of my staff, many of whom understood why I was underwhelmed with the CIRTA proposal. I also talked to some influential people in the city, including Mark Miles, then the head of the Central Indiana Corporate Partnership (a group of CEOs, university presidents, and philanthropies dedicated to the prosperity and growth of the region—a quiet but powerful group). Mark, who had traveled the world as the head of the ATP, the men's professional tennis tour, for fifteen years understood what I was thinking and proceeded to become an important force in the birth and growth of Indy Connect.

After this meeting, I often said to my team, "I can't sell a leg, but I can sell a plan." The diesel train from northeast Indy to downtown was a leg. I needed a plan I could get behind, because the mayor of Indianapolis must be behind any mass transit plan, or it would go nowhere. Indianapolis was a Democratic city, but every county around it was Republican, as was the statehouse, whose help we would need. We would be fighting years' worth of Republican ideology in these surrounding counties. If I thought better mass transit was important, then I needed something I believed in. As I was a Republican, going against type would help.

Much of this crystallized for me when a lady from Denver, an expert in mass transit, came into my office and said, "Mass transit is about economic development." That was a succinct way of explaining the value of mass transit, something that I could use repeatedly with my Republican colleagues. Most people believe that mass transit is either about traffic mitigation or a cleaner environment. From this point forward, my main argument for better mass transit was economic development because it was true. Historically, commercial and residential property development occurs organically along transit corridors. This means increased property tax.

An excellent example of this is the Blue Line in Charlotte, North Carolina. Mark Miles and others brought city-county councilors and state legislators to Charlotte to see how a new transit system operated and to show them the impressive development that occurred quickly after the southbound leg from the Charlotte downtown was built. I went on one of these trips and met with Anthony Foxx, their terrific mayor at the time. We did a press conference together in Charlotte and became friends. He later became President Obama's secretary of transportation, which proved fortunate for Indianapolis.

As the new Indy Connect team traveled throughout the region to get input from citizens, something everyone on the team felt was important, we also needed legislative help from the statehouse. For instance, it was illegal for mass transit to cross county lines in Indiana. What a ludicrous law. But it was part of the protectionist sentiment that is sometimes still evident at the Republican-dominated Indiana statehouse. It took us at least three years at the statehouse to get all the proper legislation in place to allow us to move forward. A wonderful Republican state senator from the south side of Indianapolis, Pat Miller, was finally able to shepherd the legislation through. Indy Connect had lots of roadblocks purposely put in its path by the statehouse as part of the sausage making, such as a referendum and a specific city-county council vote to approve, but we persevered and got all the approvals needed.

While all of this was occurring, the plan was developing. We eventually decided that bus rapid transit (BRT) was a more flexible and cheaper alternative to rail. It acts like rail and feels like rail, with substations. Also, with the sharing economy coming forward and the future of transportation still murky twenty years out, bus rapid transit made sense. Since I was becoming known as an electric vehicle advocate at the time, I much preferred an electric bus rapid transit.

There was much discussion about where we should start building the BRT should we get everything in place to move forward. Adam Thies, my director of metropolitan development beginning my second term, came into my office to discuss the plans for the BRT. I have said frequently that the city has never hired a person like Adam. He understands money, design, the future, and so many other facets of business and government. He is a unique individual whom I would have liked to run several city departments over a twenty-year period; he would have changed Indianapolis in so many positive ways. He closed his successful business in Bloomington and moved his wife and four children to Indianapolis to come work for the city. (I am still amazed at the many sacrifices that much of my staff made to come work with us for a few years.)

Adam believed that, since mass transit was primarily about economic development, the Red Line—the north-south spine through the heart of the city—should be the first line built, not the northeast corridor to downtown or the downtown-to-the-airport route, as many others wanted. He believed that the most density would occur as a result of the Red Line being built. The Red Line would run close to four universities, through several important neighborhoods, and of course our thriving downtown, where so many people worked. I agreed with him, as did others.

Since this was to be an electric BRT, something unique at the time, I wanted to brief the secretary of transportation for President Obama, Anthony Foxx, the former mayor of Charlotte mentioned above. I went to his office with Adam's briefing materials and explained what we envisioned. Without my asking, he gave the city $2 million for research and development and then asked us to ask him for $75 million in startup money through a federal program. That is a pretty good sign that we would be competitive for such a federal grant, and we did receive the $75 million. The Red Line had a great beginning.

The referendum in the city passed, and the city-county council passed a small, dedicated tax increase to pay for the full Indy Connect plan. As I write this book, a few Republicans at the statehouse still try to prevent more mass transit being built, but I cannot fathom why. The people and the legislative body have voted. Some Republicans even tried to stop the already-approved $75 million from getting to the city after President Trump was elected, but even they eventually saw the insanity of trying to prevent already-approved federal money from reaching the city.

Full approval of the plan occurred after I left office, but those advocating for it still wanted me to be the primary advocate for the plan. Democrats in the city did not contact me, but other organizations, like the Indianapolis Chamber of Commerce, wanted me to stay involved. I did so. For instance, the Metropolitan Indianapolis Board of Realtors (MIBOR) used me to participate in a massive group phone call with senior citizens before the referendum. I was a bit puzzled by this until Mark Fisher of the Indy Chamber and I visited Columbus, Ohio, to talk to transit advocates from Columbus, Cincinnati, and Cleveland. When we took questions after the presentation, one lady asked why the chamber is using a former mayor. Mark said something like "Because he polls at 78 percent." I did not realize at the time that, even after I was out of office, my popularity was still strong.

I do not know why Republicans are reflexively against mass transit. Mass transit makes sense in well-populated cities. Some may see it as a handout, but that is a small way of thinking. There are bigger, broader, Republican reasons for why mass transit makes sense.

- *Economic mobility.* For the poor, transportation is a big expense, as explained above. If we want people to move into the middle class, as we constantly espouse, then the small investment in mass transit makes sense.
- *Expanding the property tax base.* All municipalities should be trying to expand their tax base. Transit-oriented development, commercial and residential building along mass transit corridors, results in an increase in the property tax base. This is obvious, but many believe otherwise. Why I could not tell you.
- *Attraction of talent.* Cities and states should know that to attract businesses, they must have a base of talent. Companies move to where they can hire an effective workforce; it is their highest priority. Talent today moves to where they can experience a high quality of life, and effective mass transit is one of those amenities that is important to talent. Only those still living in 1950 believe otherwise.

Of course, traffic mitigation, less pollution, and senior citizen mobility are also factors in favor of mass transit, but so many of the economic philosophies that Republicans espouse favor mass transit. We just have to realize it.

I hope that when Indianapolis Democrats cut their ribbons and talk about the expansion of mass transit in Indy, they will remember that it was a Republican mayor who changed the trajectory of mass transit back in 2008, worked years with many partners to get the needed legislation at the Republican statehouse, got the initial federal funding for the city, and then, when asked, continued to champion the mass transit efforts in Indianapolis once out of office.

Bicycling

Before Jamison Hutchins became our go-to guy for bicycling in the administration, he was already the embodiment of what an enhanced quality of life looked like to a millennial. This was talent attraction in the flesh. He grew up in Indianapolis but moved away as a young adult seeking a different lifestyle. When he heard that our administration was growing its bicycle culture, he moved back to become a part of it.

The growth of bicycling in Indianapolis came about because the multimodal transportation mindset of millennial talent required the city to move on the issue. Almost every other major city had a growing bicycle culture, but Indianapolis did not. We had some nice pieces like the Central Indiana Bicycling Association (CIBA) and the Monon Trail, a north-south former railroad line from downtown Indianapolis north to Carmel. I was told that before I became the mayor, the city had one mile of bicycle lanes. I do not know if that was true, but it made for a funny icebreaking line: "What does one mile of bike lanes connect to?"

Before we even conceived of having a bicycle/pedestrian coordinator in public works, Jamison took me and a few others on a long bike ride one weekend. A kind, unassuming, intelligent man, Jamison was the logical choice when we decided we needed more expertise. The city was well rewarded by that choice.

With the Rebuild Indy money and as part of the connectivity we wanted to develop for the city, we set a goal of having more than two hundred miles of bike lanes and paths in place by 2015, the end of my second term. Of course, I had to get reelected to make this happen. I believe we made our goal but did not make a final check as we left. I know we were close. After I left office, trails continued to be built, so the city is well past the two hundred miles; I am very happy about that.

We also conducted multiple rides with me throughout the year, such as a Spring Fever Ride and a birthday ride. These were very popular, with hundreds of cyclists coming out for each one. Part of the attraction was that we used police escorts so that we did not have to stop at traffic lights during the rides. With the help of sponsors, we made T-shirts for each of these rides, and they became popular also. We also changed the routes every year, showing the cyclists the new bike lanes and/or trails that had been built in the last year.

The ride that became the most popular was the Polar Bear Pedal, a ride scheduled just after the new year, guaranteeing that it would be cold. We came up with this crazy idea at an October meeting, and just a few months later, we held the first one. Our team could not believe the crowd that first year. We thought it might take a year or so to catch on, but the bicycling community came out strong with the very first one. The Polar Bear Pedal easily drew the most participants of any of the annual rides. We had tremendous press coverage also; who did not want to see the mayor and other bicyclists riding their bikes in freezing weather?

More Visibility

Every year, the *New York Times* comes out with a feature on the fifty-two places in the world to visit over the next year. One year, Indianapolis was one of only two places selected in the United States. The *New York Times* told its global audience that Indianapolis should be visited because of the Cultural Trail.

A transplanted San Diego visionary, Brian Payne, planted the idea of a Cultural Trail in the minds of city leaders before I became mayor. A spider web–like path downtown, the trail uses a different type of pavement with clear markings on the ground. It connects to other trails and popular neighborhoods like Massachusetts Avenue, dubbed "Mass Ave," and Fountain Square near our downtown. Private dollars and federal dollars paid for most of this trail, with the city providing the space. The original plan was for only eight miles total (it has since been expanded), but it made a difference in these areas. Fountain Square had been an up-and-coming neighborhood for a couple of decades, but it never really blossomed until the

Cultural Trail connected it directly to downtown. Now there are tremendous restaurants and other attractions in Fountain Square. It is no longer up and coming; it has arrived.

When I won in 2007, the first leg of the Cultural Trail was being built. Of course, after election night, as I mentioned, all the arts and sustainability folks were worried about this new Republican mayor. Frankly, I do not remember if I even knew what the Cultural Trail was when I got elected. However, I was asked to cut the ribbon on that first leg once in office, and it was clear to me that Brian Payne and others were worried that I was going to cancel the rest of the Cultural Trail. As the mayor, I certainly had the power to do just that. I understood their concerns but assured them that I had no intention of canceling it. I loved trails and knew their intrinsic value to cities from my time living in varied locations around the nation and the world. Brian became a trusted advisor. Whenever I had a big idea to talk about, I usually consulted Brian. Indianapolis is lucky to have him.

Our NBA team, the Indiana Pacers, also helped the Cultural Trail and the city by creating and maintaining a bike share program on the trail. The Pacers' owner, Herb Simon, has always been philanthropic (more than most people know; he is very quiet about most of his gifts), and this was a wonderful addition to the growing bike culture. People could now travel through downtown and the surrounding neighborhoods on these familiar bikes painted a bright Pacers gold. It was particularly gratifying to see so many people using the bikes on weekend family outings.

When we transformed the City Market (see below), the east wing became a bike hub. Bicycle Garage Indy put in a small sales and repair shop. The YMCA put in a gym with showers. There was storage for bicycles and lockers for those who wanted to ride downtown to work and then clean up. This was another important piece that signaled the city was serious about the bike and connectivity culture.

Unfortunately, as often happens, new administrations have other ideas, and the bike hub is becoming apartments.

The Velodrome—A Public-Private Partnership

Another key piece was transferring responsibility for the Major Taylor Velodrome on the campus of Marian University from the city to Marian University itself. The velodrome was built for the 1987 Pan Am Games hosted by Indianapolis. Although the facility itself remained usable, the city did little with it. When I became mayor, the city paid two Parks Department employees $70,000 annually to sit around and manage a closed facility. When I asked if it was ever open to the public, I was told that it opened on Monday evenings. I was stunned. This velodrome was just sitting there.

Marian is the best cycling college in the nation, winning some sort of national championship every year. In college cycling, there is Marian, and then there is everyone else. A great Catholic university in Indianapolis, Marian wanted to control the facility, but there were some sentiments to overcome within the Parks Department. All I saw was the city had this great asset but was doing nothing with it. It was ripe for a public-private partnership. The city needed to maximize the value and use of this public asset, not just claim ownership, which was all that the city was doing. If the city could not maximize the use—and it could not—then let someone else do it. Marian had the will and a plan to use this asset for the good of the city, and, as it turned out, for the country.

Marian began hosting regional and national races and championships at the velodrome, which they used as an institutional anchor to draw road races, BMX, cyclocross, and other events to the area. It was an absolute home run for the university and the city, and Marian became a nationally recognized host for cycling events. I attended many of these events, and it was heartwarming to see the amount of activity that now surrounded the velodrome.

Transformation

One bicycle shop owner mentioned at a press conference that our administration developed decades' worth of infrastructure in just a few years. All the bicycle shop owners loved what we were doing because their revenues increased dramatically as more and more people in the city began riding bikes. The increase in riders and the excitement within the city were obvious.

The nation noticed. When we started the transformation, we went to other cities to learn; now cities were coming to us to learn. Indy received the designation of bicycle-friendly city. I received a national bicycling leadership award; was asked to speak at an important Portland, Oregon, bicycle ride (Portland is the intellectual center of bicycling in the country); and was a featured speaker at the National Bike Summit in 2013 (it is still on YouTube).

Many of my fellow Republicans had difficulty with the growing bike culture within the city. It was not one of their ideological pillars. They could not connect the expenditure for bicycle-related infrastructure with the talent attraction that would eventually expand the tax base. It did not matter to me; I was moving forward with it.

While I was deciding whether to run for a third term, my political team already had plans to use the now-robust bicycle culture in the city as a campaign item. What a change. Guess I was right.

Parking Meters

When I took office in 2008, our parking meter processes and technology were straight out of 1950. People had to carry quarters, dimes, and nickels to feed the meters. Also, parking spaces with meters were free the entire weekend: an out-of-towner could drive into Indianapolis on Friday night, park at a meter, stay the entire weekend visiting friends, and then leave Monday morning without paying one nickel for the privilege.

In areas with retail, customers had to park blocks away to shop because whoever got a parking spot by Friday evening could stay there the entire weekend. Retailers hated this because customers had to park so far away from their stores; there was no turnover of the spaces. Even during the week, retailers were hurt because the cost for meters was so low that some people who went to work actually did carry quarters, dimes, and nickels by the bagful to feed the meters every couple of hours, because the price for our meters was by far the lowest in the country.

That may sound good on the surface, but price is a main determinant in controlling supply for any commodity or service. Our pricing was not close to bringing supply and demand into any sort of equilibrium.

Other cities had already moved on to new technology; it was time for Indianapolis to do the same. We went through a bid process, and a consortium of primarily local companies called ParkIndy won the bid. It is a fifty-year deal, and ParkIndy must keep up with any new technology.

ParkIndy put in meters that could use credit and debit cards and created an app so that people could pay by phone and even find an empty parking spot. We kept the cash option also. Most parking spots now use a numbering system, and people walk a half-block or so to put in the number of the parking spot and then pay through a credit or debit card or cash, if they did not pay by phone. For those meters not on the numbering system,

ParkIndy put in a credit/debit card slot so people could easily pay that way or use cash. The legendary broken parking meter phenomenon common in cities was largely eliminated. ParkIndy has a vested interest in keeping those meters operational; they are now repaired within hours instead of days or weeks.

As with any change, there were some complaints, but for this big of a change in the city, the backlash was minimal. Within a matter of months, over 80 percent of the transactions were by credit card or by phone app. Consumer satisfaction was much higher.

In 2010, the net revenue for the city with the old technology was just over $300,000. With the new technology, the net revenue to the city in 2013 was over $3 million, a stunning increase. The best part was the city now had no expenses related to maintaining the parking meters; we just took the money. We now did not have salaries, pensions, maintenance costs, etc., and the net revenue is at least ten times what it was before, with updated technology and much faster repair times for the meters, and the citizens are much happier.

As part of the change, we doubled the rates for parking—but we were still the lowest in the country. We did not allow people to stay in parking spots for extended times; most had a maximum time of four hours. The meters became free as of Saturday night, not Friday evening. Retailers were happier.

One cannot attribute the ten times increase in revenue simply to having raised the price of the meters; that would have only doubled the revenue. Increased turnover, not allowing people to park free the whole weekend, and comfort with the use of credit/debit cards and the phone app all contributed to the increase. More people were now using the parking meters because parking spots were now more available, and they did not have to search for loose change.

A major difference in how we approached this project was how we used the increased revenues. As far as we could tell, every city that had completed a similar project took all the cash up front, then allowed the vendor to collect the cash for the term of the lease. For instance, Chicago leased their meters for a seventy-five-year term for $1.1 billion. Within three years, that money was gone, used for normal operational expenses. We did not do that.

I understand the short-term nature of politics, and current officeholders love getting their hands on as much cash as they can for their pet projects, but I did not think that was fair to future administrations and councils. By state law, parking meter money must be spent on infrastructure in the area of the parking meters. Knowing how difficult it is to maintain infrastructure, I wanted most of this money to go to future city officials.

We took $20 million for some near-term projects and then left the rest of the future money over the next fifty years of the term for future mayors and future councils to spend. Future administrations will now have at least $3 million more annually to spend on infrastructure than they otherwise would have had.

Our administration was different, always looking for the long-term health of the city. This is what mayors should be doing, not necessarily spending everything they can now to make themselves look better politically.

I received the National Parking Association for Innovation award based on this project. The primary reason for my award was that they liked what we did with the proceeds from the deal. I wish more local officials would think in such terms.

The Republican-led city-county council was skeptical at first but also knew that the parking meter system should be updated. They wanted some input into the process. A key point they wanted was an every-ten-years buyout opportunity for the city. The ParkIndy consortium readily agreed to this request, and I thought it made a lot of sense also. Every ten years, the city can look at this project and decide whether they want to buy out the contract or not. Of course, if they do that, they will give up the increased future revenues to the city, and the city would have to maintain and update the technology itself at great expense. At the first ten-year mark, my successor and the council determined that they wanted to continue with ParkIndy.

After the new parking meters were in, Democrats on the council would frequently criticize the deal or say something like, "You left money on the table." I would remind them that just a few years before, "You had the mayor's office and the majority on the council, and you did nothing." That would quiet them quickly. In reality, the criticism occurred only because I was a Republican, the change was popular, and the revenue increased tenfold. They did not do it. We did.

Another interesting part of the story was that, as this parking meter deal was being completed near my reelection, my opponent in that race called up one of the contractors affiliated with ParkIndy. She begged him to somehow cancel the deal, saying she would get it done after she had won the election with him playing a major part. He did not bite. She did not win.

There is a feeling among some Democratic officeholders that the city and the state should do everything it can with only government employees. I reject that notion. Public-private partnerships, also known as P3s, should be used whenever possible. Elected officeholders should do what is best for their citizens. Sometimes, there are private companies that can perform better for the city and the state; they can be more efficient, save taxpayer money, and increase future revenues.

Former mayor Stephen Goldsmith put it this way: if you look in the Yellow Pages (or their modern equivalent) and see that at least three firms are performing a function that the government does also, you should look at contracting that function out. Many times, a P3 relationship is better. It certainly was for Indy's parking meters.

Parks

In the first few months of our administration in 2008, the parks director, whom we retained from the previous administration, would brief me on the status of the pools that were to open that summer. He kept saying things like, "Don't worry, Mayor, the pools will be open. We'll make sure they'll be ready." It was odd how he was saying it, implying that it would take a lot of work, but no matter what, those pools would be open on the first day. I could not help but think that something was wrong, just from his tone of voice. Why would the pools not be open? Why did he keep saying this to me in the way he did? Was getting the pools open on time not a routine occurrence?

I came to find out that getting the pools open on time was a politically sensitive issue. Some advocates in the city believed that those pools opening on time was a sign that the city cared about its children, and that anything less was a signal of a failure to care. This pressure led to a patchwork of temporary repairs over the years, just to ensure that the pools were open. This proved detrimental to the overall operation of the pools.

It is hard to believe, but we found that the pools in the city were leaking about thirty-five million gallons of water every summer, thanks to that patchwork nature of repairs over the years. One pool alone was leaking seven million gallons per summer, keeping the grounds of the surrounding park moist all summer long. Apparently, the sensitivity of opening the pools outweighed the value of the neighborhood enjoying that park.

Political considerations, therefore, were more important than doing the right thing. This was unacceptable. Hiding the poor condition of so many of the pools would not stand. From my marine background, I knew the importance of maintaining equipment and the potentially disastrous consequences that could occur if equipment was not maintained.

To repair the pools, some had to be closed over the next summer. This caused a lot of consternation in some areas, and we predictably heard from some citizens that the city did not care for its children, that crime would rise, and the like. Most of it was genuine concern, but some of it was bashing of the still-new administration. However, I was firm in my belief that the city must repair the pools for the long term and that the old cycle of patchwork repairs was not going to be acceptable anymore. I was not going to let a few people who were angry at me stop me from doing the right thing. None of the dire predictions about the crime rate proved to be true.

Starting in my third summer in office and from then on, all the pools opened on time in a routine manner. The pool that was leaking seven million gallons each summer was completely redone and made into a spectacular new pool for the kids. The reopening of that pool was wonderful, and the families in the neighborhood could not have been happier.

In line with enhancing the quality of life of the city, we redesigned the pool at Wes Montgomery Park. (Wes Montgomery was a famous jazz guitarist from Indianapolis). The pool at the park was empty most days, used by virtually nobody in the neighborhood. One lady, fairly active in some community affairs, would occasionally bring some kids from a nearby neighborhood to the pool, but that was minimal use. Our parks director at the time had the brilliant idea to make the pool a spray pool for little kids so that parents in the neighborhood could bring their little ones to frolic in the water. He thought the park would be used much more frequently this way. The idea was to design the spray features in the shape of Wes Montgomery's guitar.

We had to close the pool to remake it, but it was a tremendous success immediately, and the Montgomery family, who attended the reopening, was thrilled that we had come up with the guitar design. The lady who brought those older kids to the pool was furious at us for what she believed was turning our back on "her" kids. However, our parks director was right.

The spray pool and the surrounding park were now being used much more frequently by the families in the neighborhood. Every time I drove by there, lots of little kids were playing at that spray pool with their parents in attendance. It was now a great park for the neighborhood, just as it should have been all along.

We never let just one person or one small group of people dictate what was best for a neighborhood or the city. All cities have activists, and most mean well. However, their ideas can sometimes be off track for what is best for all. Our administration did a good job of separating what was a personal agenda from the overall good.

Lilly Endowment

With the help of the Lilly Endowment, we were also able to upgrade other park amenities, not just the pools. The Lilly Endowment, one of the largest philanthropic foundations in the world with assets over $20 billion, has been crucial to the economic and physical development of Indianapolis and Indiana, but it also helps with smaller projects that can have significant value to the city and the state. They were gracious enough to give us several million dollars for needed upgrades to the parks.

A Different Way to Fund?

As in most cities, the park system has many supporters, financial and otherwise. However, in Indianapolis and several other cities, the public-safety budget overwhelms other departments and makes it difficult to find additional dollars for both operations and maintenance of the other departments. I could not get out of my mind that our city had to find another recurring source of revenue for the parks department. I explored the possibility of creating a separate endowment, but upon some research, that seemed improbable.

However, I do believe there could be a way to provide a dedicated source of funding by having commercial activities or housing in a small portion of the parks, with the tax revenue from these sources dedicated to the parks. The park purists hate this idea, believing that every inch of a designated park should be "the park." When I visited our sister city, Taipei, Taiwan, I was taken aback by the number of commercial activities in their parks; it was a vibrant and active scene. If I had had a few more years in office, I believe I could have moved in this direction, securing much-needed dedicated funding for the parks department.

Naivety

I was naive in the beginning to the sensitivity of the parks. In my first year in office, as part of briefing the *Indianapolis Star* editorial board before the annual budget presentation, I made a stupid mistake regarding the parks. In discussing the budget, I mentioned that we may be looking at cutting some of the budget. I mentioned that we may look at closing some parks.

In my mind, this made sense simply because some of our parks are just small pieces of land that have no amenities and no visitors. They are just designated a "park," which means the city must keep it up. One of the most bizarre parks is a small diagonal slice of land along a main thoroughfare, East Thirty-Eighth Street. I am sure most people do not even know it is a park. No one is ever there because it would be unsafe go there, so near to the very busy Thirty-Eighth Street. There are a few other pieces of parkland that have no value and no usage whatsoever. It made sense to me to get them off the budget.

However, the editorial board was aghast that I would mention such a thing. Closing parks was heresy, not something to speak about, and the editorial cartoonist ran a cartoon with a boy on a swing with a "For Sale" sign stuck to his forehead. I fondly remember my public-safety director, Scott Newman, in the editorial meeting with me, valiantly trying to save me from myself by mentioning that there were other cuts we were looking into. At this point, he was much more politically savvy than I was. He knew I never should have mentioned such nonsense, especially in this forum. I got pummeled publicly for quite a few days. We never closed any parks. It was not worth the aggravation; there were bigger fish to fry.

Eskenazi—The National Model for Public Hospitals

When I became mayor, Wishard Public Hospital was a collection of decaying buildings on West Tenth Street, just outside of downtown. It had a long and interesting history. The public hospital model in Indianapolis began in 1859 with the opening of City Hospital—originally a federal hospital for treating smallpox, but it became a Civil War military hospital. After the war, the federal government turned City Hospital over to the city, which opened it in 1866 as a seventy-five-bed charity hospital. The hospital, led by Dr. William Wishard, was expanded in the 1880s. It established the first nursing school in the state, graduating the first class of five nurses in 1885.

In the early part of the twentieth century, City Hospital was the only hospital in the city that would treat African American patients. In 1947, the name was changed to Indianapolis General Hospital, and in 1951, Health and Hospital Corporation was created to govern the hospital and remove it from political influences. General Hospital expanded again in the 1960s. It was renamed Wishard Memorial Hospital in 1975, and both a trauma center and a burn center followed.

After my election, Joe Loftus, our city lobbyist and also the Health and Hospital Corporation lobbyist, came into my office to discuss Wishard. At the time, HHC was run by a brilliant, caring lawyer named Matt Gutwein. Although HHC was technically free from political influences, as the new mayor, I could have replaced him if I desired. I was advised otherwise and listened to that sage advice.[1]

With multiple structures decaying at Wishard, the city had three options: simply close it, repair its buildings, or build new facilities. After a few more months and discussions with Matt, we were left with only two options: close it or build new. In my mind, closing it was not an option at all. Wishard, despite the condition of its buildings, had a sterling reputation for care, as personified by Dr. Lisa Harris, its chief medical officer. It also was important to the people in the lower-income neighborhoods, who trusted Wishard. It had a stellar history dating from the mid-nineteenth century, and I sensed that the citizens wanted it to continue.

Matt had skillfully positioned Health and Hospital to take on the debt for a new hospital, although property taxes could be used if needed. There was some financial risk, but I trusted Matt and his team, as they also knew the sensitivity of the use of property taxes. Even though a furor over property taxes had helped to elect me, I was vocal in my support for building a new public hospital. It was important to the citizens and sent a message that the city cares for its less fortunate. Also, there was tremendous philanthropic support from the beginning. The city had AAA bond ratings; Matt told me that the AAA status saved HHC about $350 million in debt service. I do not believe that property taxes have yet been used for the debt service.

Urban Republicans understand the importance of publicly serving the less fortunate. In other settings, private and personal assistance may dominate or be more appropriate, but citizens in major cities strongly desire that the city lead on helping the less fortunate. We did so.

A Work of Art

The new facility is an incredible public hospital. The design of the building, both inside and out, is stunning. There is a calming water feature outside the hospital (our babbling brook?). There is also an urban garden inside where they grow fresh vegetables for their patients. The hospital earned a silver certification from the US Green Building Council for Leadership in Energy and Environmental Design (LEED). It has 315 inpatient beds, nineteen operating rooms, two hundred outpatient exam rooms, and twelve labor and delivery rooms.

Sid and Lois Eskenazi, local and philanthropic commercial real estate developers, donated $40 million, earning the name change from Wishard to Eskenazi. HHC also opened satellite medical facilities around the city. The public hospital concept is alive and well in Indianapolis—and functioning at a high level.

What Matt Gutwein and Dr. Lisa Harris did for Indianapolis during this time was amazing.

Broad Ripple—Listening to the Neighborhood

Broad Ripple is a legendary neighborhood in the city north of downtown in what we call the Midtown area. It has some nice restaurants and bars and other mostly unique retail. Young adults frequent Broad Ripple at night and on the weekends. While running for office in 2007, I attended a meeting of the Broad Ripple Village Association (BRVA), an active group that included both residential and commercial (retail) interests. It was another of those meetings that I attended during the campaign when almost no one in the meeting of about seventy or eighty people knew who I was.

Their Republican councilor, Ryan Vaughn, spoke, and some started to complain about the direction of the city. Ryan, who would become my third chief of staff, quickly pointed out to them that if they wanted the city to improve, then they needed to elect "that gentleman sitting over there," pointing at me. I am sure that this was the first time most of them had ever heard of me. It was a nice moment that added a bit to my still-meager name recognition.

After the election, the BRVA invited me back. As this was a vocal group, I expected to hear what they hoped for from the administration. I talked to the group for a while. Then, as I always did if possible, I took as many questions as they wanted to ask. During the Q&A, it became apparent to me that the BRVA was divided by what the residents wanted and what the retailers wanted.

I stayed there for a full two hours, getting more exasperated as the meeting went on, as they squabbled openly in front of me. These were nice, caring people, but as a group, they did not know what they wanted. As nicely as possible, I told them as I left that I had no idea what they wanted and could not take anything back to my administration to work on. I could tell they had never heard that before from a mayor.

They then asked to hold an upcoming Mayor's Night Out, and we granted that request. It was clear from the beginning of that Mayor's Night Out that they had talked among themselves and had come to some sort of clarity on their goals. They wanted more development but not so much as to take away from the unique character of their neighborhood.

The retail piece was hampered by inadequate parking. As a result, people wanting to go to restaurants or bars, particularly in the evening, would park in the residential areas in front of homes. Homeowners with schoolkids were less than thrilled about this. There were parking meters in the area, but they did not serve much purpose other than providing minor revenue to the city. The city had no money set aside to help with the sort of development they were seeking.

Then the parking meter deal closed. As mentioned above, the city took a small portion of the projected revenue up front ($20 million) but left the vast majority of that revenue to future administrations. Since state law mandated that parking revenue money could be used only for infrastructure in areas where there were parking meters, we now had money to help Broad Ripple. We tore down an abandoned gas station and used Keystone Construction, a local developer, to build a parking garage on College Avenue directly across the street from the beginning of the retail area of Broad Ripple. The garage itself also included retail on the street level.

This was a bit of a gamble, but it paid off. Almost immediately thereafter, mixed-use developments, including nice apartments, sprang up. Natural foods grocer Fresh Thyme opened a store. As we learned, developers want to see some commitment from the city before they invest. Now, the local residents seemed to come out more, prouder of their already-nice area. I was invited to events a bit more. It continues to grow as of this writing.

I learned that it is much easier to deal with neighborhood groups if they are plain-speaking and detailed in what they want from the city. It provides better clarity for all concerned and saves time.

There are some who want Broad Ripple to grow even bigger, with taller buildings, but my sense is that most Broad Ripple residents wanted more vibrancy and more attention, not a major redevelopment that would take away the character of the area. I think we delivered on their desires.

Market Square

After Bankers Life Fieldhouse, the home of the Indiana Pacers (now called Gainbridge Fieldhouse), opened in 1999, the city imploded the former home of the Pacers, Market Square Arena, in 2001. Market Square Arena remains a fond memory for those who had helped build up the city since the late 1960s. It was former Mayor Richard Lugar (before he became a respected US senator) who decreed that downtown must be the vital part of the city; therefore, the new fieldhouse would be built downtown. The downtown that is now recognized nationally started from that point.

The old Market Square Arena site was prime real estate in the heart of downtown, and when it was demolished, most expected that a redevelopment of the site would occur quickly. That did not happen. When we took office in 2008, those (now) two sites remained as parking lots, not necessarily an eyesore but certainly underwhelming in view of their economic potential.

We tackled open downtown properties as aggressively as possible, with the philosophy of finding a way to yes being critical to our success. We quietly doubled the number of residential properties in downtown Indianapolis, but we also took on the task of developing the obvious, open spaces in our downtown. Market Square was a key part of this downtown development.

Once the country emerged from the Great Recession, we put out a request for proposal (RFP) for the north lot. We received several proposals and selected a stunning twenty-eight-story luxury apartment tower with retail on the street level anchored by a Whole Foods grocery store. Called 360 Market Square, it was developed by the local firm Flaherty & Collins.

Soon thereafter, we worked out an arrangement with Cummins, the forward-thinking Fortune 500 engine manufacturer, to build a beautiful, environmentally friendly structure that houses a global division headquarters. Cummins wanted more of a presence in Indianapolis (their global headquarters is in Columbus, Indiana), and this building fit perfectly in their plans—and fit perfectly in our plans for the south lot of the old Market Square Arena.

My economic development team was always stellar, but transforming these two parking lots into a pair of magnificent buildings was a major accomplishment for the city.

More property tax would be coming our way.

CityWay

The biggest gamble we made during the Great Recession was CityWay. This was another open spot downtown, just south of Bankers Life Fieldhouse. We wanted to build more downtown residential properties, and Eli Lilly wanted a nice hotel nearer their campus on the south side of downtown for visiting employees and guests. CityWay accomplished both objectives. Given the uncertainty of the length of the recession, financing was a gamble, but one that I approved. I thought that we should keep building if possible, and having the backing of Eli Lilly helped with financing.

It proved to be a great success. The Alexander Hotel is high end, with a great restaurant. It was an important addition to the other high-end hotels in downtown Indianapolis. The apartments were of high quality and filled up quickly. A fully outfitted YMCA, funded primarily by the Irsay family (owners of the Indianapolis Colts), was built across the street south of the hotel. An addition, CityWay 2, approved in the last month of our administration, started building once I left office; these apartments are across the street from the hotel to the west and have been completed.

The gamble paid off handsomely for the city. That Lilly supported the development helped make our decision easier.

Central State Hospital

Central State Hospital opened as the Indiana Hospital for the Insane in 1848 and housed more than 2,500 patients at its peak in the 1950s. Located on the near west side of Indianapolis, it remained a psychiatric hospital until it closed in 1994; the city bought the property a decade later. When we began our administration, the site was overgrown with vegetation, had unsafe structures and environmental problems, and was riddled with vandalism and crime.

In my first few years in office, I drove through the area several times, wondering what could be done with the space. Developers were interested in the property, but nothing seemed appropriate for the space until our administration partnered with some local firms to finally develop the area. The environmental issues alone made this a difficult undertaking, but it was a great space aching for a new use. As usual, developers feel more comfortable when the city puts some skin in the game. We did.

Again, our economic development team was aggressive, and 2011 began the reemergence of this area. Along with new roads, an affordable apartment complex, a senior housing facility, a charter school, and a public track-and-field site soon sprang up. An event center, micro-offices, and creative studios also were built. The site just needed someone to invest in it, and we were able to find the right fit for the property.

After our administration, development continued. We made the right call to redevelop this unusual space.

16 Tech

My predecessor's team had envisioned a life sciences corridor on the near northwest part of the city, just outside of downtown. It is a wonderful area that, if designed well, would be a spectacular addition to the already-robust life sciences businesses and organizations in the city, along with the research components at our universities. We felt that, even during the Great Recession, we should find some way to keep this project afloat. We did so.

Thanks in part to the sale of the water and wastewater assets to Citizens and the extension of the downtown tax increment financing district (TIF), we found the financing to secure land from various entities to keep this project going. Mike Huber, Deron Kintner, and Adam Collins were savvy and aggressive, as we thought 16 Tech, even if completed after our administration, would be of great value to the city and state. We helped with the design and partnered with the Central Indiana Corporate Partnership (CICP) to keep the master planning on track.

We signed a project agreement the evening of our very last day in office. My successor was able to build aggressively on this land in lockstep with the vision of the two previous administrations. It is becoming an important research component in the city.

City Market

The city running a commercial enterprise seemed odd to me, but such was the historic nature of the City Market. It was run by a board largely appointed by the mayor but was hardly a thriving endeavor. Government is usually terrible at running commercial operations because government has a different mindset than business does. When I entered office in 2008, the City Market, straight across the street from the City-County Building with the mayor's office overlooking, was battleship gray on the inside. The recent renovation of just a few years prior had made it as dull as it could be.

The building was donated to the city by the Tomlinson family more than one hundred years before and supposedly had restrictions on its use. As we looked into upgrading the market, we found that there were no restrictions on the property; that was a long-held urban myth.

It is considered a city landmark. I remember my mom taking us down by bus to buy groceries for our family fifty years earlier. When I assumed office, it was mostly restaurants with a few food vendors, a barber shop, and other retailers. It had a center hall with wings on both sides. We had problems with vendors not paying their rent and others who felt that they could dictate to us what they would do. We had different standards, however, and vendors found out that we would play hardball.

We decided to put all the retailers into the middle section of the market and use the wings for other activities. We also put in the Tomlinson Taproom on the upper floor, which became an instant hit. From about 4:00 p.m. on, the taproom was in use by downtown workers relaxing with friends and drinking a beer after a day at the office. It was a great addition to the City Market. Someone from the government had a good business idea after all.

A New Director

However, the primary problems with the market were that it was ugly and uninviting and had no programming, and the technology used by the retailers was outdated. We hired a new director, Stevi Stoesz, who understood what we were trying to do with the market. She was smart, motivated, and dynamic. She started programming events for the market that brought people in.

The market had a new energy with Stevi in charge. With help from the Lilly Endowment, we were able to remake the center hall. From my Marine Corps days traveling the world, I knew that color was important to attract people; I had in mind a European color scheme. We put in the reds, yellows, and greens that were needed and got rid of the battleship gray. We left the floor as concrete but put a paint on it that proved attractive. We also had the vendors accept credit and debit cards.

Part of Stevi's programming was conducting tours of the catacombs underneath the market. Previously unused, it is a mysterious place that is defined by handsome brick throughout. It looks like it could have been used as a speakeasy during Prohibition or as a gambling area hidden away from the cops. However, we could find no plumbing. No one really knows what the space was used for, adding to its attraction. Stevi cleaned up the space and started tours, including the annual, and appropriate, Halloween tour.

As mentioned earlier, the east wing of the market became the bike hub but has since been repurposed as apartments. We were considering turning the west wing into some sort of arts venue or maybe tearing it down and putting in some sort of green space with a small outdoor theater. Then Bill Taft of Local Initiatives Support Corporation (LISC) came to us inquiring about making this wing into a nonprofit center. That made a lot of sense to us. LISC is now in there with some other groups, along with the City Market's offices. It is also designed to be a meeting space that is used quite frequently. It seems the perfect use for the space.

After Winnie and I publicly celebrated our thirtieth wedding anniversary in early 2013, Stevi asked me if I would conduct a mass vow renewal annually at the City Market on Valentine's Day for any couples who wanted to renew their vows. It was a success, and if I recall correctly, we had about fifty couples by the second year. It was a nice, sweet event and typical of Stevi's ingenuity and drive. The market was lucky to have her.

A Precursor

There was one episode that stood out involving a friendly, well-respected tenant. A gay couple came to the cookie vendor and asked if they would make some cupcakes for their upcoming wedding. One of the owners said,

"I can't because I only make cookies," which was true. However, he then told them that even if he did make cupcakes, he would not do so because he did not believe in gay marriage. This caused quite a stir, as the gay couple made this incident public. Because the city owned the market, the words of the cookie vendor violated a city ordinance.

As sometimes happens, things that could have and should have been handled locally between the parties and the city grew into something much more. It went national. This was my first time experiencing the activism of the religious right, but not my last. They organized nationally on this issue and made harassing phone calls to our office. They told those answering the calls that the mayor was working with the devil and other such nonsense. It was very stressful for the people working the issue on my behalf. In retrospect, this incident was a precursor to a much more volatile and stressful situation that would occur a few years later and is covered in a subsequent chapter.

We gave the cookie vendor a letter of reprimand, stressing to them the requirements of the city ordinance. They understood, and it didn't happen again.

MLK Boulevard

With Rebuild Indy money, we thought it would be appropriate to refresh Dr. Martin Luther King Jr. Boulevard on the near northwest side of Indianapolis. In addition to repaving the street, we also put markings in the concrete similar to those on the Cultural Trail, ensured the sidewalks were in good condition, and built new bus stops that provided a Black history narrative at each stop. Working with neighborhood leaders and other stakeholders, we spent over $2 million improving this important corridor. The boulevard looked tremendous when we were done, and the commercial vendors on the street were thrilled with the outcome.

We held a ceremony to celebrate the new look, and Martin Luther King III was gracious enough to attend. A wonderful man, he did some local media with me to talk about the occasion. He also attended the ceremony, which had a very nice crowd as people wanted to celebrate what had occurred. As he sat next to me, he whispered that he wished all the MLK streets across the nation looked as good as this one and that our efforts to beautify the boulevard gave him renewed enthusiasm to urge other cities to do what we had just done in Indianapolis. It was a proud moment for me, but I also knew that a lot of planning, design, and construction work was done by people who cared deeply for our city.

Unfortunately, not one Democratic officeholder attended the ceremony.

Neighborhood Redevelopment

The importance of continuing neighborhood redevelopment is understood by urban Republicans. Much of our redevelopment centered on the neighborhoods. Avondale Meadows, an area near where I spent much of my younger years, was an area of focus for us. It is a poor neighborhood with too much crime but wonderful, caring citizens. Now there are several high-performing charter schools in the area, a new YMCA focused on the needs of the neighborhood, an Excel Center to help adults earn a high school diploma, and new, attractive apartments, along with other amenities.

I spoke already of Broad Ripple, but we also upgraded the Irvington and Wanamaker neighborhoods, important areas on the east and far south sides of Indianapolis. We used $29 million in Neighborhood Stabilization Funds from the federal government to attract additional investments that resulted in new housing units on the near north side, the near east side and the near southeast side. We used data to target these neighborhoods, looking at utility disconnections, police runs, foreclosures, and the like to determine where the money could be best used.

We had big plans to rehab the Riverside/northwest corridor, including the Marian University area, but could not put the pieces in place before I left office. The northwest side of Indianapolis from downtown out is topographically beautiful and deserving of more investment than it has had in the past. I wish we had had more time.

Of course, Rebuild Indy provided the millions in much-needed refreshment for neighborhoods across the city. That work will stand for decades.

Demolition

Part of redevelopment, both commercial and neighborhood, is the demolition of structures whose presence is not just lost potential, but an actual negative influence on the area. The Keystone Towers on the northeast side of Indianapolis were one such example. These were once a modern housing development, but by the time I became the mayor, they were abandoned and had become a public-safety issue for the city. They would crop up in the news occasionally because of criminal activity, with reporters asking us what we were going to do about them.

In 2011, we imploded the towers. We made it into an event with all the TV stations present; most people are fascinated by a loud implosion, and we took advantage of that. We were solving a problem, loudly. The site is now home to nice new apartments.

Another prominent site that had become dangerous was the old Winona Hospital on north Meridian Street. Meridian is the north-south spine in most parts of the city, dividing Indianapolis from east to west. I worked in that hospital while in high school, delivering food trays in a cart to the floors. Winona could not compete with the larger hospitals being built across central Indiana, and in 2004, they announced they were closing.

When the hospital closed, everyone just left, and the beds, the instruments, and most of the other equipment just sat in the unused hospital for years. The city was fearful that the site was a biohazard. We eventually sent teams inside to ensure that an implosion would be safe for the surrounding neighborhoods. Once that was accomplished, we imploded the building in 2011.

One other large demolition occurred in Stringtown on the near west side of Indianapolis. An old industrial facility that occupied a large lot (about two blocks long and one block wide) had closed, and the facility had deteriorated terribly. It was mostly an open lot with a surrounding, deteriorating outline of a building. Parents were worried not just about the unknown environmental danger but also for their kids who wanted to play in this dangerous space.

This facility was unknown to almost everyone, but I knew about it because the neighborhood ensured that I visited the site personally. It took me and our staff a while to figure out what to do. We estimated that the demolition (piece by piece, not an implosion) would cost about a million dollars. It was difficult to find that kind of money when no redevelopment was on the horizon.

The residents of Stringtown—an oft-neglected part of the city—did not go to the press complaining or making threats; they just wanted the city to help them. It became personal to me. We eventually found the money, took down the structure, and removed the pieces. A redemptive aspect was that the Department of Metropolitan Development recycled enough of the material that it almost covered the million dollars we spent on the demolition.

That was welcome news, but it was more important to me that we fulfilled a reasonable request from the neighborhood. They wanted a nicer place for their children.

Homes

No one likes to take down abandoned homes. Children grew up in these homes. Each home meant something to someone at one time. However, across America are many abandoned homes that should come down. Most abandoned homes either have or will have criminal activity in them. The neighbors knew this also, and it scared them. They did not want their children near the drugs that were common in these abandoned homes.

If a home was salvageable, we did not take it down. However, between Rebuild Indy funds and Neighborhood Stabilization Project funds, we took down well over two thousand homes. Housing activists complained to me that we were taking down too many too fast, but I never heard that complaint from residents in the neighborhoods.

Breakthrough Needed

Early in my tenure as mayor, I was visiting a senior home, and a lady asked me about filling potholes. I explained about cold patches and hot patches. Cold patches are done when the temperature is below freezing; they do not last long, only a few weeks. It takes a hot patch completed when the temperature is warmer to have the pothole repaired for any real length of time. She then asked me something only a senior citizen would ask, "You mean we can send a man to the moon, but we can't fix a pothole in cold weather?" The answer to that is yes, but she has a point.

A better road material would annually save city and state taxpayers across the country hundreds of millions of dollars, if not over a billion dollars. It needs to have the same friction capabilities for current tires while not being subject to the freeze-thaw cycle that causes potholes. Northern and Midwestern cities and states know full well how much money is needed to keep the roads smooth as spring follows winter. The same roads are frequently repatched every year until a municipality finds the funds to repave them. It is enormously expensive to do both these tasks when you include the labor and material costs. Additionally, motorists must pay for expensive repairs on their tires and wheels. Potholes can be the source of injuries and even death, although such extremes are rare fortunately. It is a headache for both motorists and politicians alike, the latter who deal with the inevitable outcry when a pothole is not filled as quickly as possible.

I do not know how much research is being done in this regard, but it would be a major benefit. I know it would hurt the concrete and asphalt companies, who can be major contributors to political campaigns, but a better road material would be of great benefit to the taxpaying citizens of the North and Midwest.

Two Projects Passed On

I mentioned above that I felt we were put into office to accomplish projects that were left undone for political or financial reasons. We had two significant projects that were thoroughly planned, but we were not able to put the shovel in the ground to begin them.

The Criminal Justice Center

The first was the Criminal Justice Center. Prior to our administration, some had talked about such a project but did nothing about it. We did. We envisioned a new campus that would be built at the old General Motors Stamping Plant just off downtown. The campus would include the jail, the courts, relevant offices like the prosecutor, and other similar functions.

There were several reasons for this. All these functions took up valuable downtown real estate at a cost that could be much less elsewhere. The jail was a series of separate buildings that could be better utilized as commercial properties, thereby expanding the tax base for the city. The prosecutor rented high-end office space in a prime downtown location, which was a waste of taxpayers' money. The courts were in the City-County Building, and the transportation of prisoners between the jail and the courts was dangerous and expensive. One time a prisoner escaped from his handlers inside the City-County Building and found his way to the council chambers. (The council was not in session.) Every day, prisoners and their handlers used the same freight elevator that I used to get to my office. Frequently I would pass by them on the way up to my office.

If we could have moved these functions onto a separate campus, it would have been much safer and cheaper for the city. The transportation of prisoners would be simpler with much less risk. With the courts moving out of the City-County Building, other city offices that were renting elsewhere, such as the Department of Code Enforcement, could then move into the City-County Building at less cost to the taxpayer. The enormous rent being paid by the prosecutor's office would now be much less. All of it made sense to us.

We created a public-private partnership (P3) to build, finance, and operate the facility. Republicans are comfortable with P3s, feeling they are less expensive for the taxpayer operationally, with costs such as salaries, maintenance, insurance, and pensions being picked up by the private sector, which tends to be more efficient than the government. Democrats philosophically tend to favor public operations being fully funded and staffed by the government. We felt our structure would be better for the taxpayer, and the estimates on the costs that we presented to the public did not even include the rent that would not be paid by city offices being moved into the City-County Building. Also of importance, the building and entire operation would be turned over to the city after thirty-five years, which I believed was a terrific bargain for the city.

Since this was to be a major project for the city, Ryan Vaughn, my chief of staff at the time, crafted a letter that indicated everyone involved agreed that this project should be moved forward. It said, in part, "The Parties will cooperate in good faith for the primary purpose of exploring, with the intent of effectuating, the Justice Facility Improvement Project." Signees to the document included the sheriff, who ran the jail; the prosecutor; the president of the city-county council; and others. They put their signatures on that piece of paper, as did I.

Nationally, this was being talked about in the P3 community. I was asked to speak at different conferences around the country on what we were doing. As the council passed bills that authorized funding for the designs and other work to be developed by the contractors, everything seemed on track. Millions of dollars were authorized by the council for the early stages of the project.

Then I announced that I would not be running for a third term. I naively believed that this would take any politics out of the project and that it would be smooth sailing. I knew I would not be around to see its completion, but I expected to put the first shovel into the ground. I was wrong.

Any power I had to move this massive project forward evaporated with my announcement to forego a third term. All those Democratic officeholders who had signed that piece of paper disappeared. The sheriff, who desperately needed a better jail, would not talk to me about it and certainly did not want to participate in a press conference with me, even though he was very much in favor of the project when it was announced. The Democrats felt they could just wait until I left office and then do the project on their own.

This is what they did. I am glad that the project went forward, in a different section of the city, although I would have liked our original P3 financial structure. However, that is not how elections work. The original designs were of help to those who eventually built the campus. I worried about the city's reputation for trust and credibility with the private sector when a project that was approved and being funded was suddenly pulled from their grasp, but it seems to have worked out. The city needed the facility, and now it is a reality. I am glad we pushed it forward.

Lugar Plaza, a.k.a. Ballard's Back Yard

The second project that we initiated and planned is now called Lugar Plaza. I called it my backyard. It is the back side of the City-County Building, which originally seemed to be designed to discourage visitors. Along the Cultural Trail on Washington Street, that space made me wonder if it was designed that way for security reasons. However, now with the stunning 360 Market and the beautiful Cummins division headquarters across the street to the east, both buildings being parking lots just a few years before, it seemed time to make the back of the City-County Building into a visitor-friendly green space.

Adam Thies, then the director of the Department of Metropolitan Development, instituted a design contest to reimagine that space. I told Adam that downtown Indianapolis needed an outdoor ice skating rink for the winter, and Adam encouraged those submitting designs to understand that. The nickname for the project as it developed was Ballard's Back Yard, but I had no illusions that that name would stick.

We had numerous exceptional designs and felt that this would be a great addition to downtown, a welcoming space on the grounds of the City-County Building. We had funding lined up, and Adam's team picked the winner. However, we soon learned that the estimated cost submitted by the winning designer was not close to the actual cost. We had to regroup, but as we did so, time ran out on the administration.

My successor moved forward with the project but with a different design and a more reasonable actual cost. It does have a water feature but not an ice skating rink. However, the original intent of having the space be beautiful and welcoming was achieved. It was named after the former mayor of Indianapolis and United States Senator Richard G. Lugar. "Ballard's Back Yard" did not make the cut.

Two Projects Talked About

There were two potentially significant projects that we talked about but never reached the point where we took action.

International Restaurant Area

I wanted to create an international restaurant area from scratch in the Lafayette Square portion of Indianapolis. Lafayette Square was already home to many international restaurants. I envisioned pulling many of them together in an area similar to Chinatown in London, where there are blocks of Chinese restaurants with other Asian shops in the surrounding blocks. I wanted the area to become a destination for out-of-town visitors from the Midwest who would come for a long weekend to sample the variety of international restaurants.

The Lafayette Square group is now redesignating their area as the International Marketplace, and it is still home to dozens of restaurants with cuisine from around the world. However, if you drive into the area, you would never know this, as the commercial area is also dotted with KFCs, flower shops, auto repair shops, and the like. I envisioned a specific area that would stand out and be instantly recognizable as an international restaurant area, a tourist attraction that would generate buzz from around the country and could be enjoyed by both locals and visitors.

The Lafayette Square area is nice enough but has struggled since the local shopping mall declined over the past few decades. Willing to use Rebuild Indy money to build this new project, I drove around and looked at specific blocks and underutilized lots where we could build it. I was even willing to help existing restaurants move in. However, the Lafayette Square organization did not seem excited by the prospect. I thought it would be a big hit and provide some much-needed economic prosperity to the area. But I also knew that if the local neighborhood organization was not enthusiastic, then the chances for success were slim.

The Electric Company

The other project was buying the electric company, Indianapolis Power and Light. We kept these discussions very quiet. Although we had sold the water and wastewater assets to Citizens Energy, a great move for the city and the ratepayers, the electric utility was an organization I would have loved for the city to own.

It would have created shock waves throughout the state if we had attempted to do so; Indiana utilities are highly regulated. However, I wanted the city to move more quickly to other fuels for electricity besides coal. The five regulated utilities in the state that control electricity wield enormous power in the state legislature and move very slowly toward anything new. That is odd because as monopolies in their designated areas, the utilities are guaranteed a profit.

Many conservative states are increasingly using wind and solar, but Indiana is not. In Iowa, over 40 percent of its electricity comes from wind. Several other conservative states have over 30 percent of their electricity coming from renewable sources. Many states are now using more natural gas than coal. Although Indiana has been using more natural gas in the last few years, an improvement over coal, still well over 80 percent of its electricity comes from these fossil fuels.

Most Hoosiers still believe that Indiana is a low-cost state for electricity, but it is not. Bills have been passed that are hostile to clean energy. It is illegal to sell solar power from one county to another; that hardly seems like a free-market concept to me. I thought Republicans were for a free market and not protectionism.

I wanted to challenge all of this. However, it was our second term when we talked about this, and we eventually did not think we could get it done in a timely manner. Additionally, I would have had to serve another term or two to set it in the right direction, and I was not sure that I wanted to serve that long. That said, owning the electric company would have been a challenge I was ready to accept.

A Final Thought about Infrastructure

The basics of infrastructure—roads, sidewalks, sewers, etc.—are critical to the success of any mayor. Insisting on architecturally significant new buildings is also important to a city's identity, though there will be opposition to building such structures.

We were aggressive during a difficult economic period in our nation's history. Urban Republicans, if we are to maintain the support of the citizenry, must show visible, physical progress in a city while maintaining a feel for the less fortunate, those who could be left behind. I think we did just that.

Note

1. In my leadership book, *The Ballard Rules: Small Unit Leadership*, I detail a leadership reality that I call "There is authority, and then there is power." As mentioned above, mayors, governors, and others have far more power than legal authority. Their words and desires influence people even without statutory authority. I was always mindful to wield such power carefully.

12

PUBLIC SAFETY

Soon after my election, a senior police officer told me, "We can't do anything about the crime rate. All we can do is arrest them" (the criminals). He was not a senior police officer much longer. Although the police are not the sole factor in the crime rate of a city, neither the police nor the citizenry should believe such nonsense. Without a belief that the crime rate can be lowered, there can be no improvement. I thought we could do something about the crime rate, and we made changes to do just that.

In my Ballard Rules for the City of Indianapolis, I said upfront that public safety is Job One. I meant it. For elected officials, especially in executive positions, safety and security should be the main priority for citizens. My marine background helped tremendously, not only in understanding the dangers of police, fire, and emergency services work, but also that those functions are a means to an end.

Public safety matters only within the context of what the city is trying to achieve. It is not the end game unto itself. The end game is a city where people feel safe enough to move to, where they can find a job, raise their families, and enjoy the quality of life they desire. Public safety is one element in that overall equation.

Also, in my mind, public safety is more than just crime. Public safety is the fire department handing out smoke detectors. It is having sidewalks where needed. It is a sense that the government is doing all it can for the security of its citizens. That is the way I think about public safety.

Fortunately, our fire department is nationally recognized because they are innovative and competent. They were a key part of our public-safety team. They host the thirty-thousand-plus Fire Department Instructor's Conference (FDIC) every year, which brings in firefighters from around the country (and sometimes the world) to hear of the future of firefighting. They are a well-led, nationally respected organization.

However, I also know that many think of public safety merely as the crime rate, particularly the homicide rate. The homicide rate is not necessarily the only indicator of crime in a city, but it is the most visible. Homicides are well documented and verified by the FBI. It is how cities are judged—not just by its own citizens but by the nation as well.

When we took office in 2008, homicides were about 115 to 130 per year over the prior ten or fifteen years or so. The range was fairly consistent. Perhaps it was my marine background, but I thought we could lower that rate.

Citizens also equate a lower crime rate with more police. That is not the case. A Department of Justice study in in the 1980s reported that "an examination of the relationships between population; number of police per 1,000 population; crime rate; and crime rate ranking for 26 major cities fails to reveal consistent relationships among these variables. Several studies have found a relationship between police organizational style and police effectiveness. Overall, this survey suggests that it is far more important how police are used than how many there are. Increased police strength alone does not make a difference."

More recent studies are mixed, but it remains clear that how police are used is far more important than just the number of officers. Just like in public works, how you do things matters. When I became mayor, it was explained to me that cops' beats were assigned by the number of historical runs; that is, calls for the police. That sounds logical to some, but not all runs are equal. A trash can missing on the south side of Indianapolis is not the same as a shooting in a high-crime neighborhood.

However, at the time, a run was a run, and the beats were assigned accordingly. That made no sense to me. The number and organization of police in an area should be determined by statistics more relevant than simple calls for the police no matter the reason.

Also, police are not the only instrument to reduce crime, and they may not be the most important instrument. Putting truly violent people in prison for a long time is important. Cops can arrest them, but the justice system must do its part by taking the worst offenders off the street. Groups like the Ten Point Coalition, a pastor-led organization of former gang members who walk the streets to talk to young men at risk, are key to reducing retaliatory murders. More emphasis on understanding mental health and how to reduce the violence around the drug trade would be of great benefit.

Taking Over

When I took office, the police department belonged to the sheriff; it did not report to the mayor. With the implementation of Unigov in 1970, a consolidation of city and county government, the sheriff maintained his law enforcement responsibilities outside of the old city limits. What was then the Indianapolis Police Department patrolled only the old city limits.

In the early 2000s, my Democratic predecessor wanted to merge the law enforcement responsibilities into one organization under his charge. The sheriff, also a Democrat, was having none of that—that is, until the mayor finally offered the sheriff the leadership of the entire law enforcement operation in the county. The then Democratic city-county council passed the ordinance to make this happen.

I believe that the law enforcement function should belong to the mayor. Citizens look to the mayor for the overall public safety of the city, and without the law enforcement function reporting to the mayor, the situation made no sense to me. Something did not feel right. As I say in my leadership book, *The Ballard Rules: Small Unit Leadership*, if you are going to be held accountable for a situation, then you should have the authority that comes with that accountability. Additionally, mayors of major cities always have control of their police departments.

After the election, I publicly made known that one of my first actions would be to gain control of the police department. Since the leadership change to the sheriff came with a council vote, this could be undone with another vote by the council, which was now in Republican hands. I am sure the Democrats never thought a vote on this would happen because they believed they would control the city far into the future. The sheriff was asked how he felt about this, and he said, "I can count." We had the votes.

Soon thereafter, I asked the legislature to put into state law that the Indianapolis Metropolitan Police Department (IMPD), as it was now called, would remain under the control of the mayor. They did so.

Changing Things

Going back at least thirty years (and maybe forty), one can find the annual murder rate below one hundred only four times: 2009, 2010, 2011, and 2012, all during my tenure. Here is what we did—all these tenets will work in any major city—and why it started going back up after 2012.

1. A STRONG PUBLIC-SAFETY DIRECTOR

I knew from my time in the Marines and my own study of leadership that if you want meaningful results in an area, then there should be a person whose sole focus is that area. This is so obvious to me, but for some reason, others cannot see it. The city has directors for parks and public works and for all the other departments. So should public safety. If public safety, the safety and security of the citizenry, is the first priority, then someone must be tasked with this responsibility. It sends a signal to everyone that this area is important.

Whenever I spoke of public safety on the campaign trail and after the election, I would mention that I wanted the public-safety director (PSD) to be a general, not a figurehead. I said this because I heard the designated public-safety director from the previous administration talk one time, and without going into details, it was clear he was in charge of nothing. I believe they had someone else performing the public-safety director's functions quietly.

The director cannot be the police chief, because he is leading just one area of public safety, that of law enforcement. The police chief has an organization to manage, and he is busy with law enforcement, administrative and discipline issues, and a myriad of other duties that police chiefs are responsible for.

Police are about law enforcement. In most cases, they do that well. Addressing the larger questions involved with public safety can be a frustrating experience, which necessitates the need for a public-safety director. The police chief cannot possibly drive public safety in a city. Neither can anyone else, including the mayor, who has other duties besides public safety. A designated person must be in charge. Otherwise, public safety, and the crime rate, will be far from optimal.

The public-safety director must be competent and self-driven, not a political friend of the mayor. The PSD must be given the resources to succeed, including a staff. The PSD needs the freedom to use the resources as he or she sees fit and have autonomy within the framework of the mayor's goals.

As an example of why the PSD is important, early in my administration, I asked the police chief the target number for murders for the upcoming year. That may sound like an odd question, but it is actually a resource question. In most organizations, having a target begins the conversation on how many resources are needed and how they are to be used. He said, "Zero."

I knew he did not understand the question. In fairness, it is an odd question, and I knew what he meant by his answer, but I wanted our administration to think in terms of prevention, saving lives, and not just arresting after the fact.

What will a public-safety director do that the police chief or anyone else does not have the time for? The director can work with the prosecutors and judges (within the bounds of the law) and help them realize the factors or people that are contributing to a higher crime rate. He should also act as the single point of contact with state and federal agencies, coordinating and directing action with the other levels. He has the time and wider knowledge to be much more effective at this than anyone else. He can also use data, spotting crime trends much more rapidly. The police are so busy looking at what is in front of them that connecting data to determine trends at the local, state, and federal levels is impossible. Only the public-safety director and his staff can do this.

The PSD can also serve as the point of contact for the public, informing them directly and calming them when necessary. He can do this routinely through the media and through other means like community meetings, which would allow the police chief to concentrate on his important law enforcement, organizational, and administrative functions. In cities without an effective PSD, reporting to the public usually defaults to the police chief, who can only do it on a situational basis versus routinely.

I knew about safety and security as concepts, but Scott Newman, my first PSD, knew these areas in depth when it came to Indianapolis. One of the first things that Scott focused on was getting the open-air drug markets to operate inside, not on the street. That sounds like we just moved the problem along, but in truth, violence can erupt from these transactions, and if they were going to occur, then we wanted them away from the public. It is a perception but one that is important. We wanted people to feel that they could walk the streets safely.

He also started to use the police differently, insisting that they were in force at events or hot spots as they arose. They did not always like this, but no one could credibly question Scott's tactics or intelligence on these matters. He made a difference, and the city started to see the results by 2009.

We had four public-safety directors during my eight years in office. Scott was followed by a protégé of Bill Bratton (the New York City police commissioner), Frank Straub, whom the fire department loved but the police department hated. Frank instituted a lot of reforms, some at my insistence, that I will discuss later. He was data driven and hard nosed. He made the police uncomfortable, holding them accountable much more than they were used to. Although there was friction at times, including with other members of my administration, I thought Frank brought some much-needed new thinking to the police department.

Frank was followed by Troy Riggs, who was a Louisville policeman before he moved to San Antonio and worked in broader areas than just the police. He had a bit of a national reputation; he was religious and a strong family man. Data driven and community minded, he was beloved almost immediately throughout the entire city. He was the first in the city to identify the data surrounding mental health runs. He was the first in the state to act on the opioid overdose problem, providing Narcan to police officers before anyone else had thought about it. He wanted to save those lives. His data identified six areas in Indianapolis where most of the public-safety problems occurred and then started to provide remedies for those areas, not just having the police arrest the troublemakers. If he had been able to do this for ten or twenty years, it could have made a huge difference in those neighborhoods and the city. However, administrations and tactics change over the years.

When Troy left about six months before I left office, David Wantz, another former policeman who took temporary leave of a high-level academic position at the University of Indianapolis, filled the position capably. He knew he had been brought in to ensure a solid pass-off to the new administration, and he did so, closing all the loose ends possible. I thank UIndy for allowing David to fill that position.

All my public-safety directors were wonderful public servants who knew that I did not want to play politics with public safety. I cannot thank them enough for their service to the city of Indianapolis.

2. COORDINATION WITH AGENCIES

We made a major effort to coordinate with the prosecutors, who should be completely focused on putting the truly violent criminals, the repeat offenders, behind bars. There are individuals and groups (or gangs) who are well known to the police, prosecutors, and sometimes the FBI. The public-safety team should be energetic and adamant about getting these people off the street. There are too many minor offenders behind bars, but the truly violent people should be identified, and there should be a multiagency focus to put these people away for as long as possible.

There are legal ways for prosecutors, the FBI, and the police to tell the judge that the person in front of them must be put away. All the agencies should know the difference between the low-level offenders, whom we should help, and the truly violent. Also, the public-safety community should be attuned to mental health issues and the drug culture, so as not to confuse the lower-level criminal with the truly violent. Most of the criminals on the street also want to get the worst people off the street; it is too dangerous out there with the real crazies on the loose.

Two stories still stick with me. One evening, during a large event downtown, a young man shot nine people; no one was killed. The public-safety director, Frank Straub, happened to be downtown still monitoring the event, and he and the police got the situation under control quickly. It took only a few days to apprehend the shooter. About two to three years later, the police, during a traffic stop, found this young man in the back seat of a car. He was already out of prison—after having shot nine people. He went back to jail for a parole violation. I was told later that the rearrest saved his life; other violent people were looking for him.

The other story is heartbreaking to me. A young married man, his wife pregnant with their first child, routinely walked along a street on the west side of Indianapolis for exercise in the early morning. He was shot and killed by a sixteen-year-old. This sixteen-year-old had twice before been arrested for illegal gun possession. One time the charge was dismissed, and the other time the charge was pleaded out. Twice we had this teenager for illegal gun possession. The system had told him that illegal gun possession was just fine.

There was video of the young married man walking along the street. I saw him walk up the street to a certain point when the teenager called the young man off to the side, out of range of the camera. I next saw the young husband stagger back to the street, doubled over after being shot. It was gut wrenching to watch. I have never forgotten it.

I went to the calling to express my sorrow to the pregnant wife. But I just felt helpless, empty inside.

People who use guns in an offensive manner need to be put away for a long time. The police cannot do this by themselves. They need coordination with others.

3. DATA

All cities use data, but some do it more effectively than others. Understanding the data that feeds crime, interpreting it correctly, and then acting on it is key. This is something the police cannot do by themselves. They are not organized for this and do not train for it at the level needed. This is not a slight; it is just that the police do not have the time or background to do this sort of work.

My first two public-safety directors, Scott Newman and Frank Straub, collected more data than ever and used it effectively, as the homicide data reflects. Straub was very aggressive in his use of data, and the police were not fond of him. However, the police needed to see something else besides what they had been doing for decades.

The third PSD, Troy Riggs, took it to another level. As mentioned above, he was the first to point out the areas where mental health runs were prevalent, which allowed the city to change its strategy handling these types of runs. No one had even thought of this before. Again, he was way ahead of anyone in the entire state in the use of Narcan, used to prevent the death of opioid overdose victims. His data identified those six areas in Indianapolis where we could make the most difference, and the remedies included food and better health practices, not just more policing. I cannot help but think what twenty years of such efforts would have produced.

Troy's efforts were significant. Unfortunately, some elements of our administration's strategy were taken away by the city-county council, beginning in 2012. The homicide rate drifted up. Even so, the first five months of 2015, my last year in office, the homicide rate was low again before Troy and his excellent deputy director left the administration. (It is common for staff to leave for other positions before the end of an administration when an officeholder announces he is not running for reelection.)

David Wantz, widely respected, became the final PSD of my tenure, but he had no deputy director, and he was correctly focused on ensuring a smooth turnover to the incoming administration. The police, as I have indicated, could not carry the ball by themselves, and other elements of our strategy had been taken away. The last half of 2015 had high homicide rates, once again proving the importance of having a cohesive public-safety team and keeping the entire strategy in place.

4. CRIME PREVENTION MONEY/PARTNERING WITH RESPECTED, ORGANIC STREET-LEVEL ORGANIZATIONS

The prior administration discussed using public funds for crime prevention efforts but never moved forward. We did, and quickly. We allotted $2.5 million to go to nonprofit organizations that we felt could help reduce the most violent crime. These funds had to be approved by the city-county council, but for the most part, the mayor's office, in coordination with the public-safety director, picked the organizations who would receive the money. This was not a slush fund for friends; the focus was on reducing violent crime.

We never looked at these organizations from a political perspective. We just wanted people who were passionate about reducing violent crime in the city but also had the capability to do so. Two of these were the Ten Point Coalition and Young Men, Inc. As many people in Indianapolis know, Ten Point uses former gang members who know the street to patrol at night in high crime areas, talk to those prone to committing violence, and tamp down retaliation on the street, including going to funerals.

The results were outstanding in the areas Ten Point patrolled, and the model has been adopted in over two dozen cities. I believe that such organizations must be organic to the community, not subject to police or other city influence. Ten Point worked with the police closely but maintained their street cred because they were former gang members who could talk to the kids on the street. They were not cops, nor were they working for the city.

Another great organization was Young Men Inc., who worked with at-risk kids up to their teen years. They did a tremendous job with these kids, who largely stayed out of trouble. We also funded organizations that helped ex-offenders stay on the straight and narrow. Most citizens have no idea how much crime is committed by those who have already been in prison.

Another aspect of these organizations was that accurate intelligence was being passed on to the police. On one occasion, we had intel that riots would happen in Indianapolis; positive action was taken to prevent the rioting. I know this also happened with a previous mayor. We knew when funerals might be the point of retaliation. Any number of small details were passed along to us to prevent further violence.

Unfortunately, in 2012, the council, now led by a Democratic majority, took the money away from the mayor's office completely. My then chief of staff was able to convince the council to let a nonprofit decide where the money should go instead of the council administering the money directly. This task went to the Parks Foundation, who had no experience in public safety. I believe that the council leaned on the Parks Foundation to give the money to council "friends," although some did find its way to ex-offender groups. However, the organizations that had the most direct influence on stopping violent crime, like Ten Point and Young Men Inc., did not make the cut. They were defunded.

The expected happened. Homicides started to rise. Although some former gang members were able to stay on with Ten Point, they had to eat too and could not continue with little to no funding. There were fewer people talking to the gang members on the street; there were fewer people trying to tamp down retaliatory murders. The numbers went up. It was inevitable.

Proving the point about relationships, there were no murders during the ten-day period of our Super Bowl in 2012. Ten Point asked the violent groups in the city to hold a moratorium on violence during this ten-day period, and they largely did. This is the value of relationships on the street, which we had.

Many of the criminals on the street do not like their lifestyle; they are in it almost by default. Many have never seen any other way of living. Ten Point set up a meeting for me to talk to a couple of them. The young men's demeanors were anything but what most people would imagine. They were embarrassed and ashamed of their lifestyle. Their heads hung low. They were human, and they wanted help. I also learned that most of the kids on the street carry weapons for defense, not to attack people. It's a lifestyle that most want out of.

They need help to do so.

5. DETECTIVES WITH STREET CRED

If the city wants to solve homicides and get the violent bad guys off the street, it needs true manhunters—cops with the aggressive dedication to make the streets safer. The leader in the detectives' section must have this attitude, as well as the street cred to talk to the gangsters and the families, earning their trust.

I was lucky to have Bill Benjamin as chief of detectives for several years, and he solved many of the worst crimes, because he was relentless and had credibility. While in charge of the detectives, his clearance rate in solving crimes was in the top echelon nationally.

If detectives pursue solving the most violent of crimes through standard, school-taught methods, the clearance rate will plummet, and the most violent will stay on the street. There must be an aggressive attitude and a willingness to talk to bad people. The streets are safer this way.

6. WORKING WITH EX-OFFENDERS

I learned while campaigning in 2007 that there was almost no path for ex-offenders to survive except by committing more crime upon release from prison. There have been nonprofit organizations to help ex-offenders (my wife was the bookkeeper for one for years), but the government was mostly absent. I set up an office to help ex-offenders, and now, many others in government, including at the state level, are starting to realize that they need help. Most citizens do not want to talk about helping ex-offenders, but providing a valid path for them upon release from prison is a critical part of reducing crime.

Most government agencies across the country do not want to spend the time, money, and energy to improve the situation. This is sad, because not only would we live in a safer environment, but individuals who were never given much of a chance in life could have their lives turned around. They could be paying taxes instead of using taxpayer dollars to arrest and incarcerate them.

However, too many people dismiss helping them, essentially implying, "Let them fend for themselves." Fending for themselves means going back to what they know best: committing crimes to live. I talked to ex-offenders all the time; the common sentiment was that they want to go straight and succeed. I often said that the best compliment I ever received while mayor was an ex-offender telling me that I was "the only mayor who ever cared." Not quite true—but I did make a very public effort to highlight the need to assist ex-offenders.

There are wonderful organizations to help them, like Recycle Force, run by Gregg Keesling, who does e-cycling (phones, computers, etc.) and hires only ex-offenders. There are other groups that provide counseling, addiction help, job training, and other services. Lots of elements are in place.

However, the organization that could provide the most help is the state. Most states talk about the "first day out" for those in jail, helping them prepare for life on the outside, but these programs start very late in the prison term. We should change that dynamic to "first day in." So many of these men and women have addiction, behavioral, and violence issues stemming from childhood. Some scientists are now theorizing that many of them had PTSD as children, just from living in their neighborhoods. They never had much of a chance.

The state could address these issues early in their prison terms because these men and women are going to be in prison for quite some time. It seems the right thing to do, because their living conditions as children failed them. We should want them to succeed once they assimilate back into society. It makes perfect sense—but the bureaucracy is not built this way yet. If we want less crime on our streets, we should work with prisoners early in their sentences and then help them intensively upon release.

Our administration made minimal progress, but I do believe we were successful in getting many people in the city and the state to think differently about ex-offenders. However, I made an important hire: I brought on an ex-offender as a deputy mayor, sending a very strong message about how I felt. Olgen Williams, by the time I met him, was a legend on the west side of Indianapolis in an area called Haughville and running Christamore House, an organization that provided educational services to youth and a place to socialize, keeping kids off the street. While campaigning in 2007, I talked to him about his feelings on crime in the city. He was then known as the "mayor of Haughville." He stayed with our administration all eight years and was a force in the city.

7. WORKING WITH HELPFUL ORGANIZATIONS

I frequently said that I was President Obama's favorite Republican mayor. He never actually told me that, but I claimed it nonetheless. He was laser focused on helping young Black men and boys with his My Brother's Keeper initiative. I was the lone Republican mayor on his advisory board. On one occasion, he invited eighteen mayors to the White House to discuss these matters. I was the lone Republican present, and he seated me directly across the table from him. He also asked specifically that I inform the group what we were doing in Indianapolis.

Forty mayors across the country joined Cities United to address the issues concerning our urban youth. This was helpful, and much like My Brothers's Keeper, mayors could talk about their issues with other mayors and could learn what others were doing.

I was similarly focused in Indianapolis on our own Your Life Matters (YLM) initiative. The leaders of the Indiana Black Expo and the Indiana Civil Rights Commission led a task force in 2014 that focused on evidence-based problems and solutions. They addressed five areas: education, justice and reentry, employment, health, and mentoring. It was very well done and provided well-researched information that the city and other organizations could address. It was illuminating to many people.

YLM was very direct with its guidance, such as "We do not have a youth unemployment problem; we have a youth work readiness problem." They also specifically pointed out that once a student drops out of school, it is very difficult to reach that child. There was so much great information provided by the Your Life Matters task force—and they recommended solutions, rather than just point out problems.

8. SHARING INFORMATION

I learned a long time ago that sharing information is important to everyone's success, no matter the endeavor. Those who hold information tightly are generally not good people to work with and are not to be trusted. There are exceptions, such as in a business with proprietary information, but generally, information should be shared by people who work with each other.

We did this. We worked closely with the prosecutors, our Ten Point Coalition partners on the street, other police departments, our own city agencies, the FBI, schools, and many other community partners who also shared information with us. As mentioned above, we frequently had intelligence on events that were about to happen so that we could prevent or mitigate the damage.

Whenever an event in another city had national media coverage with the potential to cause protests or riots in cities across the nation, we already had collaborative relationships in place to effectively counter any violence that might occur. Indianapolis has a history of this sort of preventive activity. There were no riots in Indianapolis after the 1968 Martin Luther King Jr. assassination, after the 1991 Rodney King beating, or the unrest in Ferguson, Missouri, which occurred during my tenure. The organizations in the city came together to protest peacefully, making their feelings known, but did not escalate into violent activity. Intelligence gathered from information sharing played a large role in keeping the protests peaceful.

Long-Term Solutions

All the above are short- to medium-term solutions that worked for us. However, no one in the country has successfully come up with a long-term (twenty-plus years) solution that works. The most obvious reason for this is that politics gets in the way of a long-term solution. Each new mayor campaigns on better ideas and then tries to implement them. This makes for a revolving door of ideas that never fully work.

There are many wonderful organizations doing good work, but they tend to be specialized, spurred by the interest of an individual or a small group. Of course, fundraising is always an issue for these groups. And potential funders are drawn in different directions, not knowing who is really making an impact. At times, the funding efforts are competitive, hurting the overall effort.

Regional Goodwill organizations have much autonomy in how they pursue philanthropy within their area. In the last few years, the Central Indiana Goodwill folks have been implementing a holistic model, helping at-risk families for long-term success. It is captured well in Jim McClelland's book, *Toward Greater Impact: A Path to Reduce Social Problems, Improve Lives, and Strengthen Communities*. He is the well-respected forty-year-plus former director of the Central Indiana Goodwill.

The organization came upon this model accidentally through its Nurse Partnership and Excel Center programs. Goodwill's Nurse Partnership pairs low-income mothers pregnant with their first child with a registered nurse for ongoing home visits. The Excel Center is a mayor-sponsored charter school focused on getting high school diplomas for adults, which has been very effective and has expanded throughout the state. Central Indiana Goodwill realized that helping adults succeed is not a one-off event but a multigenerational effort to ensure that families are fed and educated and feel secure in their lives. Most of us take our upbringing for granted, but poor people usually do not realize how to become more productive—how to overcome their situation—because they have not seen it. It has not been modeled for them. Education, counseling, transportation, food access, parenting help, and addiction help are just a few of the areas that could be coordinated to help individuals and families overcome multigenerational poverty, erasing the need to resort to crime for subsistence.

Goodwill has incredible success stories, and bringing these efforts to scale over a long period of time could be revolutionary. In my last year as mayor, I began something called the 360 Coalition, similar to the Goodwill effort. I wish I had figured out the need sooner and was more aware of what Goodwill was doing. Perhaps together we could have begun to bring this effort to scale. Most cities and states have incredible databases that could guide the effort.

States may be able to help, but they are prone to the same "going in a new direction" efforts with each new election. A nonprofit/private/corporate organization that had government buy-in (and funding if possible) would be most effective over a two- or three-decade period. All the other programs collectively have failed—the result of disjointed, political, and haphazardly funded efforts.

Money Matters

Many local politicians, especially candidates, clamor for more money for public safety. In some cases, this is a legitimate need, but often such rhetoric is used to get votes. It worked for me. However, municipal budgets in most major cities are tight, and the dollars allocated to public safety must be balanced against other needs. In Indianapolis, the public-safety complex, including fire and courts, dominates the budget—well over 80 percent. This is done at the expense of infrastructure, parks, and other legitimate requirements. In the middle of the Great Recession, this became even more of a problem.

Through innovation and a different focus of effort, we lowered the murder rate dramatically by our second year in office. To this day, the only years over the past four decades where the murder rate was below one hundred are 2009, 2010, 2011, and 2012, during and shortly after the Great Recession, when finding money for cops was difficult. Hiring was at a near standstill, yet we lowered the murder rate.

When Troy Riggs became my third public-safety director, he too wanted more money. I told him that money was too tight at the time. He asked that if he could find savings within public safety, could he then use that money to hire more cops? I said yes.

He created efficiency teams consisting of public-safety personnel, other city personnel, and citizens from the community. This combination brought some much-needed business acumen to the table and instilled a sense of ownership and accountability. At this time, no one was complaining about waste in public safety; indeed, over the previous few years, the citizens and I were pleased with the performance of the public-safety team in Indianapolis.

He found $10 million in savings based on how he would operate and directed that money into putting more cops on the street. His use of data combined with regular community meetings then resulted in millions of dollars in grants coming to the Indianapolis public-safety team. He also created the Public-Safety Foundation, which raised additional funds.

Before citizens and politicians ask for more money, an analysis of how current revenues are being spent is in order. Again, no one accused the previous public-safety team of being wasteful; there are just different ways of conducting business. David Sherman saved the water and wastewater ratepayers over $800 million by redesigning a federally mandated sewer improvement. Similarly, Troy Riggs put more cops on the street with his analysis. Government personnel, if given the opportunity, can be both efficient and effective. Citizens should insist on this.

Community Policing

Be wary during election season when candidates use the term community policing. It is a catchall phrase that is often used by officeholders and candidates to signal that a new direction is needed, as in, "We are going to institute community policing." If one looks up the definition and objectives of community policing, you would find such items as partnerships with the local community, being proactive in problem solving to prevent crime, and organizing the police force to carry out these tasks. In truth, almost all major city police forces employ community policing in some way. Almost any tactic used, other than just arresting people, falls under the umbrella of community policing. A good indicator of solid community policing is whether the self-initiating activities by individual cops, such as quickly acting on tips or observed suspicious behavior, is high. If so, there is competence and high morale within the force, and community policing is occurring.

Police Reform

Cops get upset when someone like a mayor tries to impose reforms. On some level, I understand that. I know that people are generally resistant to change, but agencies that do not have a tradition of organizational self-improvement are doomed to a poor culture and frequent failure.

Most cops perform well. They certainly did in Indianapolis. I had cops in other parts of the country help me out when traveling, and they were uniformly professional and fun to be around. However, there are organizational flaws in police forces around the country that grow over the years. Each city has its own oddities. Some are obvious, others not so much.

One of the oddities in Indianapolis when I assumed office was that the police department was not allowed to use the internet. The sheriff had been in charge of the police department since the merger with the police in 2006. He was being heavily criticized online, and many people believed much of the criticism was coming from the police themselves. The content of the criticisms would certainly indicate this.

The sheriff's response was to forbid the police department from using the internet. I found this bizarre. How does a detective put a case together without the internet? How does the patrolman do any research on a neighborhood without the internet? That policy changed instantly when I found this out.

Performance Evaluation or Lack Thereof

When I came into office, the police had no performance evaluation system. I could not believe that a 1,600-person paramilitary outfit did not rate the performance of its personnel. When I would tell business groups this, they were aghast. This is so basic to these types of organizations, but the police did not want to be rated, and they were not happy that I insisted on a performance evaluation system. It took a few years, but we put a system in place. They did not really know what to do with it, nor did they understand its importance, but I am hoping that it is still in place and they are taking it seriously.

If an organization does not have a performance evaluation system, the inevitable question is "Who gets promoted?" This also was bizarre to me. When I came into office, cops could put themselves up for promotion. There was no system mandating that only the best cops were eligible; of course, that is tough to do without a performance evaluation system. Cops who wanted to become sergeants were given books to study and then went before a panel to be evaluated. Do a good job in front of the board, and you were promoted; it did not matter if your fellow cops knew you were not up to par.

When we instituted the performance evaluation system, I insisted on something the Marines call the "truth teller." The person writing the evaluation had to rate, by number, the cop being evaluated, as in three out of ten or five out of twelve. The intent was that only those cops who were rated in the top half would be eligible for promotion. Did they actually do this? I do not know, as it took quite a few years to get these basic reforms in place, and I was nearing the end of my time in office. I left it to the police themselves to ensure that these changes were made.

Other Reforms

We brought in CompStat, a performance management system that helped New York reduce crime through data sharing and accountability; it became famous under police commissioner Bill Bratton. District leaders had to brief their areas to the entire command staff. I doubt that it got as tense as the New York sessions were reputed to be, but at least the commanders had to prepare and really look at their areas. Again, this took some getting used to, as it was not part of the Indianapolis police culture.

As we had to do routinely in the Marines, an internal organizational "gut check" can be helpful. In Indy, we created a Professional Standards Division in the police force to help with these reforms and to help hold cops accountable.

Of note, we instituted a Leadership Academy that was very well received and is ongoing to this day. Our team hired a retired marine lieutenant colonel to teach the class, and he related well to the police. After a few classes, other law enforcement agencies in the area asked to attend, a sign that the academy was well respected. I am hoping that after fifteen or twenty years, the lessons learned in this academy become second nature to IMPD.

There were items I did not get to that I also believed were obvious reforms. These included the police chief being a terminal appointment; once a person becomes the chief, the next stop should be retirement. But that does not happen in Indianapolis; chiefs go back into the ranks when they are done. This brings up potential conflicts, the most obvious one regarding discipline. If a police chief must discipline a cop, particularly a senior cop, will the chief go light on the punishment, knowing that when he is done being chief, he will be going back into the ranks where retaliation could occur? Can you imagine a four-star general in the military going back to become a colonel once his job was done? Of course not.

Also, the command staff, the most senior cops by rank, still hold second jobs. This is ingrained into police forces around the country, but it should be eliminated. There is an obvious conflict of interest if a command staff member works for an organization where an employee gets arrested. There should never be a risk of a senior cop being perceived as exerting influence to help an employee of an organization where that cop works at a second job. Pay command staff police better if you must, but they should not have second jobs. They must be focused only on their duties as a cop.

Despite the wonderful work of our individual police in Indianapolis, their organization is less than optimal. It is not pleasant to wake up in the morning and see the pictures of over a dozen cops on the front page of the local newspaper with a story recounting their recent misconduct. How does the police union support a drunken cop that ran over motorcyclists, killing one and injuring others? Such incidents invite reform. Most cops are wonderful people, but organizationally, they cannot see this.

Defund the Police?

The defunding the police movement has been political gold for the Republican Party. Many Democrats make the mistake of believing that the egregious behavior by some cops toward Black citizens means that most people who live in these neighborhoods want no cops around. It has been my experience that most who live in Black neighborhoods want to be treated with respect by cops but do not want them to go away. In Indianapolis, and I suspect in most large cities, there are daily efforts by the police to reach out to those who are living in high-crime areas. They want cops in their neighborhood to deter the violence, but they want a good, respectful relationship with the police also.

Pay for Cops

Many people believe that cops are underpaid. Just like the military, the public cannot possibly pay for the entire sacrifice that cops endure. That said, in Indianapolis, I believe the police force is paid fairly. A third-year cop with a high school diploma makes significantly more than the average income, with benefits that include a car they can use for personal matters and a retirement package.

That seems fair to me.

A Bad Day

My security team always consisted of great cops. My worst day in office was when I publicly admonished one of them near the end of a sporting event. They always wanted me to leave such events early, but I never wanted to. I am usually low key and level headed, but something set me off that day. I still feel bad about it to this day.

A Cautionary Tale

When I came into office, it seemed I had the complete support of the police department, including the local Fraternal Order of Police, the police union. They were not fond of my predecessor even though he is a good man. I visited the FOP hall a few days after the election to celebrate with them. I like cops then and now. I honor those who put on any uniform in service to their fellow man.

Before I won the election, my predecessor had promised the police generous raises. Some of my team, knowing we were going to have budget troubles during the first few years of my administration because of the Great Recession, recommended that I rescind the final two years of the contract they had signed—which would be my first two years in office. I refused to do so.

We not only gave them those raises, but also, Scott Newman, the public-safety director, found money for an increase in the police clothing allowance, something they did not even ask for. The police chief also asked me if it was OK for the patrol officers to start using their utility uniforms daily instead of their dress uniforms. I had no problem with that.

When I took over the police department a few months into my administration, I held a ceremonial roll call with hundreds of police officers present. They were ecstatic that I had wrested control of the department from the sheriff, but I also told them that "attempts to curry favor with the mayor's office will be counterproductive." I wanted them to concentrate on work and to be proud of themselves. Self-initiated activities by the cops rose immediately, and everyone seemed happy, including me.

Four years later, the FOP was loudly and publicly campaigning against me. I knew that some of the police had trouble with my then-public-safety director. Still, I was surprised that the FOP endorsed my opponent after I had worked hard to give them what I thought they deserved.

The FOP always complained publicly about needing more pay and needing more cops (who pay dues to the FOP). During one of the budget negotiations, my chief of staff asked the FOP if they wanted a raise in pay or more cops on the force. They said more pay. Once the budget was complete and passed by the council, they went back to loudly complaining about the need for more cops.

I believe that the FOP is always looking for the next candidate in its attempts to gain leverage. It is easier to gain leverage during a campaign, using that leverage against the sitting officeholder and publicly asking for more benefits. Still, after all I did in support of the police, seeing the FOP leadership actively work against me at campaign events seemed odd.

That said, I still think that most of the police force voted for me on my reelection. Most of the Indianapolis police force belong to the FOP only to support contract negotiations and to tap into legal funds if they need to defend themselves in some way. Other than that, most police do not pay attention to the FOP. In fact, I do not think it represents how most cops feel about many different subjects. It's just the way it is.

Other Public-Safety Improvements

As I mentioned earlier, public safety is about more than policing. Putting the public's safety at the forefront of our administration's thought process was paramount. Other actions needed to be taken; we took them.

A New Emergency Operations Center

After being in several command centers during operations in the Marine Corps, I knew that our Emergency Operations Center (EOC) was terrible. The former EOC was located on State Street, a couple of miles east of downtown. It was small with tiny areas for one person to represent the various agencies (police, fire, EMS, weather, public works, etc.) that might be involved in an incident. It had minimal technology and unacceptable conference room space.

It took a few years, but we were able to secure some land on the old Eastgate Shopping Center on the far east side. Eastgate was an outdoor shopping center before there were indoor shopping malls. My mother shopped there regularly.

The new EOC is now an ugly, nondescript building on the old Eastgate land, surrounded by two stacks of huge concrete blocks for security purposes. Thankfully, it is not near anything or anyone that might long for a better-looking building. Inside, though, is a large, spacious area with advanced technology, plenty of meeting space, a huge briefing room, and separate offices as needed for outside agencies like the FBI. It is a vast improvement over the old EOC on State Street.

Predatory Towing

Predatory towing, where towing operators use questionable tactics and business practices to take advantage of unknowing citizens, was increasing in Indianapolis around 2010–11. The towing operators were becoming aggressive, waiting in private and public parking lots and taking advantage of poorly worded signs. Once they towed your car, you were at their mercy. Many of them charged exorbitant storage fees, and some accepted only cash.

Ryan Vaughn, who became my third chief of staff but was then the president of the city-county council representing the Broad Ripple area, kept hearing about this from his constituents; predatory towing was rampant in the Broad Ripple area. He was preparing legislation to address the issue when the four TV stations in the city started picking up on the increase in predatory towing and began running stories on it. One local TV anchor became a victim of predatory towing, and she upped the coverage dramatically.

All this publicity helped make the legislation flow quickly through the council. If there were any towing companies who were lobbying their councilor to vote against the legislation, such efforts were drowned out by the extensive TV coverage. The legislation passed easily; it included requiring better signage in parking lots and limits on towing costs, and it also required that towing companies accept credit and debit cards. The media was terrific in their coverage, but Ryan was months ahead of them in addressing the issue. We kept that to ourselves.

Updating Towing Practices

Other issues with towing included the disparity in business practices among the towing companies and that a police officer could call any tow company he wanted. This latter issue is obviously open to fraud, although I do not recall any instances of people alleging fraud in this area. As in all cities, most of our police are hard-working, caring citizens, but the potential for abuse of the system was there. Also, most of the towing companies were honest and doing good work, but there were some bad actors. Additionally, people who had their cars towed would have to go to the City-County Building downtown to begin the retrieval process. This was obviously an uncomfortable process for the citizen, but it was also inefficient for everyone else. In addition, the only reason the City-County Building was open twenty-four hours a day was to process towed vehicles.

Rick Powers, heading up our code enforcement unit, brought AutoReturn into my office. They were a national though fairly new company at the time, but they were in the business of making the towing experience much easier on the citizen and more efficient for the city. What they did made sense. They had a software system that enabled dispatching to become routine, and it standardized prices and practices. AutoReturn had no towing equipment of their own, just a new system. Because we knew the local towing companies would be unhappy with any change in the city's practices, we decided to bid this out.

We were specific in what we were asking for, essentially a digital layer on top of the towing companies that would standardize almost everything in the towing process—with the bonus of not having the citizen go to the City-County Building downtown in the dark of night to begin the process of retrieving the vehicle. Also, the bid required the process to be online so that the citizen could find the car quickly and pay standard fees. Twenty-four-hour service was also required. A few of the towing companies submitted bids, but they did not have the tools that AutoReturn did.

The local towing companies were not happy with us changing the system. However, I believe that government practices that affect citizens should be looked at from the point of view of the citizen and not the one providing the service. There can be too much protectionism if private companies or even a government office are allowed to completely dictate how a service is provided. Make it efficient for the consumer and prices tend to go down while service levels rise.

Despite the outcry from the towing companies and from some councilors who suddenly now seemed to have their favorite towing companies in their respective districts, this legislation got passed. It was a big win for the city but an even bigger win for the citizens. The good towing companies also benefited from the change.

13

MONEY

Money always matters. My Democratic friends too often fail to realize that tax money comes from successful businesses and people. The more successful they are, the more tax revenue comes into the government.

Despite the oncoming recession in 2008, I wanted to be responsible with the people's money and to be seen as doing so. Of course, there are always different paths to success.

Six Sigma

Anyone who has worked in government knows that there are ample opportunities to improve processes, thereby saving taxpayer dollars. Government workers are not always inclined toward the goal of improving their processes, as many feel that "cost-efficient" sounds too much like "I am losing my job." This proved not to be the case in Indianapolis. There is also the feeling that those who can direct such processes to be improved (such as mayors and governors) do not want to do so because then they cannot hire more people whom they want to reward in some way (known as patronage). I just wanted to be efficient and effective for the taxpayer.

I say frequently that when I hear "That's the way we've always done it," my antenna goes up. Before I attended my first US Conference of Mayors meeting three weeks after inauguration in 2008, I was already concerned about pothole repair. Something did not seem right. I knew we had a large population and a large area to cover (about four hundred square miles), but something seemed off to me. My antenna was up.

When I went to that first USCM meeting, I asked several other mayors from around the country how long it took to repair a pothole. All of them said about two days. I brought this back to Indianapolis and asked my public-works director to look into it. He did. The workers and the union said, "There is no way other cities repair potholes in two days." But surely, all those mayors were not lying to me.

I knew I wanted to bring Six Sigma to the city. Six Sigma is a set of tools and techniques that improve processes. It was originally used in manufacturing but can be adapted to other organizations. The intent of Six Sigma is to develop the most cost-efficient and effective processes. That seems reasonable to me.

We did not have a Six Sigma program that first year, so I asked Eli Lilly, the global pharmaceutical manufacturer based in Indianapolis, to lend us some Six Sigma experts from their company. Through the Six Sigma process, we found out that Indianapolis then had twenty-three steps to fix a pothole, and it took around eleven days. We reduced the number of steps to eleven and from then on fixed potholes routinely in two or three days. Nobody lost their job.

We started our own Six Sigma program in the city and grew our own experts. The program measures the relative expertise of its participating individuals by designating them with colored belts, as karate does. Participants earn yellow belts, green belts, and black belts. We eventually had many green belts and even a few black belts. It was an important certification for those employees and made them more valuable in the job market if they ever left the city's employ.

Manny Mendez ran the program for us through his Office of Audit and Performance and did a remarkable job. He solicited jobs from the various departments and agencies and received mostly positive responses, which resulted in savings for the taxpayer. However, he was frustrated that some offices, particularly other elected officials, were reluctant to use Six Sigma. Some government officials either do not understand how commercial processes can help government or just want to do what they have always done.

By my sixth year in office or so, Manny and his team were saving about $15 million annually over previous practices through more than a dozen Six Sigma improvements.

One of my favorite Six Sigma stories is actually a very simple one. Replacement of trash carts for homes went from 142 days to 2 days. This is a classic example of listening and looking at what can be done. "That's the way we've always done it" is the signal to investigate an issue.

The Budget

The reason we needed programs such as Six Sigma was the budget situation when our administration began. When we took office in January 2008, it was a tense period. The state was experiencing a property tax crisis, the Great Recession was around the corner, and local governments had little clue as to what their revenue would be over the next few years.

The annual budget for the city was around $1 billion. The projections from the previous administration, and we agreed, were that the city budget on its present course would have a deficit in 2012 of over $150 million. This was scary to me with the oncoming recession and the property tax crisis in the state. There was work to be done.

If we could cut from the 2008 budget (which was passed by the previous administration and council) and then pass our own budget in 2009, we could make a significant dent in the projected shortfall. This meant that some items in the budget had to be reduced or eliminated, upsetting many people who had counted on the city to provide services. That first year of dealing with the anger of people whose money was either being reduced or eliminated was not pleasant, but it had to be done. Otherwise, the city was heading toward a financial disaster, putting the most basic of services in jeopardy.

The property tax reform/reduction being proposed by the statehouse in 2008 was soon upon us. I supported the statewide property tax reform when I was running for office and still believe it was the right thing to do. As a new mayor, I even went to the state legislature to lobby for it. The ability of citizens and businesses to live and operate comfortably in the city and state was paramount. Otherwise, they could just move somewhere else, and many talked of doing so. The property tax situation in the state at the time was that bad.

In the near term, there would be a reduction in property tax receipts for the city. Additionally, the oncoming recession would mean lower income tax receipts over the next few years. The income tax increase the previous city administration had passed mitigated these reductions somewhat, but in early 2008 the citizens were still upset at the combination of unknown—but mostly skyrocketing—property tax expectations and an income tax increase being forced on them at the same time. The financial picture for the city was not for the faint of heart. It was a tense time in the city.

Thankfully, my first controller, David Reynolds, was brilliant. He was a calming influence on everybody, including me, despite the difficult situation. We found some budget items that could easily be cut; other items were more difficult to cut but were acceptable. We cut legal fees from about $8 million to about $4 million almost immediately. We eliminated some obvious patronage jobs. We eliminated the Department of Administration.

Some money was rerouted to other offices, but that also signaled that business as usual with city money was changing. We brought the budgets into balance, improved the cash flow of the city's receipts and payments, and even reduced the income tax by .03 percent. That may be a small sum, but it was symbolic, showing that we had the situation well in hand. The city's bond ratings were at least AAA across the board through almost my entire administration (an important signal to businesses and investors), and when one of the rating agencies put the rating one rung lower, it was not because of the city's financial picture but because of another municipal entity in the city that had a potential shortfall.

This was one of the great victories of our administration. But as happened with the massive ratepayer savings when we stared down the EPA and the Department of Justice to reengineer our mandated sewer improvements, no one in the city even knew we did this. It was not sexy enough to be covered by any media. Still, I was proud of our entire team for working through this.

David Reynolds was an incredible public servant, an unsung hero, who used his immense talents to benefit all of the citizens of Indianapolis.

Reducing the City Debt by Two-Thirds

On top of getting the budget under control, reducing the city debt by two-thirds during the Great Recession was another major accomplishment. When I entered office, the debt was $330 million; when I left office, the debt was $110 million. Doing this despite the awful budget projections and the national economic climate was remarkable and an achievement of which I am very proud.

Reducing the debt was important to me. It helped keep our bond ratings at AAA, which allowed other entities (like the new Eskenazi public hospital) to borrow at reduced rates. The then-CEO of the Health and Hospital Corporation—which ran Wishard, the old public hospital, and built Eskenazi, a marvel of a public hospital—told me that our bond ratings saved HHC about $350 million over the life of the debt. Bond ratings matter, and our focus on reducing the city debt contributed to that. It saves money for the taxpayer over the long run.

I was committed to reducing the debt. A mayor finds out quickly that he and the council are the only ones who care about the overall budget. The city agencies under the control of the mayor wanted more money but also knew that they reported to me, so we worked out the budget together. However, some other elected officials could not have cared less about the city budget; they only wanted more money. Those negotiations were more tense.

That said, we had a great team who worked tirelessly to come up with a workable and funded budget every year. It was a difficult task during the Great Recession, but we were steadfast in reducing the debt.

This also was never made public.

Pre-1977 Public-Safety Pensions

Prior to 1977, cities were solely responsible for the pensions of public-safety personnel. This was a major budget issue for most cities in the state. The law was adjusted in 1977 so that cities and public-safety personnel would both input into the pensions, eliminating an ever-increasing burden on the taxpayer. However, in the 2000s, the pre-1977 pension burden on cities across the state was still on the increase. Cities were given a levy (an ability to tax citizens) by the state to pay for these pensions, but it was still a nervous part of the budgeting process for Indianapolis due to the increasing tax burden on citizens.

The 2007 statewide citizen revolt surrounding property taxes resulted in a significant percentage of incumbent mayors losing reelection battles, scaring the state legislators into necessary property tax reform. Somewhere in the 2008 legislative session, an off-budget year, I had asked our lobbyist, Joe Loftus, if the pre-1977 public-safety pensions could be addressed also. This was an almost naive request from a new mayor considering the statehouse's laser-like focus on property tax reform.

Joe is quiet about everything. He is one of the most respected lobbyists in the state, serious but with a wry sense of humor. Unbeknownst to me, he had been silently working on the legislators about this issue and was able to slip in a provision that the state would pick up the pre-1977 public-safety pensions, not just for Indianapolis, but for all cities across the state. It was a remarkable achievement that went largely unnoticed. Cities lost their levy, which made sense, but it was off the table as an annual budget issue for cities in Indiana. It was a tremendous accomplishment, however silent.

Trash Truck Rerouting

When you are in an executive government position such as governor or mayor, you realize quickly that two levels below you as officeholder are supervisors and workers who have been through multiple administrations. While most are dedicated to their jobs, the long-term workforce can make change difficult for an eager new administration. On some level, these workers just want to retire from their positions with the city or state. Most understand that there will be some changes with each administration, and they accept it. Some have been beaten down or keep their profile low so as not to upset the incumbent administration; they want to survive.

Occasionally someone will stand out—someone who has been waiting for an administration to listen to their ideas. Indy had such a man in John Williams. He had worked in the Department of Public Works and for years had an idea to reroute our garbage trucks. It made a lot of sense, but he could not get anyone to listen to him until David Sherman became the public-works director.

John's idea was to work the garbage trucks in quadrants within the city on the same day. Previously, on each day there would be garbage trucks in neighborhoods all across the city (about four hundred square miles). However, if all the trucks on a particular day worked in the same quadrant, not only could gasoline be saved, but if a truck broke down, then another truck could cover that area within a few minutes instead of using one from thirty to forty minutes away. It made perfect sense.

Because many citizens would have their trash day changed, we used the media to announce the change but also held public neighborhood meetings to inform as many people as possible. I went to a few of these meetings; as expected, many people were upset. However, the only reason they were upset was that the day was going to change; there was no substantive objection whatsoever. We also wanted to provide free carts and recycling services for the elderly and disabled.

We made the change. It went smoothly and saved us a million dollars that first year, which we used to buy new trucks.

Ideas can come from everywhere. You have to be open and listen.

Money for My Successor

Along with reducing the city debt by two-thirds and having strong bond ratings, which lowered the city's debt service, another major part of leaving the city in better shape than I found it included leaving money to my successor. We knew there would be some structural financial issues to be worked through the year we left, and we wanted to position the incoming administration as well as possible. That meant cash.

City budgets are always tight. There is very little wiggle room for a mayor's priorities, as salaries and other mandatory items must be paid. As mentioned, the public-safety apparatus alone (police, fire, etc.) takes up well over 80 percent of the Indianapolis budget.

Even though Indianapolis has AAA bond ratings much of the time, it has never had much in the way of reserves. We tried to get the departments to sock away 5 percent of their annual budgets for reserves, but that was difficult even for those directly reporting to the mayor's office, and the separately elected officials were, to be kind, less than gracious on that request. A mayor learns quickly that very few elected officials care about the city budget; they just want more money for their offices.

However, with the transfer of the water and wastewater assets to Citizens Energy, of the $425 million in cash that we received, we put away $80 million into a newly created Fiscal Stability Fund, a fancy term for reserves or rainy day money. When the council turned Democratic in 2012, they tried spending that money, and we fought them off as best as we could. When I left office in January 2016, there was still $78 million in that account.

Also, a few years prior, the state paternalistically passed an onerous law that allowed the state to keep a portion of a city's income tax in state reserves. This was a silly law especially as cities were still reeling from the Great Recession. The state claimed that this was a safety measure in case cities went bankrupt, but there was no evidence of any such thing happening in anyone's memory. The state likes to claim they give cities "home rule," but nothing could be further from the truth. The state was keeping our money for no reason.

I wrote a letter to the governor asking for the city's own money, but he wrote back saying it was the law, even though the withholding was not mandatory. I was furious but unable to do anything about it. The state was withholding $17 million annually from Indianapolis. They did that for my final three years in office, with a total withholding of about $51 million dollars that the city was owed. They never gave it to the city while I was in office. Our administration could have used that $17 million annually to good effect.

We knew this was the city's money, and we counted it as something like accounts receivables. Sooner or later, the city would get that money. By the time the state realized the error of its ways sometime in 2016, the figure was around $60 million. The state gave that money to my successor. I was angry, but I was also out of office. I was nevertheless happy that the city finally got its own money.

Between the Fiscal Stability Fund, the delayed state-held money, and the few million that was actually in reserve accounts, I left my successor around $140 million in cash, a handsome sum indeed. I was proud of that. We knew there was a structural deficit in his upcoming budget, but he had multiples of that amount in cash to work with over many years.

A Little Help?

All across the country are cities that are paying for police, fire, and other services, on their dime, for people who work and play in those cities but pay their taxes elsewhere. I took seriously my charge as the mayor of the capital city of Indiana. I wanted people from all around the state and the country to visit, and I always wanted Indianapolis to put its best foot forward. There is only one big city in the state, and it needed to be a warm, clean, and welcoming one.

That said, there are more than one hundred thousand people who come to work in Indianapolis daily but live in the neighboring suburbs. This is fine, but they use our roads, our public safety, and other amenities that cost millions of dollars to maintain. However, their property and income taxes go to the county they live in. Many likely moved to the area because of Indianapolis, but the citizens of Indianapolis must pay for the use of city services by these neighboring suburbanites.

Our team brought this up to our local state legislators, who listened well and understood but were unwilling to act. We were not asking for anything as dramatic as a fifty-fifty split on taxes, but a small percentage of income taxes could be split so that counties providing services to nonresident workers could have some help in maintaining the municipality. Seems fair to me. It would not be hard to enact.

A Secret

The secret in Indianapolis finance is that the school systems combined have several hundred million dollars of debt. Very little attention is paid to this phenomenon, most likely because there are eleven different public school systems in place with no one paying attention to the cumulative debt total. With referendums now in place for school systems to raise additional revenue (a by-product of the property tax reform in 2008), a few people are paying attention, but not enough for anyone to act. Still, no one seems to notice the accumulated total. There is little pressure on schools to look at their spending.

When I left office, the only school system that did not have debt was the Speedway school system. Speedway also has far and away the best graduation rate among high schools in the city. It is stellar. It is not, as most people outside the city would suspect, a rich area of the city. It is typical middle class with caring people. I wonder if the lack of debt is related to their great performance.

5

GOOD GOVERNMENT

MANY PEOPLE HAVE LOST FAITH IN GOVERNMENT. But I still believe that good government, responsive to citizens' needs, can and does happen. I certainly believe that most officeholders start out wanting to serve their citizens well, but many get lost along the way. I like to think we never lost our way.

Ethics Reform

In our first year in office, we passed an ethics reform bill. Indianapolis has not had a whisper of corruption from the mayor's office that anyone can remember, something of which the city should be justly proud. However, the existing city law was behind the times. In addition to requiring lobbyists to register with the city, we updated the law regarding gifts, patronage, the use of city-county property for nonbusiness purposes, conflicts of interest, whistleblower protections, nepotism, and other items. We also mandated that city employees and board appointees be trained to these higher standards.

Information about the Indianapolis boards and commissions, their members, and their terms were made available online. Additionally, we put all the city contracts online, a move that I thought was extraordinary at the time as so many government critics openly complained about contracts being signed with a veil of secrecy.

I naively believed that these updated ethics reforms would be talked about and heavily covered by the press. When we held the press conference to announce these reforms, the interest was minimal at best. It was still the right thing to do.

Mayor's Action Center Upgrade

The Mayor's Action Center (MAC) is the city's call center. Citizens can call to ask questions or request service from the city, report potholes or high weeds and grass—any number of issues. All major cities have such call centers. Ours takes over one hundred thousand calls annually, and the telephone operators are unfailingly polite and patient. However, as a call center, it was not up to industry standards in 2007. It took about two minutes for a call to be answered. As a result, calls were abandoned at an unacceptable rate. It is easy to say, "This is government; that's the way it is," and just continue with current practices, but we knew what the industry standards were, and we wanted to at least match them.

Sarah Taylor spearheaded these improvements. It took time, money, and effort, including a software upgrade, but the time to answer a call fell from two minutes to less than ten seconds. Ninety-eight percent of calls were answered before they were abandoned, well above the industry standard. As a bonus, the operators loved the system as well. They did not like having abandoned calls.

We then took the unprecedented action of calling citizens back to check if their problem was solved. This was in line with our listening philosophy, ensuring that the proper actions were taken. As I remember, we followed up with about a third of the calls made to the MAC. Few governments at any level would take this sort of action. I would occasionally drop by the MAC to talk to the operators, and when we started calling citizens back to check if the issues had been resolved, I would ask the operators what the response was by the citizens. Many people thought it was a prank call initially, but the callers became used to this practice and were very appreciative. The MAC would have me make some of these return calls personally on the milestone of every twenty-five thousand calls or so. It was fun to hear people respond to the mayor making the call back to a citizen to see if that pothole was filled.

There were other improvements using digital technology. We began Request Indy, where people could submit their request online and track it. This method of requesting services became about one-third of the MAC's intake. We followed up with a mobile application, allowing people to take pictures and send them in with their request. Both these actions had the added advantage of being available twenty-four hours per day. This seems normal today, but for the Indianapolis MAC at this time, it was revolutionary.

The impetus for all of this was that we wanted our citizens to feel comfortable and listened to when they called in or submitted online. The callback feature told us that the upgrades in service and technology were recognized and appreciated. Sarah and her team were tremendous, and the citizens of Indianapolis benefited.

Stability for the Capital Improvement Board

Despite the continuous stress of being the mayor, at only one time during my administration was my physical health affected by stress.

My blood pressure went up enough that I knew something was wrong. My body was acting differently, and for a while, I routinely visited the medical clinic in the City-County Building to check my blood pressure. We had installed this clinic as a perk for city employees, but I never imagined I would be needing its services.

The Capital Improvement Board (CIB) was created in 1965 by the Indiana legislature. Its mission is to finance and manage such capital improvements as sports facilities like Gainbridge Fieldhouse, where the Indiana Pacers play; Lucas Oil Stadium, where the Indianapolis Colts play; the Colts' headquarters; the convention center; and a few other buildings. It is funded by a special set of taxes that allow these facilities to bring in tax revenue for the construction and maintenance of these facilities.

It has been a tremendous success for the city and the state. It has allowed the city to build wonderful facilities that were a catalyst for the city's sports strategy of prior decades. However, in 2009, the situation was so dire that we were warned by an auditing firm that the CIB might soon not be able to operate. Lucas Oil Stadium had just opened in 2008, but the higher operating costs compared to the previous stadium were only a part of the problem. The CIB had a large structural deficit, other debt was coming due, and a shortfall of $40 million was anticipated in a few years. Urgent action was required.

Although the CIB operates within the city, it was created by the state, and the state must approve the special taxes that fund the operation. The CIB did what it could to lower expenses while we worked through the statehouse, but some members of the statehouse either did not understand or did not want to understand that these facilities brought in massive tax revenue for the state.

Failing to grasp the importance of the successful sports strategy in Indianapolis, some legislators wanted to kill the CIB altogether, which would have been disastrous for both the city and the state. There is a feeling among some in the state legislature that "Indianapolis gets everything." It is a nice political slogan that helps them get elected in their rural areas, but it also could not be further from the truth. Indianapolis and the surrounding counties in central Indiana account for one-third of the state's economy and are net contributors to the rest of the state. Roads in the rural areas of Indiana would not be paved if not for the economic activity generated in central Indiana.

My team and I worked the issue hard. I had appointed Bob Grand of the law firm Barnes and Thornburg as my first CIB head in 2008. That proved to be one of my best moves during our administration. Bob was not only brilliant and forceful when necessary, but he also had enormous influence in the statehouse.

Early in the process, it looked gloomy to me. It was the first time, but not the last, that I felt the weight on my shoulders of the good work from the previous mayors (Lugar, Hudnut, Goldsmith, and Peterson) who worked so hard with the business, philanthropic, and nonprofit entities to build the city up from the 1960s to where it was now. The pressure came from not being able to control the outcome, although it was going to affect my city. It was in the hands of others.

Cooler heads prevailed. The funding formula was amended to allow the CIB to continue. My blood pressure went down and has remained normal ever since.

Unigov Reform

In 1969, the Indiana legislature voted to consolidate the city of Indianapolis with the rest of Marion County. Taking effect in 1970, it was called Unigov. This was a difficult political achievement that geographically made Indianapolis, wholly contained within Marion County, and the rest of the county into one government.

It was hailed nationally as a model for future municipal government, but cities and counties around the nation did not follow suit. Many in the state commented, then and now, that it enabled Republicans to control the city for decades. Indianapolis in the 1960s was becoming more Democratic while the rest of Marion County remained staunchly Republican territory. Eventually, however, all of Marion County became more Democratic than Republican, and the first Democratic mayor in decades won election in 1999. Most political observers believed that the citizens of Indianapolis would not elect a Republican mayor well into the future, but I was elected eight years later, in 2007.

There were significant consolidations as a result of Unigov, but there were also a significant number of "carve-outs" that made passing the 1969 legislation possible. There are four "excluded" cities within the county that maintain their own government. Three of these cities elect their own mayor; the residents of these cities actually vote for two mayors, their own and the mayor of Indianapolis. There are also some "included" cities that have some autonomy but largely rely on Indianapolis for their services.

Many of us wanted to continue the consolidation. Indianapolis continues to learn the lesson, though, common around the country, that officeholders do not want to give up their turf, no matter what is best for the citizens.

In Indianapolis after Unigov, there were still fire departments under the control of the township trustees with some of the excluded cities also maintaining both police and fire services. Why township trustees have fire departments in Indianapolis is beyond my comprehension. Over a period of years, some of the township fire departments consolidated with the excellent Indianapolis Fire Department. My predecessor was courageous in pushing for some of these fire departments to join IFD, and our administration also brought a few more departments into IFD. However, when I left office in 2016, the three western townships still had their own fire departments, even though this was more expensive for the taxpayers in these areas. The trustees did not want to give up control of their departments.

Some of the excluded cities kept their fire departments. One excluded city mayor, whose fire department was having budget problems, had the gall to ask me to help pay for his department. In other words, he wanted the citizens of Indianapolis to pay for his excluded city's hyper-local fire department. I declined the offer by asking directly why the citizens of Indianapolis should pay for his department.

We consolidated the emergency medical services organizations (that is, ambulances) of the Indianapolis Fire Department and Wishard (now Eskenazi) Hospital. We placed this new organization under the Department of

Public Safety, and this turned out to be a great partnership that was both efficient and effective. It was also a very proud organization with a great leader in Charles Miramonti.

We were successful in eliminating the township assessors. Assessors in Indiana were not held in high regard in most places because of the property tax fiasco in 2007 that helped usher me and other new mayors around the state into office. When the state provided an opportunity to eliminate the assessors, I jumped at the chance. Graciously, my predecessor joined me in a press conference to call for their elimination. Assessors are now largely only at the city and county levels in Indiana.

Most of the township trustees and township board members are good, civic-minded people. I was friendly with them and supported them when asked. That said, I am not fond of township government. I understand the concept of government closest to the people but feel that the city is close enough to understand the concerns of the citizens. The city-county councilors and the neighborhood liaisons from the mayor's office can fulfill the "closest to the people" concept. Without fire departments, township trustee duties are minimal (maintenance of cemeteries, assistance to the poor) and could easily be covered by the city.

When Mitch Daniels was Indiana governor, he created a bipartisan commission to look at local government structure throughout the state with an eye toward consolidation, but there was little appetite at the legislature to change the current structure. I am sure that the legislators felt kinship and loyalty to those in township government in their respective districts, despite the additional expense to the taxpayers. Many people like township government, and it does get more people involved in local government, but I am not sure these intangibles outweigh the additional cost and bureaucracy.

A few in our administration felt we could consolidate almost all the elected offices in Indianapolis, mostly under the purview of the mayor's office. Our most radical example was that Indianapolis needed only three elected officeholders: the mayor, the prosecutor, and the clerk. The rest would be appointed positions. It will not happen anytime soon.

Enterprise Resource Development

Mayors and other officeholders can tell some unbelievable stories about built-in, systemic inefficiencies in government. Some even like them; it is usually very hard to reverse such inefficiencies as workers are comfortable with the way things are, despite the obvious savings to be had.

Enterprise resource development (ERP) is a fancy term for centralizing financial reporting within the city. Prior to my taking office, there was no central method for accounting, purchasing, budgeting, or tracking spending. The different departments did their own thing, making it more difficult for the city's financial team to make decisions. We made the multimillion-dollar, multiyear investment to update and centralize the systems for greater efficiency and transparency.

This was the brainchild of my first controller, David Reynolds. I was again lucky to have the right person in the right spot when needed. David was brilliant and dedicated, but he also knew all the financial systems at the city and state levels. The city is much better off now for the long term.

Office of Audit and Performance

When I took office, I was aware of the CompStat system used by the New York City Police Department. It was begun by the legendary Bill Bratton and was very successful in helping Bratton significantly reduce crime in his city. I also knew that a few cities used a similar concept for their police departments.

Early in our administration, we created the Office of Audit and Performance. Part of OAP, run by Manny Mendez, was the creation of IndyStat, based on the CompStat principles. Departments reported on their performance to an executive panel and me about twice per year. My past experiences told me that some sort of accountability, some measure of performance, improves people and organizations. I do not believe this had ever been done before in Indianapolis. People in government are usually uncomfortable reporting on their department's performance publicly, but we did not make it a grueling experience; we just wanted to ensure that progress was being made.

A routine part of IndyStat was reporting on the status of city contracts with minority, women, veteran, and disabled business owners. This was a common thread throughout the sessions as it was important to me that contracts were not just awarded to larger, more established contractors. Our administration did well in helping these smaller companies.

Six Sigma, detailed above, was a part of OAP. In addition to the green belts and black belts trained in the city, we also trained more than one thousand employees in the basics of Six Sigma. Manny's team saved over $15 million annually. Projects included such items as cell phone usage analysis and arrestee healthcare processing (which saved over $1 million). Many different processes were studied that resulted in nice savings for the city.

Department of Code Enforcement

Early in 2008 upon assuming office, we eliminated the Department of Administration. Its only purpose seemed to be employing people. We also created the Department of Code Enforcement (DCE).

DCE consolidated the licensing, permitting, and inspection functions of multiple departments into one organization. Previously, people who wanted to improve a property, host an event, get a needed inspection, or conduct similar activities frequently had to visit different city departments for the required approvals. This changed with DCE. Such a wide-ranging organization needed a leader with an eye for detail for numerous responsibilities but also one who understood that these functions should be carried out with an eye toward quality of life, not just penal enforcement. Rick Powers, a friendly former marine with an appetite for detail and doing the right thing, was the right guy for this job. It is hard to be the first leader of a new organization, but Rick performed exceedingly well.

DCE now covered everything from building permits, boarding up abandoned homes, cleaning up illegally dumped trash, and regulating taxi companies. Previously, the costs of many of these functions were borne by the general taxpayer rather than the people or organizations that required these services. That changed with DCE. People or organizations that needed these very specific services were now required to pay for them. This took some massaging of feelings, but Rick and his team worked through the concerns.

DCE was a success, but it was the aforementioned Richmond Hill tragedy (the gas explosion that destroyed homes, damaged a neighborhood, and took two lives) where they showed how a great team responds. The public-safety investigators, including the late Gary Coons, a great public servant, were diligent and thorough in finding the cause of the explosion. They were outstanding in every way and ensured that their investigation put the perpetrators in jail. The rest of the recovery was left to DCE, which performed the months-long, immense, and detailed work of helping that neighborhood recover after the explosion.

Snow Fleet Upgrade

Mayors in large cities routinely hear about snow removal efforts being less than perfect. Indianapolis was no exception.

Just before every winter, the city holds a press conference to tell the citizens that the snow fleet is ready to go. That first year in our administration, we parked our snow fleet for all the press to see, but to the operators of these vehicles, this was merely putting lipstick on a pig.

Some rust was visible, but much of it was painted over. I learned that some drivers had to use cardboard or rags to cover holes in the floorboards to prevent the cold and snow from entering their vehicles. Overall, the fleet looked ragged. One driver sidled up to me away from the press and told me he did not think some of the trucks would make it through the winter.

From the Marines, I knew the importance of keeping vehicles in operational condition, not just to be effective and save money, but also to ensure morale within the ranks. No one wants to drive a poorly maintained vehicle. It is unsafe, particularly in the winter, when freezing temperatures can become a real danger. A poorly maintained vehicle also tells the driver that the city does not care enough to provide him or her with safe equipment.

David Sherman, my public-works director, located money somehow to upgrade the fleet. Within a year, he had bought a whole new snow fleet of more than eighty trucks, this time with stainless steel cargo beds so that the salt would not rust them. New trucks improved morale greatly within that section of public works. And of course, the downtime for maintenance on the new trucks was minimal. David upgraded our overall fleet in the city so much that we became nationally ranked, in the top fifty fleets in the nation. We had never been ranked previously.

David also reorganized the snow fighting plan. He prioritized them as follows:

- Primary routes—The main thoroughfares, because they link the police, fire, and EMS routes and are the main routes for people to get to work.
- Secondary routes—The sometimes highly traveled routes that feed into the primary routes.
- Residential—We instituted a policy of clearing snow in residential areas when the snow was six inches or more. We hired about three hundred contractors, mostly businesses and individuals who put a snowplow on the front of their pickup. They did a great and quick job of moving snow. Citizens loved this plan.

I mentioned to someone in public works that they should look into upgrading a small sliver of Forty-Eighth Street on the west side of the city, near my house, as it was a feeder lane for several neighborhoods leading to the very busy Kessler Boulevard. A mayor must be careful when asking such things because it could be interpreted as favoritism. However, I thought it was a legitimate request, and when public works looked at it, they agreed.

Soon after, a snowfall occurred, and the snow removal drivers plowed all the snow right up to my house, about a mile from Forty-Eighth Street. Although my nearby neighbors loved it, I put a halt to it. It was a funny moment.

I appreciated so much the efforts of the drivers of our snow fleet. In any situation involving snow, it is the mayor who takes the brunt of the criticism. That is just part of the job; I knew that. However, when people publicly complained about the snow not being cleared well, the snow fleet took it personally. In almost all cases, it was not the snow fleet's fault. Fortunately, the press understood how difficult it was to predict snow or ice on the roads, and how difficult it was to clean up during and after a snowstorm.

One time, though, even I got upset at the criticism coming my way. Temperatures between thirty and thirty-four degrees make the situation tricky enough, but when combined with a muddled precipitation forecast, it is very difficult to decide whether or not to use the snow fleet as a preventive measure. As part of our decision-making process, we looked at several forecasts to get an overall picture. On one particular night, we thought a preventive coat of salt might be needed in some places; we sent out half the fleet. No other county in the area sent anyone out at all. The state, responsible for the highways, sent no one out.

Just before rush hour the next morning, the temperatures dropped below thirty-two degrees, and a freezing rain fell. The roads, particularly the untreated highways that were the responsibility of the state, were very dangerous—so dangerous that the state closed the highways leading into downtown Indianapolis, just before rush hour. The state did not tell us they were going to do that; they just did it. Those thousands of cars that normally used the highways during morning rush hour heading toward our downtown were now using overcrowded city roads, only some of which had been treated. Predictably, there were dozens of accidents on the city roads, because the thousands of cars that came by highway were now jammed together in a freezing rain on icy streets not designed to handle that volume.

Indy took the brunt of the criticism. We never heard a word from the state. We were the only municipality that had put trucks out the night before, yet we were taking the hit. I was not happy.

Another difficult time for the snow fleet, during my second term, was the "polar vortex" that sent temperatures to forty below zero after the wind chill was factored in. From my marine training, I knew how dangerous this was. Near zero is cold enough, but forty degrees colder is extremely dangerous. We essentially closed the city for two days. In Indianapolis, the press on these sorts of occasions was always stellar. They did everything they could to inform people of the danger. We knew we could count on them. I was scared for people's safety, and I was particularly worried about acts of bravado—maybe some father, bragging about how he had toughed it out in the cold when he was a kid, would take his son out sledding, and they would not make it back home. Minus forty is different than zero.

Snow came just before the temperature dropped to forty below, so our snow fleet had to go to work to accommodate those vehicles that might have to use the streets, such as emergency vehicles and those used by essential workers. On one street, because of the extreme cold, ice bumps took shape. The snow fleet is not equipped to shave down ice bumps in the road. In fact, I do not know of any piece of equipment that shaves down ice bumps on a street in forty-below weather.

One Democratic councilor loudly complained about the snow fleet's performance during the polar vortex. This councilor had a shop in downtown Indianapolis, and a member of the snow fleet asked me if I wanted the piled-up snow moved to the front of his shop so no one could get in, sending a strong signal to that councilor. I told the snow fleet that would not be necessary.

I got along well with the drivers. I knew they worked hard, and I knew that going to see them and thanking them was important. Many politicians do such things when the TV cameras are rolling. I made a point to go there routinely when the TV cameras were not present.

Department of Metropolitan Development Restructuring

Sometimes one person makes a dramatic difference in a city. Indianapolis had never hired anyone like Adam Thies before and probably will not for quite some time. If Indianapolis could put him in charge of multiple departments for at least twenty years, the city would be dramatically improved well into the future. He brought a holistic design perspective combined with practicality and fiscal discipline. He is unique.

Adam closed his successful business in Bloomington and moved his wife and four young children to Indianapolis to become the Department of Metropolitan Development (DMD) director at the beginning of my second term. He stayed for three years.

Before Adam, DMD managed some city properties and completed some neighborhood design plans that largely sat on the shelves. It was full of good people, but "innovative" and "dynamic" were not words that would describe the department. Adam changed the thinking of DMD as much as he could. He brought in younger, bolder talent that looked at city development differently.

Adam also was a sounding board for me on many projects and the driver of many initiatives. It was Adam who came into my office while Indy Connect was being planned and told me that the Red Line, along the north-south spine of Indianapolis, needed to be the first bus rapid transit line built because that route had the most potential for economic development. (Prior to Adam, either the line along the northeast corridor to downtown or the line from the airport to downtown was presumed to be the first line built.) He put together the briefing for me when I traveled to Washington, DC, to talk to the secretary of transportation personally about the all-electric BRT. This resulted in $2 million immediately for design and engineering of the Red Line and $75 million for the initial construction, both grants coming from the federal government.

Indy Rezone and Others

Adam was critical to the Indy Rezone efforts that updated the zoning laws and requirements put into place decades before, when the city was still expanding to fill out Marion County. Indianapolis needed new regulations for redevelopment, with modern standards to include mixed-use development, integration with natural features, and connectivity with multiple modes of transportation, not just the automobile. We needed to both protect current property owners and preserve some historic areas while looking to the future.

Many people and organizations, realizing the scale of what we were trying to achieve, felt a need to weigh in. This was a multiyear effort, and again, our administration's listening skills helped as we held over one hundred meetings to get ideas from all angles and hear the concerns of the citizens. This was a massive effort, handled expertly by DMD and others. It became law in 2015. It never made the newspaper or TV in any meaningful fashion, but this was a major accomplishment of which I am very proud.

Adam was also critical in developing Massachusetts Avenue (known locally as Mass Ave.), a commercial district just off downtown with a trendy urban vibe. We decided that the Indianapolis Fire Department's headquarters, Fire Station #7, and the Firefighters Credit Union should move from Mass Ave. New development replaced the IFD buildings, and we found better homes nearby for the IFD offices.

I was hoping for a more modern design for the new Station #7 but received pushback from IFD, which wanted a traditional fire station design. I thought that would not fit in with the surrounding architecture. Adam stepped in and made the design acceptable to all.

Adam came into my office one day with an idea to attach apartments to a parking garage in downtown Indianapolis. The plan would include removing a lane from the street. I told him that I could not imagine removing a lane from a downtown street, but he had examined the traffic patterns in the area and thought removing the lane would make no difference. I was skeptical and told him so. I appreciate people who have ideas that seemingly come from nowhere, develop them, and then present them for consideration. This was just such an idea, but the lane removal was too much.

He worked on me for about a year advocating for this project, and I finally relented. The lane was removed. Sure enough, it had no impact on traffic. The residential development looked great, making a dull, gray parking garage sparkle with an orange exterior for the apartments. It fit right in with its surroundings. It really is something to see. The old Department of Metropolitan Development, as good as it was, would never have presented such an idea to me.

KIB Great Indy Cleanup Reorganization

Cities across the country have annual cleanups. Some are local to neighborhoods; others are more ambitious. Indianapolis is lucky to have an aggressive organization that partners with the city to conduct such cleanups.

Every year, the city (mostly public-works) partners with Keep Indianapolis Beautiful (KIB) on a spring cleanup. It is conducted over the four weekends in April and is a fun, celebrated event in the neighborhoods. I would attend two or three of these cleanups each weekend to show support and talk to as many people as possible. Much like the initial garbage pickup routes we inherited, the Great Indy Cleanup was all over the city every weekend in April. Historically, neighborhood groups (of which there are several hundred) would choose which weekend they wanted to have their cleanup, and the city and KIB would accommodate. It was hardly a model of efficiency.

However, there were only so many DPW trucks and drivers available. In our view, it made sense to organize the cleanups by quadrants each weekend to maximize the trucks and drivers. This sounds like an easy thing to do, but it was very difficult. The neighborhoods treasured the weekend they historically had in April because the weekend cleanups were a time for neighbors to come together, not just to clean up, but to mark the arrival of spring. The neighborhood groups felt we were failing to recognize their historical time for spring cleanups. All we wanted to do was use the DPW trucks more efficiently to make the whole process far more effective.

Mitzi Hurst, an unsung hero of our administration, took charge of this effort. It took Mitzi ten months of working with KIB and the neighborhood groups to reorganize the spring cleanup. Dave Forsell, head of KIB at the time and a wonderful man, told me that because of the reorganization, the number of tons of trash picked up was dramatically higher, well over a 100 percent improvement. It was a big success. The DPW drivers liked it also.

A few years into our administration, I mentioned to Dave that every winter there seemed to be a lot of trash in plain sight. I asked him to investigate doing fall cleanups so that citizens didn't have to look at so much trash during the dreary days of winter. He organized this, and now many neighborhood groups do October cleanups also.

Dave Forsell is a tremendous, caring citizen. He has battled cancer most of his adult life and is still winning that battle. Dave told me that on election night in 2007—when I was declared the winner, and Carl Brizzi made those public comments that Indianapolis citizens could look forward to no more arts and sustainability and the like—he curled up in a fetal position on his floor and cried.

Eight years later, he told me that my administration was the best friend KIB ever had.

The Central Indiana Council of Elected Officials

After a trip to Denver, I began an association of central Indiana mayors, the Central Indiana Council of Elected Officials (CICEO), and their equivalents to discuss common issues and potentially save money through combined purchases of supplies. I was visiting Denver with the Indianapolis Chamber of Commerce in 2008, and the Denver area had success with just such a group of elected officials. Several metropolitan areas around the country have similar organizations. I thought Indianapolis should have one also.

I led the group for the first couple of years but also realized that the Indy mayor should not dominate the discussions over the long haul, so I passed off my leadership role to the Westfield mayor, Andy Cook, who helped me start the group. Several individuals have led the group since. CICEO discussed issues of common interests like mass transit and collective economic development. It also attracted a lot of attention; various organizations wanted to address the group, a promising sign of its collective power. Legislative leaders in particular wanted to know what we were thinking. We also brought in guest speakers to keep us informed on some issues.

CICEO continued after I left office, but has since morphed into another, larger group that is still very effective.

Merging Develop Indy and the Indianapolis Chamber

Almost every week when I was mayor, our economic development team, Develop Indy, would meet with me to discuss businesses looking to move to or expand in Indianapolis. By the time this team would brief me, they had already talked to the companies, met with site selectors and other entities, and come to some possible terms. I was the final deciding point.

I wanted to know primarily how many jobs were anticipated and at what wage rate; that was our main priority when it came to incentives to move to Indianapolis. Many people assume that cities are too generous when it comes to incentives, but most of the time it is just some level of reduction in future taxes. The state can help with additional benefits such as job training, and frequently the state was a great partner with us. Cities and states do this because there is real competition for businesses. The benefits that these companies can bring include jobs for our citizens and a broadening of the tax base overall.

The head of Develop Indy came to me to discuss merging his organization with the Greater Indianapolis Chamber of Commerce. At first, this made no sense to me. I was afraid that the influence of existing businesses belonging to the chamber might result in new businesses being disapproved so that there would be less competition for the existing businesses. I also believed that citizens voted for the mayor to make these types of decisions.

He tried to convince me that this would not be the case and that having potential new businesses working with elements of the chamber early on would be better. It took some time, but I came to be convinced that the synergy of the chamber and Develop Indy could in fact be an improvement. Many of the functions were merged, and I believe it was the right call. It took a few months to get the right language for the merger mainly because I insisted that the mayor make the final call as to the incentives. I still believe the mayor should be accountable to the citizens for those decisions.

The Smoking Ban

In my first term, the media kept bringing up that Indianapolis did not have a smoking ban in public buildings, particularly in bars. I did not pay much attention to this early on because I did not hear that sentiment at all in the monthly Mayor's Night Out during my first term, except for one time after a media outlet had pushed that issue. Most buildings, other than bars, already forbade smoking indoors. I was in the public all the time and rarely heard anything about it.

I hate smoking. Being around cigarette smoke makes me ill for days. I do not know why tobacco is legal; it seems to have no positive effects at all, only negative ones. We ban most things like that. However, tobacco as a crop was foundational to our nation at one point, and the culture of using tobacco continues to this day, despite its obvious harm and subsequent massive effect on our healthcare costs.

That said, it is a legal product. I did not feel comfortable having the government ban a legal product in buildings. Customers who frequented bars that allowed smoking knew there were health risks. However, people did not have to go to bars that allowed smoking; it was a personal choice. Also, bars did not have to allow smoking—again a personal choice of the bar owner.

Many laws are compromises between dueling principles. A good example is government transparency versus national security. During wartime, do we want the government to be totally transparent, knowing it could kill our service men and women, or do we want to protect much information so that it does not get into enemy hands? Remember the World War II slogan "Loose Lips Sink Ships"? The level of government transparency in national security affairs, even during peacetime, is still a matter of significant debate.

Another example is the energy we use, particularly as clean energy becomes cheaper and more readily available. Do we want to continue to use dirty energy like coal, that may (or may not) be slightly cheaper but is harmful to the health of people—again adding to our healthcare costs while lessening our gross domestic product because of sickness and the premature deaths of workers?

There are always trade-offs between competing philosophies. In the case of smoking in public places, my thought was that tobacco is a legal product, and we have free will; individuals can choose whether to step foot in a bar or not. It was health versus free will. Even though several cities had already moved to ban smoking in public buildings, including bars, I thought it was government overreach, limiting free will. People are allowed to eat terrible food and drink to excess, knowing that it will shorten their lives, but they do it, and it is legal. It seemed the same principle to me.

Some of the media kept up the onslaught. My political team thought it was an easy throwaway issue—just pass it and move on. Bar owners would tell me they appreciated my stance, but part of it seemed to be that these owners mainly wanted a level playing field. They were afraid that if they banned smoking in their own bars, it would be detrimental to their profits as long as other bars continued to allow smoking. I understood that. Finally, I got a sense that the bar owners were going to be OK if the law changed because the smoking ban would apply to all of them. There would be a level playing field.

There were still two issues to deal with. I had a Republican-led council at the time, and many of their sentiments were in line with my thought that it is not the government's business to limit freedom of choice. There was also the debate whether this would be just for buildings that accommodated the public, or would private buildings be included also? I wanted it just for public buildings.

This issue came up during the televised debates for my reelection. When I said something like, "There is room for discussion on this issue," it took the wind out of the sails for any contentious debate. Still, I did not think this was major issue at the time, and I rarely heard it on the campaign trail. Some media outlets were still pushing it, but not the general public. In the last days of my first term after the election, the still-Republican council tried to pass a bill that I would have signed, but it was scuttled in a committee meeting. With the new Democratic-led council after my reelection, they passed a bill immediately, including the private building ban. I vetoed it. Not having the votes to override my veto, they passed a new bill a few weeks later with the private building clause removed from the bill; I signed it.

The Democrats were mad, but before I was elected in 2007, they had the mayor's office and the council yet had done nothing on a smoking ban. I think the final bill was a good compromise.

Being Quiet to Get the Job Done

Sometimes, even as a mayor, being quiet is a more effective way to get things done. Two instances come to mind.

Early in my administration, we were trying to fix the CIB financial mess. The Capital Improvement Board has been critical to the success of Indianapolis and central Indiana. As mentioned above, it is a quasi-governmental organization that has built and managed the main sports properties over the last several decades, enabling the sports strategy employed by the city to be so effective. The finances were no secret to those paying attention, and the previous administration was upfront about the upcoming difficulties from the combination of building the spectacular Lucas Oil Stadium and other debt from various sources.

The city, though, did not have the dedicated resources (a combination of local taxes) to correct the situation, which meant the state had to get involved. Previously, the state had taken over the responsibility for building the stadium from my predecessor, but I would not consider that much of an issue. However, it does indicate that some at the state level know just how important the sports strategy is to the state's financial picture.

In going through old records, I noticed a trend in the newspaper that constantly criticized me for not being more out front, telling people what needed to be done. "He should lead on the issue" was the common refrain. However, if one is asking for help from others, publicly telling them what they should do makes little sense. It would only upset them, risking further damage. We had to work this quietly, and I had to take my public lumps as needed.

I took them, and the situation got resolved.

The second time was when the musicians' union at the Indianapolis Symphony Orchestra went on strike. The symphony is a highly regarded organization in the city with much support, but this situation dragged on for weeks, putting the symphony schedule in doubt. Again, I was being publicly flogged for not stepping out to make my views known and urging a quick solution.

Unknown to the press, a board member whom I knew well called me during my public flogging asking me to stay quiet. She told me they were working through the issues well and would come to a solution soon. I did and they did. Any public pronouncements on my part would have hurt the situation.

As good and fair as our local press was, some of them thought that I should have weighed in on every subject. They were used to politicians being more than eager to do just that. After all, I was the mayor; I made good copy. However, I just wanted situations resolved. Sometimes that was a public stance; sometimes it was a quiet stance.

The Land Bank

Unfortunately, two young men whom we hired to work in Metropolitan Development at a lower level betrayed the trust of the citizens. No city money was involved at all, but they took some money from private citizens on the side for special information (about $2,000 total, if I recall correctly) about land bank properties that were designated to be put back on the tax roll. That was a function of the land bank, to get distressed properties back into livable conditions by working with partners, usually in the nonprofit world. It was a minor crime but a breach of trust. The irony of this story is that, despite the greed of the young men, the land bank actions were increasing the city's tax receipts.

A member of my staff had knowledge of this crime because he was given a heads-up from some former colleagues. He told me and the DMD director about four days out from the arrest. We were cooperating with the federal authorities to arrest these two men, trying to make the feds' job as easy as possible. My staff told the FBI that there is a loading dock in the parking garage underneath the City-County Building where the documents they were seeking could be loaded onto the FBI trucks. They could also take these two young men out through the garage. What happened next is an example of the federal government not at its best.

The federal prosecutors, not the FBI, decided to turn the arrest into a dog-and-pony show, alerting the media to what was about to happen. A member of the federal prosecutors' staff had an early-morning breakfast with a print reporter from the local business newspaper, with that reporter subsequently being present outside of the DMD office around 7:00 a.m., before anyone from DMD was at work. How odd. The TV media were also alerted and were on hand outside the City-County Building, filming the FBI truck and the agents performing their duties.

The FBI special agent-in-charge in Indianapolis had actually called me the day before to apologize for what was about to happen. The dozens of agents involved (just a few could have done the job) were upset they were part of such shenanigans, but they had to follow orders also. It was over the top and unnecessary. They could have quietly picked up these two young men at any time, with our cooperation. Instead, there was a media show.

We read the federal prosecutors' report; it was full of inaccuracies, which we corrected and then gave back to them. One of the young men pled guilty, was crestfallen at his mistakes, and has since led an exemplary life. The other went to court. Unfortunately, it probably cost a hundred times more money to prosecute him than the $2,000 they took. He was found guilty.

It hurt. I liked both these young men.

One must wonder why the feds insisted on such a big show when all the parties were cooperating.

The State Following Our City

One of the points that gives me great satisfaction (and I am probably a little too smug about this) is that we led the state on several issues. Most states have far more assets and capabilities than even their largest cities, and that is true for Indiana and Indianapolis. However, we were ahead of the state in many areas, and they followed our lead.

Even though education is a state responsibility, Indianapolis took the lead, along with corporate help, to begin a pre-K program in Indianapolis. The state soon followed with its own program, though it is still not as robust as it should be.

We created the largest citywide VEX robotics competition in the nation, which grew into the largest state robotics competition in the country. Although schools from throughout the state participate now, the state government is barely involved in one of the great workforce development tools in the state.

We initiated goals for veteran-owned businesses to receive at least 3 percent of the city contract dollars. To the best of our knowledge, no cities in Indiana had done so, nor had the state. Many cities followed our lead, as did the state.

We created a sister city with Hyderabad, India, which led to Infosys, a massive Indian IT firm, choosing Indianapolis as its North American hub. To its credit, the state jumped on the opportunity and brought some of those more robust assets to seal the deal. The state now has a sister province in India.

We highlighted the need to address ex-offenders and their needs, both while they are in prison and once they are released. The state has instituted a coding program in one of their prisons and is starting to realize that it must do more.

The state is now looking at a trail system throughout the state. More than ten years ago, Indy began spending Rebuild Indy money to create a two-hundred-mile system of bicycle trails and lanes that is still expanding. The state has had excess funds for over a decade but did little. Again, quality of life and talent attraction.

The state is now looking at electric vehicles and the enormous economic possibilities from battery manufacturing. We were ten years ahead of the state on this, but to be fair, Indianapolis was several years ahead of most of the country when we first acted.

I kept these thoughts mostly to myself, until now—but I still derive satisfaction from them.

15

EDUCATION

I FREQUENTLY SAID THAT EDUCATION, public safety, and economic development, over a generation, are the same issue. Mayors usually have some control over public safety and economic development, but as American society developed, schools became their own entity, seemingly separate from the rest of our institutions. To be sure, my experience with teachers while mayor was extraordinary; whether I visited a school on a scheduled visit or unannounced, teachers were focused on the tasks at hand. Inspiring is not too strong a word.

However, many school systems are entities unto themselves and may or may not fill the needs of the community in which they are located. This can be a problem. I knew of instances where employers outside of Indianapolis mentioned they could not find qualified employees (as in high school graduates) in their hometowns. Community colleges would tell you that most of their students need supplemental schooling to meet the minimum enrollment requirements, as in basic math and English. One school superintendent instituted a trade school program to supplement regular schooling. He did this so that his high school graduates could have high-paying jobs right out of high school, but he shut it down quickly when he could not find students who were interested.

Something else is going on. Some school systems are stellar in educating their students while others go through the minimum motions required. When schools produce less-than-capable workers, when students drop out and are essentially lost to everyone but themselves, then the public-safety aspect of a city comes into play much too often. These situations are related in outcomes, as in poorly educated students who cannot find a job turning to crime for subsistence, but are not related during the time when these problems could be solved. There is a disconnect.

Mayors across the country are aware of this problem but statutorily can do little about it. It is a frequent topic of conversation at the US Conference of Mayors meetings. Indianapolis is fortunate that the mayor has chartering authority (and may still be the only city in the nation where that is the case), thanks to the courage of my predecessor and several people working in the statehouse at the time. Also, during my time in office, there was a silent but forceful push for the mayor to take charge of the Indianapolis Public Schools system. I thought about it, but I could not get past my internal conflict of being in charge of only one public school system in the city when there were ten more such systems in Indianapolis. If all of them had been offered to be under the charge of the mayor, I would have jumped at the chance.

Mayors want to influence education in their communities but feel hamstrung. They do not like having robust police forces who arrest people, and they do not like companies bypassing their cities because the city's workforce is not capable. They want their cities to be full of educated, community-minded citizens who pay taxes, rather than people who drain a city's resources through the public-safety apparatus.

As I have said previously, mayors and others in office have influence and power beyond their legal statutory authority. Below is how we used our influence to improve educational outcomes in our city and state.

Charter Schools/Office of Education Innovation

I was lucky that Karega Rausch, Beth Bray, and Christine Marson chose to stay in the charter school office when I became mayor. A few years earlier, in a display of bipartisanship, the Democratic mayor of Indianapolis and the Republican statehouse passed legislation that enabled the Indianapolis mayor to charter schools, unique among cities in America. Mayor Peterson courageously partnered with the state, upsetting some long-held Democratic constituencies. I made a point of publicly giving him credit for that courage every chance I got.

Karega, Beth, and Christine were all intellectually gifted with a strong sense of public service, wanting to do better for the city's children through better schools. They could have moved on when I won the election, but we convinced them that our administration had the same goals for this office as Mayor Peterson. They continued their high-quality work.

When our administration began, the office was the gold standard for chartering authority in the state, and it still was when I left office. Organizations wanted their charter schools to be authorized by the mayor's office. The standards were extremely high, and the routine inspections were thorough. Just getting a charter was difficult; our education office not only thoroughly checked the academic approach but also checked for financial viability and the quality of the board. Fewer than a quarter of the organizations wanting to charter a school from the city of Indianapolis were granted the authority to do so.

Our team believed in school choice, so expanding the number of schools made sense to us. Informed parents should be able to decide where their children go to school and should not be restricted by their geography. Despite the purposeful disinformation routinely used against charter schools, the mayor's office charter schools grew in number and performed significantly better than public schools in the same area. I believe we tripled the number of children that attended charter schools under the mayor's charter.

We also expanded the concept of what a charter school could be. The city already had a unique charter high school in Hope Academy, which serves only addicted students. It is a very small school, operating under its own supportive guidelines and a curriculum that meets the Indiana standards. Teaching these children in this environment could not have been possible in a regular public school setting. I spoke at a graduation ceremony, and it was a special experience. I visited the school often.

We opened the first Excel Center operated by Goodwill of Central Indiana (now Goodwill of Central and Southern Indiana) in 2010. This was another unique concept that allowed adults to get a high school diploma, not a GED. The overwhelming success of this concept belies the initial risk for this charter school. Now, however, there are several Excel Centers in Indianapolis and throughout the state serving a special population. In a subsequent chapter, I will talk more how about this concept developed into something much more meaningful.

Similarly, we opened the Damar Academy in 2011, a K–12 school that addressed students with significant behavioral or developmental challenges. Previously, the parents of these children spent around $20,000 per year on private schooling, the only option available until we opened Damar. It took much effort by many people to get this school open, but when we cut the ribbon on that school, it was one of the most emotional moments of my time in office. Tears flowed freely that day. So much of a burden had been lifted from these parents.

Being Tough

We were tough on our schools because we wanted them to remain the gold standard for charter schools in Indiana. Our inspections remained rigorous and led to our office becoming the first chartering authority in the state to close a school for academic reasons. This too was risky, because no one had ever done this before; we did not know what the fallout would be, political or otherwise. However, two schools' performance became untenable. I was willing to close them.

We closed a school on the near northeast side of Indianapolis because its students' performance was significantly worse than the state averages and were not in line with the other charter schools' results, despite a similar student population. They also had poor financial management practices. Although the school's performance was among the worst in the state, the administrators of the school refused to change their approach. They thought their academic model was just fine; however, the minority students' averages were abysmal—totally unacceptable.

Trying to protect me, my education team was not sure closing the school was a good idea. They knew these kids had little to no chance of receiving a good education at this school but were worried how it would play out publicly. I asked them, "What's the right thing to do for the kids?" I also told them I was willing to go through whatever was coming. I could tell they did not expect that sort of response.

On July 23, 2012, the school sued us in state court to stay open. We took it to federal court three days later. Again, a gutsy move. Fortunately, Beth Bray had compiled a thorough, well-researched document on the performance of the school. The federal judge agreed with us, saying, "Faced with such dismal results respecting (the school's) academic and financial health, Mayor Ballard's decision was factually reasonable and legally permissible. His revocation of [the school's] charter was justified not only by concrete facts, but also by statutory law, which clearly afforded him discretion in the matter." The school closed.

The education office has a procedure in place to ensure that students of closed schools would be able to attend nearby schools. Our people worked assiduously to ensure just that.

We investigated another charter school for cheating on standardized tests. The school made huge, unexplainable gains in its ISTEP (the annual Indiana standardized exam) scores in 2013, placing it among the top schools in the state. The school attributed the jump to curriculum changes and a better use of data.

In reality, according to *Chalkbeat Indiana*, an Indiana education newsletter, in an August 21, 2014, article, "On standardized exams (the school) staff erased and changed some students' answers on the state reading and math exams, wrote essay responses for students to copy into their own handwriting, and allowed them to practice in advance on real test questions, according to investigators from Mayor Greg Ballard's office and the Indiana Department of Education."

The article went on to further claim:

> A member of (the school's) staff alerted Ballard's office of concerns that others at the school might have prepared students for ISTEP by letting them practice on actual test questions before taking the exam. . . . Students interviewed by investigators from Ballard's office told them they knew some of the ISTEP questions from review sessions. "For reading, some were new and some we had already done," a third-grader said of ISTEP, according to the investigators' report. "I remember reading the story about ants before. The questions were the same." A teacher who was interviewed described finding evidence students had prepped on an actual ISTEP essay question, called a "writing prompt." . . . "On Wednesday, one of my students opened her book and pulled out a piece of scrap paper," the teacher told investigators. "She said, 'Is this supposed to be here?' I looked closer and it was a handwritten copy of the (ISTEP) writing prompt that had been left in the book."

We also found that the students' grades were not accurate. At a parents' meeting to discuss the school's performance, one of our staff told the parents that their kids were given fake grades to make them feel better. Some parents seemed more concerned about their child's self-esteem than that their children not being properly educated.

That meeting turned ugly. Democratic state legislators representing the area attended the meeting and privately told my staff that they were doing the right thing in closing the school. However, in the public meeting, these same legislators sided with the angry parents. It got heated, and the state legislators did not use their influence to calm the meeting. A member of my staff needed a police escort out of the building. He was justifiably scared. The hypocrisy of those legislators has stayed with me. I respected some of them before the meeting, but after the meeting, my respect for them was never the same.

After the overwhelming evidence of academic fraud, the school's board closed the school before we acted.

I mentioned earlier about the disinformation about charter schools. One popular notion was that charter schools enrolled only the very best from other public schools and that this was why charter schools performed better. Of course, this is not true; most charter schools have lottery systems for enrollment because the demand is so strong. Another mistaken idea is that anyone can open a charter school because standards are so low. This is comical considering how rigorous the mayor's office has been in ensuring quality. Less than one quarter of those who applied were given the green light to open a school.

One curious incident occurred when some Indianapolis Public Schools educators applied to open a charter school. Their application was shoddy, with pages turned upside down and multiple obvious spelling errors. We did not know whether their work on the application was the best they could do or if this was a test case to see if the mayor's office would allow just anyone to open a charter school. We never found out the answer to that question. The application was rejected at the earliest stage of review.

The team that I inherited (Karega, Beth, and Christine) moved on to other opportunities. We were very fortunate to find Jason Kloth from the Teach for America (TFA) program, whom we named the first-ever deputy mayor for education in Indianapolis. TFA hires outstanding young teachers and initially places them in public schools with low-income families. It is a nationally respected program and very effective. Jason was a stellar former teacher in another state and opened the TFA office in Indianapolis in 2008. He later had a great job opportunity in Chicago, but, heading into our second term, our team convinced him to stay in Indianapolis. Our city and state have benefited ever since.

Jason is data driven and knows how to get the most out of people. It is remarkable to watch. Renaming the charter school office the Office of Education Innovation, he became an education force within the city.

Before our administration, former mayors tried to force IPS into improving their academic results, and the relationship was tense for decades. I mentioned to Jason that nothing had changed from three mayors back, and maybe we should relook at the relationship. I paraphrased the Dr. Phil (of TV fame) saying with, "How's that working for us?"

A master at building relationships, Jason understood that. I tried to be supportive of Indianapolis Public Schools even when the results were not what we wanted. I felt we had a good working model to lessen the former tension between the city and IPS. Jason took it even further, to the point that the IPS superintendent asked me (but really Jason) to bring the larger community together to talk about education in Indianapolis. Jason organized a community-wide conversation that included two dozen ninety-minute small-group conversations, knocking on thousands of doors, calling tens of thousands of people, and filling out thousands of questionnaires along with other measures. The resulting database was of value to every school system in the city and to us.

Jason's influence was so strong that he convinced IPS to allow charter-like schools within the IPS system. This was revolutionary. Still a part of IPS but free from the bureaucracy of a standard school district, these schools are called Innovation Schools. Their early performance has been encouraging. Some traditional public school advocates were not happy, but poor results for those using taxpayer dollars invites reform.

We needed the state to approve the measure. To do so, Jason engineered a partnership with IPS and the Mind Trust, a local, highly respected, nationally known education reform organization chaired by my predecessor. Jason got them to front the bill and lobby for it at the statehouse so that it did not look like it was the city's initiative. In truth, it was our initiative, and Jason and his team wrote the state legislation that authorized these schools.

Pre-K

In 2014, I gave a speech at the old City Hall, primarily about public safety and our youth, but I included the need for pre-K to launch our kids in the right direction. I said that the city was going to step up with pre-K dollars, even though education funding was not our responsibility. The state is responsible for education funding in Indiana, not the city, but there was no publicly funded pre-K in Indiana at the time.

Too many Republicans believe pre-K is childcare dressed up, but this is not even close to being accurate. They also believe taxpayers should not pay for it, believing it to be solely the parents' responsibility. In other words, pre-K is not kindergarten-through-high school education, so it should not be paid for with tax dollars. This is a mistaken notion.

High-level, publicly funded pre-K was common in other states, and studies had been done for decades about the importance of pre-K in a child's life. Republicans like to point out a few studies that say that the education gains of pre-K are largely lost by the first grade. Even if this proved true, the studies also say that the intangible factors of pre-K—sociability, perseverance, conflict resolution, problem solving, and others—do stay with the children and are a key to success through school and into adulthood. The failure of children to master these intangible qualities at a young age are precursors to public-safety issues in the future. There is little doubt about this, but Indiana Republicans had their head in the sand on this subject.

When I announced that the city was going to find a way to fund pre-K, the private sector and the philanthropic sector were thrilled. Eli Lilly stepped up and spearheaded a fundraising campaign, with the CEO of this massive international company personally making phone calls to raise the money. As I recall, I committed $2 million from the city, and Lilly committed to raising another $8 million from the business community. We were off and running.

The city-county council was another story. Now led by Democrats, and with every Democrat in the nation being in favor of publicly funded pre-K, our council was nonetheless threatening to veto the funding for pre-K. Here was an issue they all believed in, but they did not want me to have the victory, as they perceived it. It was more important to them to embarrass me than fund the pre-K they all believed in.

Two things happened. First, Lilly, with a prominent Democrat on their staff who had worked for my predecessor, tried talking to them. Lilly was working hard to raise the $8 million they had pledged and was excited about pre-K finally coming to Indiana, even if funded by the city of Indianapolis and private dollars. This Lilly executive called a meeting with me and two Democratic leaders of the council. The councilors would not commit to vote for the funding. Then the Lilly executive asked me to leave and had the councilors stay. I do not know what was said after I left, but I understand it was loud and forceful.

Second, I played a round of golf with another Democratic member of the council. I played with this gentleman about once a year, which would surprise most people in the city of Indianapolis, but we got along fine, and we were both pretty good golfers. After the round, I hit him up on supporting the pre-K funding, and he gave me the runaround for an hour. I would not relent, shooting down every one of his arguments. But I still had the unfortunate roadblock of being a Republican mayor while he was a Democrat. He did not want to be seen as supporting me. He knew I was right, but that did not matter. Finally, he told me that he would not vote for the pre-K funding—but he would ensure that it passed.

I do not know if my postgolf conversation made a difference, but it happened just as he'd pledged. This councilor did not vote for the funding, but it passed with significant Democratic support. I am quite certain that the Lilly executive having that private conversation with the two councilors had a significant impact on the final vote.

We started to fund pre-K within the city, and then, like magic, the state started looking into funding pre-K. They started with a pilot program saying—unbelievably to me—that they had to study the effects of pre-K to see if it would work. This, despite so many states that had already funded pre-K for many years and had completed the studies that let everyone know its importance. The state was implying that Indiana's four-year-old children were different from Michigan's or Illinois's four-year-old children. Ridiculous. The state has provided more funding since but still not at the level it should be.

Robotics

Indiana has the largest VEX Robotics (a robotics program for elementary through university students) state competition in the country. Held in Lucas Oil Stadium, the home of the NFL's Indianapolis Colts, over ten thousand people attend this championship. Indiana sends more teams to the VEX Robotics World Championships, which includes more than seventy nations, than any other state in our nation. I am in the VEX Robotics Hall of Fame. It is quite the story.

Early in my first administration, I was invited to a weekend robotics competition for high schools. I had no idea that such organizations or competitions existed. As my schedule was usually packed with invitations to events that far exceeded the time available, I did not expect to attend another robotics event.

However, in this case, I asked to attend another one. I was fascinated by the possibilities. I saw students actively engaged in an endeavor that was preparing them for their future careers—and having a blast doing it. They were not only learning the technical skills but also were learning teamwork, strategy, playing to your strengths while working on your weaknesses, getting along with each other, how to communicate, and how to win and lose gracefully. These were all attributes that most athletes learn as they develop, and here were students who may not have been the most popular or recognized in their schools, but they were clearly the ones who had a greater chance for success as adults than most students. I saw it as a workforce development tool, producing talent that would be comfortable not just working in STEM fields as adults but also *leading* in STEM fields.

At this second event I attended, I gathered the adults who were running the event and asked if they had plans to expand robotics within Indianapolis. They liked the idea of expanding robotics in the city but did not think any other schools would be interested. Still, I could not help thinking that the city should help expand this opportunity to other schools and their students. They estimated that there were seven or eight high schools doing robotics in Indianapolis. I had no idea of the actual number, but there were about sixty high schools in the city, counting the public, private, and charter schools.

I proposed having a city championship downtown. While they were thrilled with the idea, within a few minutes they had decided that the best they could do was to have such a championship in a church auditorium somewhere. They were terrific parents and supporters of robotics, but I envisioned something much different than they did.

I did not make this a priority with my staff immediately, but I started asking around the city to some high school robotics coaches and an occasional IT firm if they would like to help me develop a city championship. This went on for well over a year. While all expressed interest, no one had the time to do the legwork required to develop the concept. I decided that the city had to do the initial work.

I went to see Jeff Roeder, a bright young man in the office on the twenty-fifth floor where the mayor's office resides. I told him that "we" were going to hold a city robotics championship. He looked at me like "What is that?" I am not sure he was thrilled about it, but he went to work with my guidance.

First, we had to determine the robotics platform to use. At the time, there were three robotics platforms that schools were using throughout central Indiana. Through some quick questioning, we determined that the

VEX platform had the lowest cost of entry and equipment costs, plus it had a robust international organizational infrastructure. We chose them.

Next, we had to find a place to hold it. I went to the late Jim Morris, whom I called the "great convener." If Jim called you, you either take the call or call back at the first opportunity. This applies to everyone up to the governor. Jim was a former top aide to Senator Richard Lugar when Lugar was the mayor of Indianapolis. He was a warm, friendly, and philanthropic man, but he was also the head of the Lilly Endowment for years, was the executive director of the United Nations' World Food Program for five years, was the United States representative to UNICEF, and so on. He did all this while being a Hoosier through and through with a selfless heart and always wanting to help.

Jim was employed by the Indiana Pacers when I went to talk to him. When I explained my vision to him, he insisted that the city championship be held in the Bankers Life Fieldhouse (now Gainbridge Fieldhouse), home of the Indiana Pacers, our NBA team. I could not help but think of those robotics coaches who thought a church auditorium was the best they could do.

I wanted the city to find money for the teams so that they could buy their robots. I did not expect the schools to spend their precious dollars on a new extracurricular activity, but I wanted as many schools as possible to participate. I cannot remember how it came about, but Roche Diagnostics, whose North American headquarters is on the northeast side of Indianapolis, donated a significant sum of money so that the teams could be funded. I promised Roche I would never reveal how much they donated that first year, but it covered the cost for the teams.

Randy Decker, then with Warren Central High School on the east side of Indianapolis, was the head of the Digital Goats robotics teams. (Teams do not use their school's name; they all use a fun, made-up name.) He offered his facility at Warren Central and his expertise to teach schools who had never done robotics before.

This was a magnanimous gesture. I attended some of the sessions where he helped train students from other schools. He was training them to compete against his own teams; such is the nature of robotics. Competing teams help each other, especially in the early parts of the robotics season when teams are still learning the new robots and the new game, both of which turn over every year. I call it "coopetition." It is magical to watch. Randy now works on the national level with robotics tournaments.

We had a robotics platform, money, and a place to compete. Now we needed teams. I knew most of the eleven school superintendents pretty well but did not think each would be the deciding person whether teams competed or not. However, we had to inform them of what we were doing, and we did. We then made a pitch to the high schools themselves, through the principals when possible. As I recall, we sent a letter informing them of what we were planning, and Jeff followed up with a phone call. Jeff and I were flying blind on this trip, but we made it work.

We had great partners in the Pacers, Roche Diagnostics, Warren Central, and a few others. But VEX and the REC Foundation, who helps run VEX events, also were unbelievably helpful to us considering we were putting on a city championship for the first time—with no one in the city having any experience in doing so. VEX and REC helped with the organization and setup of the championship and, much to our surprise, brought in their announcing team that did the world championships every year. Along with the individual matches being shown on the huge Pacers scoreboard, this made our first-ever city championship look like we had been doing it for years. There was a sense of excitement in the fieldhouse all day long.

Early on, I insisted to Jeff that I wanted the winning trophies to be bigger than any sports trophy in a school. I wanted to send a message that it was not just robotics that was important, but also the STEM subjects in general. I wanted those kids to be celebrated in their schools. The normal VEX trophy is a nice piece of metal with a plaque on it; it is less than a foot in height. Jeff listened well. He went out and purchased four-foot trophy stands and put the small VEX trophy on top of it. It was hilarious, and it worked. The overall excellence award (for having a great robotics program) that first year went to Warren Central's team, captained by a young female student about five feet tall. The picture of her holding that massive trophy is still in my mind. It was a wonderful moment.

I also made a point of presenting the trophies again at the winning schools. I asked the schools to have this ceremony in front of the entire student body. Some schools did this; others did it in front of smaller audiences. I heard back from students that when I presented the trophy to them with the student body present, they became celebrities in their schools, much like athletes. Just what I wanted. One year, I had a very fun presentation at Bishop Chatard High School, a great Catholic high school on the north side of Indianapolis. I presented the trophy and then took questions from the students on anything they wanted to ask. Their robotics team then challenged me to a robotics contest in front of the student body. I was badly beaten. That made sense; they were state champs.

We had thirty-eight high schools participating in that first city championship (called the IndyVRC) in 2012, which meant that thirty high schools were participating in their first-ever robotics season. Indianapolis had gone from seven or eight high schools having robotics teams to thirty-eight. That was more than I could have hoped for. We had tapped into a pent-up demand for such activities, much like bicycling and the Latino Expo (mentioned in other chapters). The participants were thrilled and wanted more robotics for their schools.

It helped that Rose-Hulman in Terre Haute, long considered the finest undergraduate engineering university in the country, offered $10,000 scholarships to members of the winning teams if they chose to attend the university. This told the students, and the schools, that this championship meant something more than a trophy.

When I briefed some educators on all this, a middle school representative stood up and said, "What about us?" That was a great question and indicative that we had hit on something that would only grow. And it did, dramatically.

I frequently say that mayor is the highest elected office where one can directly make a difference in a person's life. We changed thousands of students' lives with our robotics initiative. So many of them now had an outlet where they could learn and compete while having fun with their friends. Many changed the focus of their studies because they saw the possibilities for their future, while others just saw that someone cared about them and started working harder in school. Girls became a focus of our robotics initiative; we had staggering numbers of girls participating on robotics teams, and with subsequent funding, we incentivized schools to have even more girls on their robotics teams.

However, the most poignant moments for me were when the parents would come up to me the first few years, thanking me and saying things like "My daughter now has friends," or "My son studies now." These were tender, heartwarming moments for me. The one I remember most was when a lady approached me in the Pacers fieldhouse but could not face me out of embarrassment because she was crying so hard. Through her tears, she told me how she had "lost her son"—he had no friends, did not want to go to school, and could not get along with anybody. But the new robotics team at his school had changed everything.

"I now have my son back," she told me. Then I started crying.

In the second year, when Stephanie Bothun from our Education Innovation office replaced Jeff as the city's main representative, the IndyVRC was the largest event of its kind in the nation. More high schools showed up, the middle schools joined in (as would elementary schools in subsequent years), and sponsors were more than happy to help. Roche, thanks to a great senior executive, Tom Adkins, remained the primary sponsor, but a long list of other companies and organizations joined in: the Lumina Foundation, Eli Lilly, USA Funds, Employ Indy, Rolls Royce, Project Lead the Way, the Techpoint Foundation for Youth, the NCAA, Ivy Tech Community College, IUPUI, Butler University, Rose-Hulman University, Collina Ventures, ms consulting, Allison Transmission, United Consulting, Health and Hospital Corporation, Conexus, the Capital Improvement Board, Interactive Intelligence, and others. We had tapped into something important for our city.

Only a year before, I had been worried how we were going to pull this championship off and where the money would come from. Those worries were now gone. This was already a prominent event in the city in its second year, with people and organizations wanting to be a part of it. While Jeff and I struggled to get outside support that first year, which is not unusual for an untried idea, Stephanie was magical when dealing with organizations outside the city administration. She created an advisory board to help drive the championship, setting the organization in stone. I never worried about the event after that second year. I knew Stephanie had this event on rails.

Because of the impact that IndyVRC had on students, TechPoint, the organization that manages the still-burgeoning tech ecosystem in central Indiana, presented me with the Bridge Builder Award at the annual Mira Awards. This was validation for what our team had accomplished in just a few years and what we would continue to accomplish in the future.

TechPoint Foundation for Youth (TPF4Y) became a prominent player in the execution of the IndyVRC. The success of the championship allowed TPF4Y and the advisory board to think bigger; with the help of sponsors, the IndyVRC became the State Robotics Initiative (SRI). It included not only a new state championship in 2016 (replacing the IndyVRC) but also the expansion of VEX Robotics throughout Indiana. Through my partnership with a low-key philanthropic man named Dan Towriss, his company, Guggenheim Life and Annuity (now Group 1001), became the main sponsor of the SRI. The other sponsors stayed with the program.

The increase in robotics activity across the state exploded. By 2020, over half a million dollars in grant dollars had been awarded to schools to form robotics teams. As just one example, the number of VEX IQ teams (a simpler version of the VEX model for younger students) had increased from 196 teams to 1,833 teams—a more than 800 percent increase in four years.

Again, an emphasis on girls was included, as was an emphasis on minority students. We quickly became the largest state competition in the country. Prior to the expansion of SRI, there were a few pockets of robotics teams scattered throughout the state. As of 2022, all ninety-two counties in Indiana had a VEX Robotics team, and 51 percent of schools were participating. These are unbelievable numbers, considering where we started ten years before.

As a result of these events, I am in the VEX Hall of Fame. George Giltner, the current head of TPF4Y, calls me the "Godfather of Robotics." My successor has called me the "Vince Lombardi of Robotics" because the team trophy in each category is named after me, just as the Lombardi trophy goes to the Super Bowl champion every year. Most importantly, the sponsorship of Group 1001 and others has been so strong that every school in the state that wants to participate in VEX Robotics will have the money to start a team through TPF4Y—*every school* in the state. They just have to ask.

It is difficult to put into words how much Jeff Roeder, Stephanie Bothun, Tom Adkins, Randy Decker, Laura Dodds (of TPF4Y) and others changed the trajectory of so many young students' lives. Their help in organizing and running the IndyVRC in the early years was crucial to fulfilling the vision of what has become an important educational event in the state. Indiana owes them a debt of gratitude not only for providing a tremendous, enduring annual competition, but also for developing the workforce of the future.

Other than chartering schools, the Indianapolis mayor has little authority in education. However, pre-K, robotics, and the citywide conversation are examples of a government official responsibly using his power beyond statutory authority. Thousands of kids and families benefited as a result.

A Bold Idea

Another initiative was the idea of a charter school that covered pre-K through 14. Jason and his team conceived this idea hoping to send a message to the community that education does not begin at first grade or kindergarten, and it does not end at high school graduation. Much of the workforce gap today centers around the need for post-high-school education short of a four-year college degree. Associate degrees and certifications are critical in today's economy, and there are workforce gaps to be filled with this level of education.

We needed an organization to take this pre-K through 14 idea to reality. Purdue University seemed interested. They opened a campus of Purdue Polytechnic in an old industrial building on the east side and followed up with another school in the Broad Ripple area. They now have a third school in South Bend. They are all wonderful schools, as to be expected when Mitch Daniels is the president of Purdue University, but they all remain high schools as of now. The pre-K through 14 school is still to be opened somewhere.

A National Failure

I think the greatest failure of our country in the last sixty or seventy years is the failure to recognize what low-income children need from birth to succeed. Should the government play more of a role? This is a great question, but I hope Republicans will not default to "It's the parents' job," failing to realize that many parents are not equipped for what many of us learn growing up.

Failure to realize this plays out violently in our urban centers around the country. We made tremendous progress in the city's overall education model despite having just a charter school office when we began the administration. I cannot help but think, though, that despite the tough battles and the improvements in education in Indianapolis, we could not overcome the persistent obstacles that low-income students face every day in America. They start so far behind, and few ever catch up despite the tax dollars expended.

Just one example: The annual ISTEP (Indiana's standardized exam) is a source of concern for almost all public schools. Teachers, under pressure from administrators, take weeks to "teach to the test," hoping that as many students as possible pass the math and English exams. My children, when we came back from Stuttgart to Indianapolis, attended a high school where no teacher did any such thing. The few days that it took to administer the ISTEP at my kids' high school was considered an obstacle to learning, a waste of valuable time, and just something that the state said they must do. All the students in my children's high school passed both the math and English exams, 100 percent of the students—with no preparation at all.

There is a difference in how kids are raised. I was a marine, so I was not rich, but I knew what to do to ensure my kids had the best chance in life that they could have. This is not true across society. It is easy to blame parents, but parents cannot pass on what they do not know. There is a gap. It starts at birth.

We need to understand that the cost of not preparing our children for success is higher than the cost of taking the time and money to prepare them appropriately. And it is not just schooling. A holistic, multigenerational approach would be most effective, but most politicians have trouble seeing past the next election.

16

THE GOVERNMENT MUST CARE

Before becoming the mayor, I volunteered at the Lilly Boys and Girls Club, helping elementary school students with their homework after their school day was done. I had one conversation that I will never forget. I was sitting at a round table with two six-year-olds, a girl and a boy. The names are fictional, but the story is not.

> Marsha: This is my cousin, Jimmy.
>
> Me: Oh wow. You're cousins.
>
> Jimmy: Yeah.
>
> Marsha: Jimmy lives with us.
>
> Me: That's neat. Why are you living with Marsha?
>
> Jimmy: Because both my daddies are in jail.

The nonchalance of the conversation was heartbreaking. Family business as usual. I got up and walked away for about twenty minutes before I regained my composure. I had seen and heard of bad situations while growing up and in the Marines. I know that many kids have little chance to succeed because of their circumstances, but this conversation drove it home a little more directly.

Mayors must do what they can, but using taxpayer money to benefit only one group can be fraught with peril. When that group receives public money, there are others who will complain that "they are getting my tax dollars. I don't want my money going there." Some will complain, "Where's mine?" It is true that the general public benefit is where most of tax dollars should go. As always, there are trade-offs, and as the old political saying goes, "Elections have consequences." Those in office have their own priorities and will fund areas they think are important. That is why people elected them. It helps, though, if people know that their government cares.

I came to find out that there were an incredible number of caring, competent, and well-meaning people who wanted to help the city in this regard. Although there were some who just wanted to have their pet project funded or claim to be close to the administration, others had a decades-long record of helping administrations of both parties. These were the people we worked with, as their motives were pure. My excellent staff helped me in partnering with the right people. It also helped that the Lilly Endowment, one the largest endowments in the world, resides in Indianapolis. This quiet organization has had an immense impact on Indianapolis and beyond, particularly with economic development and education.

As I have said repeatedly in this book, elected officials have far more influence than their statutory authority would suggest. When it came to compassion for others, we used that influence repeatedly and sometimes forcefully throughout our eight years.

Eliminating Backlog in the Office of Equal Opportunity

The Office of Equal Opportunity (OEO) handled cases of discrimination for people in the city when a case could not be worked out privately. When I took office in 2008, OEO had a backlog of more than 240 cases, with an average adjudication time of seven hundred days—almost two years. The city had stopped accepting new complaints, instead referring them to state and federal agencies for adjudication. If people had violations not covered by state or federal law, they were left with no recourse.

Early on in our administration, we transferred OEO to the Office of Corporation Counsel, the city's legal department. Chris Cotterill, then heading OCC, put Maxine Russell on the case. Within a year, the backlog plummeted from 240 cases to 0 cases. The average adjudication time dropped from seven hundred days to fewer than two hundred days. This was a remarkable achievement in such a short time.

We held a press conference to announce the vast improvement, but it was clear few cared about this extraordinary success story. Criticizing Republicans for being insensitive to minorities is common, but at this time, one had to wonder how much people cared about addressing discrimination claims. Still, we did it because it was the right thing to do.

Chris was a bulldog at times. I was lucky to have him, and he was lucky to have Maxine.

Minority/Women/Veteran/Disabled Business Participation

Greg Wilson, an army veteran (and a man who never smiles for a photo), came to me when I was running for office in 2007, upset that the current administration seemed to be favoring only certain minority businesses and using gatekeepers to keep other businesses away from bidding on city business. Greg had a distinguished but almost silent career working with utilities and private-sector companies. He had a focus on helping disadvantaged companies become bigger players in working with government and prime contractors. After I won the election, he came back in to talk to me to see how he could help, bringing in several business owners to tell their stories. Greg had worked previously with David Sherman, our public-works director and someone who championed minority- and women-owned businesses for decades. We wound up hiring Greg as our minority and women business development head. He and David proceeded to change the dynamic for minority- and women-owned businesses in Indianapolis.

Greg and his team embarked on a path that is difficult to believe in retrospect. He increased the dollar amount awarded to minority contractors by the city more than fourfold—and for the women contractors, much more than tenfold. It was an unbelievable success story. He did this not only by making it fair for everyone but also by conducting outreach events. Two to three times each year, Greg and his team would hold conferences to teach small businesses how to bid on contracts with the city, including subjects like bid evaluations, contract compliance monitoring, and others. This was extremely helpful to those businesses looking to bid on contracts.

There were numerous success stories. Two stand out for me, probably because I came to know the owners well. One was a woman-owned engineering business. She started her company in 2008, during the depth of the Great Recession but also before the initial phases of Rebuild Indy. She was given an opportunity by public works, and her business continues to this day. Another was a minority contractor wholesaling trucking and industrial equipment. Both were young, entrepreneurial owners who delivered their products and services in a professional manner. Both then proceeded to give back to the Indianapolis community by serving on nonprofit boards.

Many minority- and women-owned companies were either formed or expanded in the city because of our efforts.

As mentioned, we were also the first city in the state to adopt a goal for veteran-owned businesses. That success is mentioned in the Veterans section below. The state of Indiana soon followed.

In 2013, I signed into law a disability-owned business program similar to the minority-, women-, and veteran-owned business programs. Over half the people with disabilities live in poverty, and we wanted to send a signal that entrepreneurship is a legitimate career choice for people with disabilities.

Greg Wilson went on to become a very successful Indiana Civil Rights Commission head. He is a remarkable man.

Veterans

The veteran community had little organization in the city of Indianapolis prior to our administration. We went about changing this in short order.

Veteran Service Officer

It was state law (I believe from the 1930s) that each county in Indiana have a veteran service officer (VSO) to help veterans with their issues. As far as we could tell, Indianapolis, which is also all of Marion County, never had one.

We hired Russ Eaglin, a Vietnam veteran, who did a magnificent job in supporting our veterans and in representing the mayor's office at veterans' events when I could not attend. He was followed by Carlos May, who continued the excellent job that Russ began.

Mayors' Advisory Council of Veterans

One of the initiatives of the VSO office was to form the Mayor's Advisory Council of Veterans (MACV). This group met quarterly, usually with me in attendance so that I could keep abreast of veteran issues in Indianapolis. Veteran service organizations such as the American Legion and the Disabled American Veterans joined our organization, which gave it needed clout. Issues discussed included homelessness, reintegration, employment opportunities, benefits, and communications among veterans. They also collectively advanced the cause of veterans and provided real help when needed. This group remains very active to this day.

Veteran-Owned Business Goals

By executive order, we instituted goals for veteran-owned businesses to receive at least 3 percent of the city contract dollars. This sort of initiative had been started in some cities and states, and some larger companies, but to the best of our knowledge, it was not in place anywhere in Indiana. Several Hoosier cities followed suit, as did the state.

Although Hoosiers have been supportive of veterans (Indianapolis has the most land dedicated to veterans in the country and the second-most monuments dedicated to veterans; only Washington, DC, has more), in Indianapolis, the actual help to veterans had been lacking. I believe we made great strides in addressing these issues. I also think the state noticed and upped its game.

As an example, we were able to partner with a private company to provide shelter for homeless veterans at what is now called the Lincoln Apartments. The city owned the land, a former brownfield site, and we paid for the remediation with state and federal grants. An $11 million project, it houses up to seventy-five veterans.

In the last couple of years of my administration, I asked Carlos May, a wonderful young man who was then our veterans' coordinator, to wade through the various organizations that help veterans to see if we could provide a special service. A homeless veteran could make one phone call, wheels would turn behind the scenes, and that veteran would have shelter and food that very night. It took Carlos over a year to put all the pieces together, and it only became operational in the last few months of our administration. It was a remarkable effort by many people, and one that very few cities have.

I do not know if the effort is still in place.

A Powerful Day

The most powerful day in my life was when we held a Welcome Home event for Vietnam veterans. Younger people may not know that the phrase "Welcome Home" is especially meaningful to Vietnam vets because of the all-too-common, deplorable reception so many received from their fellow

Americans when they returned from Vietnam. It is a stain on our nation's history. Citizens confused their opposition to the war in its later years with the valiant warriors who fought on our behalf. (This, in fact, was the starting point for citizens now routinely saying to veterans, "Thank you for your service," never again confusing the warrior with the civilian leadership that sends the military off to war.)

We held the event at the beautiful World War Memorial downtown, which held around five hundred people in its main auditorium. About eight hundred people showed up, both vets and their families, including Vietnam vets from surrounding states (eight states, we think) when word got out that the city of Indianapolis was holding a Welcome Home for them. We had to use the other rooms in the building to accommodate the overflow.

The ceremony lasted an hour. I was the last speaker, and with my arms outstretched, I concluded with "On behalf of the city of Indianapolis, 'Welcome Home.'" The crowd response was overwhelming, and tears flowed freely. The phrase "Welcome Home" means that much to this group of veterans. However, it was what happened afterward that sticks with me so clearly.

In the lobby after the event, family members lined up to talk to me, saying things like

"You healed our family. Thank you."

"I never understood my grandfather until right now."

"I never knew. Now I do."

I stayed there another hour and a half. I cannot recall what my original schedule was after the event, but those appointments were pushed back or rescheduled. I was not going to leave until every family member of a Vietnam vet that wanted to talk to me got the opportunity to do so. The word "closure" seems inadequate for what happened that day.

Guardian Ad Litem Backlog

A guardian ad litem (GAL) is a specially trained volunteer whom a court will appoint to investigate and represent the best interests of a child in various types of legal cases. These can include child custody battles, child abuse cases, or other cases where the welfare of the child can get lost in the proceedings. To me, GALs are heroes in the court system.

Ryan Vaughn, former president of the city-county council and then my chief of staff, informed me that the local funding that helps with GALs was falling behind. Although GALs are volunteers, there are program costs, and now there was not enough funding. The program needed about $1 million; how it got to that point I do not know. What I knew was that the city had to act quickly.

Ryan, being the brilliant and compassionate man he is, had already secured the funding within the city budget to fill the gap. That was a lot of money to come up with on such short notice, but Ryan had it solved if I agreed. I agreed.

Indy Hunger Network

In mid-2008, I could feel a change in the economy coming. Business signs like "Now Hiring" were going away, and citizens' comments at Mayor's Nights Out and other forums carried a more worried tone. I would occasionally check in with places like Wheeler Mission and the Salvation Army to see how they were doing and what they were hearing. Maybe my economics degree was kicking in once again.

The Great Recession was around the corner. Food for the lower-income population becomes a critical issue during a recession. I wanted the citizens of Indianapolis to be aware of what was coming, believing that we could accelerate the natural charitable instincts of the people in our city by appealing for additional food donations. After talking with Olgen Williams, our deputy mayor for neighborhoods, and Douglas Hairston, the head of our Front Porch Alliance, we settled on a public plea, attempting to bring attention to the issue.

I cannot remember who came up with the slogan "Pack the Pantries," but it worked. We wanted to hold a press conference, but the initial Pack the Pantries event became much more than that. We held it at my children's high school alma mater, Brebeuf Jesuit, on the north side of Indianapolis, where the motto is "Men and Women for Others." The high school turned out its entire student body. Ministers from all faiths wanted to attend. All the TV stations were present. It was a standing-room-only event in the Brebeuf gymnasium. When I spoke, I choked up, as I usually do when speaking about the less fortunate. The entire event was simultaneously festive and somber. It worked.

Indianapolis already had a strong foundation for antihunger initiatives with large, effective organizations like Gleaners Food Bank and the Midwest Food Bank, along with other organizations like Second Helpings (a food rescue network) and St. Vincent de Paul. However, individual citizens became more engaged, thanks to the Brebeuf event. Schoolchildren began collecting cans of food. There was a palpable sense of mission.

Soon thereafter, utilizing the mayor's convening power, many of the hunger organizations came together in partnership with the city to discuss what could be done collaboratively over a longer term. This sounds easy, but it was difficult initially. Food banks like Gleaners and Midwest were not at odds with one another, but their missions were slightly different. Second Helpings rescued food from restaurants and created special, delicious, healthy dishes for the hungry. St. Vincent de Paul had a food pantry but also provided wraparound services, such as legal help, for those they served. However, nonprofits can be reluctant to share donor information so as to preserve their own funding streams. Despite all this, they were talking to us and to each other.

Programs developed. Through expanded partnerships, including the federal government, the Indy Hunger Network increased the number of meals provided by tens of millions in a four-year period from 2010 to 2013. Examples of the expansion included Gleaners providing 5,500 "BackSacks" of nutritious food to schoolchildren every weekend during the school year. Also, the Summer Servings program provided meals to children in low-income areas when school meals were not available. The Fresh Group convened in 2012 to explore ways to systematically increase the supply of fruits and vegetables available through food assistance programs. Fresh Bucks doubled the federal SNAP dollars (Supplemental Nutrition Assistance Program) that can be spent on fruits and vegetables, up to twenty dollars a day.

The annual Pack the Pantries press event continued through my administration just to bring awareness, but it is the innovative Indy Hunger Network that continues to this day. Douglas Hairston was a key part of this initiative and the collaboration between the hunger organizations continue to make this effort effective. Some of the programs have been replaced with others, but it is still the major player in the city's antihunger efforts.

The Polar Vortex

Sometimes caring is not a program but an event. During the minus-forty-degree weather period, named the polar vortex by the weather people, the Mayor's Action Center closed, as it would have been too difficult for the workers to get to work. My staff, completely on their own initiative, manned those phone lines for two days. They brought in pizza and seemed to have a great, fun time answering those phones. I had an incredible staff throughout all eight years.

360 Coalition: One That Developed Too Late

I mentioned this in the Public-Safety chapter and the Education chapter. In my last year in office, after much consultation with Matt Gutwein of Health and Hospital Corporation and many others in the city, we began the 360 Coalition. It was an attempt to bring together various strategies to help the poor on their journey to self-sufficiency and to reduce crime. It was a holistic approach (hence the 360 moniker) to poverty and crime, combining many separate efforts that help in more narrow ways. Unfortunately, I was too late in this attempt and could not build enough support for the effort.

A few years out of office, I learned through Jim McClelland's book *Toward Greater Impact: A Path to Reduce Social Problems, Improve Lives, and Strengthen Communities* that the local Goodwill Industries was doing something very similar. From 1974 till 2015, Jim served as president and CEO of Goodwill Industries of Central Indiana (now Goodwill of Central and Southern Indiana) and was innovative in his approach to helping the less fortunate. Until I read his book, I did not know that local chapters of Goodwill have significant leeway in how they choose to operate.

Goodwill, using the charter school authority from the mayor's office, opened an Excel Center, a school designed to give adults a real high school diploma, not just a GED. It was an instant success. Goodwill did not stop. They now have fifteen Excel centers in central and southern Indiana. Realizing the difficulty of providing this sort of education to working adults, Goodwill adjusted its strategy and started providing other services as well. They have on-site childcare; flexible schedules, including accelerated courses; transportation assistance; life coaches; employment counseling; college credit courses; and industry certifications—all cost free to the student. This became the multigenerational focus, not only for the Excel Centers but for much of Goodwill in Central and Southern Indiana's work today.

The Excel Centers have graduated in excess of six thousand students, and those students have earned more than seven thousand industry certifications. Amazingly, 99 percent of their students have earned college credits or industry certifications. They tout a 280 percent wage increase one year after graduation.

As a result of his work with the Excel Centers, Jim could see more clearly the obstacles that prevent the less fortunate from achieving a stable lifestyle. He positioned the local Goodwill to address these obstacles, providing a more holistic approach to the reduction of poverty and crime.

Here is an excerpt on his book (from Amazon.com):

> Many major social problems—poverty, low education levels, crime, and a host of health issues, including alcohol and substance use disorders—are frequently interrelated and often reinforce and compound each other. Yet, in the U.S. we tend to treat those problems individually in isolation from the others. The public sector often does this through large bureaucratic silos, while the not-for-profit sector—a large part of which focuses on alleviating social problems—is incredibly fragmented. While many good programs and services do exist, we have generally not done a good job connecting them. We tend to be program-rich and systems-poor, and siloed and fragmented approaches to complex problems frequently fail to result in lasting impact.

My experience as mayor of a major city compels me to concur. Children do not grow up hoping to be poor or live life as a criminal. Somewhere along the way, these children were failed by the adults in their lives. When they become teenagers and adults, they are not contributing to society. They are expending resources paid for by tax dollars, such as police, the courts, poverty programs, and the like. Those committing crime put fear into the citizens who are contributing positively to society, those who pay taxes.

These solutions are cheaper than keeping the less fortunate hungry, living in substandard housing, or worse, doing time in jail. We should help them to be successful and pay taxes, rather than using other people's tax dollars to address temporary solutions.

Republicans should look at this as an investment, especially if we can reach these people at a very young age. It is not just about better schooling. If we cannot reach them at a young age, then reaching these men and women in their twenties would still be worthwhile. I know that most want to live a decent life; they just do not know how to do that. The holistic, 360-degree approach is the best opportunity to address poverty and crime over time. Scale the approach city by city. I wish I had figured that out earlier.

17

GOING GLOBAL

When I ran for office, I knew that I wanted to make the citizens of Indianapolis more aware of the global economy and its potential for Indianapolis. By the time I became mayor, I had lived in or visited large parts of Asia and Europe, the Middle East, Canada, and Panama. I knew that most young people in all the places I visited could speak English well. I suspected that most of them knew of New York and Los Angeles (because of Hollywood) and were mostly not aware of cities in the Midwest.

I did not campaign on this topic. It would have been portrayed as if I wanted to visit other countries on the citizens' dime. However, I thought it was important to the future of the city. In office, I said frequently that our competitors are not only Kansas City and Nashville, but Stockholm, Sweden, and Auckland, New Zealand. I knew that both capital and talent were already mobile.

If we wanted to attract talent and the companies that wanted to hire that talent, then we should ensure that Indianapolis has some sort of an international feel. We did not have any relationships with three of the largest and still-growing economies in the world: China, India, and Brazil. Based on my marine background, I also felt that the more countries talk to each other, even on a city-to-city or person-to-person level, the chances for a more stable and peaceful world are enhanced.

We did get more attention. A study in 2014 ranked Indianapolis in the Top 10 nationally for job growth from foreign-owned companies. Also, Indianapolis was chosen for a prestigious Brookings Institution program to help local companies export overseas and attract new investment from abroad.

I still feel strongly that Indianapolis should participate in the global economy and make it known that it is open for global business.

Sister Cities

We inherited an office of Latino affairs, but I wanted to expand that to a more international focus. We kept the Latino aspect but also created an Office of International and Cultural Affairs and initially filled the slot with a Latina, Carolin Requiz-Smith. She did a wonderful job, particularly in establishing a protocol for adding more sister cities. The Sister City program is an international program that facilitates cities around the world forming relationships with each other.

When Jane Gehlhausen took over the position, she took it to a level I never expected. She ensured the committees for each of the eight cities were solid and functioning and even instituted an annual awards program to honor the best-run committees. Of course, she asked me to attend every year, and I did.

When we were considering other possible sister cities, she became a trusted sounding board. When a French mayor visited, I hoped to create a sister city relationship, but Jane told me she could not find local support for a committee to ensure a strong connection. We looked at Mexico also, but the options did not make sense to her; therefore, they did not make sense to me.

Jane told me this was her dream job, and I was happy for her. She did the big things and the little things. The city was rewarded with winning the prestigious Sister City national award in 2013 for best overall program for cities with a population above five hundred thousand people. I never dreamed that could happen for Indianapolis when we started the International and Cultural Affairs Office. It was a nice reward for pursuing a course of action that most elected officials shun.

When I became mayor, our sister cities were Taipei, Taiwan; Cologne, Germany; Monza, Italy; and Piran, Slovenia. We doubled the number of Sister Cities to eight, adding Hangzhou, China; Hyderabad, India; the County of Northamptonshire, United Kingdom; and Campinas, Brazil.

We picked these four primarily for economic reasons, trying to match these cities' strengths with those of Indianapolis. Hangzhou had a strong industrial and manufacturing base; Hyderabad was strong in pharmaceutical and IT, the County of Northamptonshire was the home of Motorsports Valley in England (Britain refers to sister cities as "twinning"), and Campinas was a university town with some renewable energy initiatives and was right next to Rio de Janeiro. I visited all eight sister cities, some of them multiple times. I am confident that I am the only mayor to have visited all the sister cities, and I doubt that any mayor in the future will do so. Most politicians are afraid they will get criticized for traveling. That is true; they will get criticized. I certainly did but brushed it off. It was that important to me because it was important to the future of Indianapolis.

We were funded privately by those who wanted to travel with us, paying the bill for Winnie and me. I was very appreciative of all those that traveled with us, and they added perspective and fun to the trips.

India

All the cities were gracious, but the warmest reception we received was on our first trip to Hyderabad. After fifteen hours of flying, we arrived around 3:00 a.m., a few hours later than planned. We had a meeting scheduled for noon. It took about an hour to get through customs and to get our bags. As we departed the airport about 4:00 a.m., we were met with bright lights from four or five TV cameras, dancers performing for us, and a band—all to greet us. They had waited there for four or five hours in the middle of the night to ensure we felt welcomed.

I did interviews for the TV stations. Winnie and I were presented heavy leis made from beautiful, rich flowers. It was as warm and as friendly a reception as one could imagine. I had no idea any of this was planned for us; it was a great way to kick off the trip.

The Indian business community was very gracious and treated us like royalty. Several receptions ensued, and we became friends with the mayor, Banda Karthika Reddy. She hosted a wonderful ceremony for the signing of the sister city agreement. She reciprocated our trip by coming to Indianapolis and attending a Mayor's Night Out, where I asked her to speak. The people attending were astounded they were meeting an Indian mayor and treated her with kindness and respect.

We took two trips to India. We visited several federal offices in New Delhi and Mahatma Gandhi's tomb, Raj Ghat. We were able to see the Taj Mahal—a very impressive structure with a love story attached. We also visited several businesses; one was Infosys, a large international IT firm based in India. Winnie and I planted a tree on the Infosys campus in Hyderabad; the picture is still on Facebook. This began a relationship that culminated in Indianapolis becoming the national hub for Infosys—a big economic win for the city and the state. Much of the credit for this must go to Raju Chinthala, who not only headed up our sister city committee for Hyderabad but also kept in contact with Infosys officials through the years, prodding them to consider Indiana as their home in the United States.

This is one reason that personal travel is important. If Infosys was looking at a US hub for their operations in America, there is no possibility that they would have considered Indianapolis on their own. None. On our overseas trips, which were always a sales pitch, they learned that there is more to America than New York and Los Angeles. Because of our travel to India, Infosys officials learned of the potential workforce in Indianapolis, of the robust logistics posture of the area, and of the business-friendly climate in Indiana. Also, we found out later that they were highly impressed that my business card was written in Hindi on one side. Thanks, Raju, once again. After I left office, the state was able to seal the deal with Infosys.

Conversely, on one of our trips, I was able to cut the ribbon on an Indianapolis-based company that was opening an office in Hyderabad. The economic benefits went both ways. Also, Columbus, Indiana, has a sister city relationship with an Indian city, Pune, and an Indian company subsequently expanded to Columbus. Raju played a major part in this economic development also.

We began India Day in Indianapolis, celebrating India's independence from Great Britain on August 15, 1947. On a Sunday in August, we would gather on the Circle in downtown Indianapolis, hold a short parade, and then enjoy singing and dancing from all age groups. The young children dancing in Indian dress were always the highlight of the day.

I became very close to the Indian community in central Indiana. After I was out of office, an Indiana-India Business Council was formed, and Raju asked me to become the first chair of the organization. I gladly accepted. The group holds an awards ceremony every year to announce the Indiana Ratna (Jewel) award. I missed the meeting that decided who should be the recipient in its second year; they were gracious enough to present the award to me.

The Indianapolis-Hyderabad relationship has benefited both cities and is a textbook example of what can happen if cities will just reach out.

Germany

Cologne, Germany, was already a sister city when I became the mayor. I believe we made that relationship even stronger, as both Cologne and Indianapolis had strong local committees. I visited Cologne twice, and members of their committee visited Indianapolis.

The most famous aspect of Cologne is its magnificent cathedral. It is the third-tallest church in the world and is Germany's most visited landmark, receiving twenty thousand visitors per day. It contains some relics of the Three Kings and has been declared a World Heritage Site. Construction began in 1248 and was halted in 1560, still unfinished. Work restarted in the 1840s and was completed in 1880. It is hard to imagine such dedication over centuries. It survived World War II mostly intact, though some repairs had to be made. Because of its age and constant need of repair, there is visible scaffolding in place almost every day.

What I remember most about Cologne is the impact our administration made regarding our city's recognition of the global economy. Every year, the Indianapolis Chamber of Commerce conducts a leadership exchange (LEX) with another city. It is an opportunity for civic, business, and nonprofit leaders to see how other American cities conduct their affairs. I attended every one of these if possible. It is important for the mayor to interact with leaders of different organizations and to meet future leaders of Indianapolis. These visits are casual and informative but always fun. It deepened our appreciation of just how good the city we lived in was. Other cities do the same thing, with Indianapolis being visited routinely by delegations from other American cities.

There are usually forty or fifty attendees at a LEX. I asked Brian Payne of the Central Indiana Community Foundation if going to Cologne would be a good idea. The LEX had never visited any city out of the country before. He thought it would be a good idea, and because both he and I were afraid that not enough people would go, he offered to fund some of them as an incentive.

The Cologne LEX was by far the most attended in history. About a hundred people signed up. I was thrilled. I planned my trip separately, as I had some business to conduct in Paris before flying to Cologne. While I was in Paris, however, an Indianapolis policeman was killed in the line of duty, and I had to fly back immediately. I never got to attend the LEX in Cologne, but the reports were very positive. The chamber scheduled another LEX in Toronto soon thereafter. I could not have been more pleased that others began to embrace the notion of a global economy.

China

I visited Hangzhou twice, once staying in the Shangri-La Hotel overlooking the beautiful, famous West Lake, a World Heritage Site. I am a quirky eater, and with my strange diet, I have some fond memories of food events. The Chinese would want us to try some of their more exotic food, like duck tongue, but I was reluctant. Thankfully, my wife would try almost anything, so it was not so embarrassing for me.

On our first trip, Carolin, who organized the schedule, told our hosts that I had some food allergies and that I could eat only beef, chicken, and potatoes. At one epic meal, the guests were served an entire banquet while the chefs prepared ten courses of variations of beef, chicken, and potatoes for me. At another dinner, after we had otherwise seen little meat on the trip, our hosts brought out roasted chicken. Most of our party could not wait to enjoy that chicken. However, our hosts proceeded to cut off the skin of the chicken, take away the meat, and serve us the skin.

Our sister city committee for Hangzhou was strong, and our Chinese counterparts seemed pleased with our efforts. In their main public library, Hangzhou created a two-thousand-square-foot display about Indianapolis, including a replica of Andrew Luck in his Colts uniform. We were also able to visit other cities such as Shanghai and Ningbo, visiting a university in Ningbo that has a relationship with the University of Indianapolis.

The Chinese Festival that we held annually in Military Park downtown was always well attended, with introductory ceremonies (sometimes including the Chinese consul from Chicago), dancing, and of course tremendous quantities of great Chinese food.

We entertained a friendly Hangzhou businessman in Indianapolis, even taking him to a Pacers game, hoping he would open a facility in our city, but it did not come to fruition. However, having a warm relationship with a prominent city in China was still important.

England

Racing was the main reason to have a relationship with the County of Northamptonshire. The county is home to Motorsports Valley, a collection of racing factories, Formula 1 teams, and the famed Silverstone raceway. We created some solid relationships with British racing folks who always attend the Performance Racing Industry (PRI) annual convention in Indianapolis.

The connection should be obvious. Every year, Indianapolis hosts the "Greatest Spectacle in Racing": the Indianapolis 500. It is the largest one-day sporting event in the world and has been for decades. The pageantry associated not just with the race but also with the city for the entire month of May is unlike anything else in the world. It is a magical feeling for Hoosiers. In my marine career, I tried to watch the race every year, no matter where I was stationed. If you were a Hoosier serviceman overseas, hearing Jim Nabors sing "Back Home Again in Indiana" was emotional. In addition, IMS hosts other racing events throughout the year, and Indianapolis has several racing teams and racing manufacturers in the city.

While visiting England, I was able to visit the Rolls-Royce International HQ in London. Rolls-Royce has a prominent engine manufacturing plant in Indianapolis that always invited me to their annual Marine Corps birthday celebration. I made a point of thanking them as much as possible because Rolls makes equipment that the military relies upon. It was clear to me that they take this responsibility seriously.

Taiwan

The first-ever sister city for Indianapolis is Taipei, Taiwan. The relationship began in 1978, when Bill Hudnut was the mayor of Indianapolis. Taipei is now an incredibly modern city with several world-renowned technology companies.

When we visited, we were treated well by our hosts. We visited Taipei 101, once the tallest building in the world with its 101 floors above ground and five floors in the basement. It has a steel pendulum ball (called a "tuned mass damper") weighing several hundred tons and hanging between the eighty-seventh and ninety-second floors. This allows the building to withstand typhoon-level winds by acting as a counterweight when the building sways in the wind. It is fascinating to see. The building is certified Platinum for LEED (Leadership in Energy and Environmental Design). We also visited a multistory mall that has only global premium brands, from clothing to jewelry to chocolate. Taipei is a rich city.

The most fascinating part to me was Taipei's public parks. They acted as great gathering spaces for the citizens but were far more than green space.

They had several commercial activities in the parks, including restaurants and bars. Too often in America, we feel parks are just for green space. But I believe we should broaden our perspectives of what parks can be. They are meant to serve the public. Combining green space with other activities can attract more people and provide an additional source of funding for parks.

Brazil

We had a nice trip to Campinas, visiting a university and some renewable energy technology sites. However, the funniest moment we ever had on any of our trips happened here.

We always tried to meet as many mayors and other federal, state, or province officials as we could. Our trip to Brazil included a meeting with the mayor of Rio de Janeiro. Our delegation was gathered in his office waiting for him to arrive. When he walked in, the mood changed. He was the classic tall, slim, sultry Latin man. Three women were a part of our delegation, including my wife, and all three were instantly mesmerized, unable to speak, and just stared at him in admiration. It was so obvious and so funny. I will not embarrass the other two women who were with us by naming them, but we laughed with them about this incident for years afterward. It was hilarious because they were all so noticeably taken with him and did not hide it at all.

Italy/Slovenia

The final two sister cities—Monza, Italy, and Piran, Slovenia—were inherited by our administration. In our last year in office, we combined both these cities into one trip. It was a terrific experience.

In Monza, the mayor invited me to an outdoor gathering where we held a very public press conference, followed by a ceremony that included dancing in the town square. We had timed the trip so we could attend the Formula 1 race in Monza, sitting in the mayor's suite for the race. We also spent a day at the World Expo in nearby Milan.

Another funny moment occurred when we left Monza to head for Piran. At the train station in Monza, we were on the wrong track waiting for our train. Those who have been to Europe know that in many places, you must walk underneath and then back up some stairs to get to another track. We had several people with us and lots of luggage. I was still recovering from meniscus surgery, and while my knee was fine for normal walking, going up and down stairs with heavy luggage was another story. As we were late in realizing our mistake with the track, we had to hurry, and it appeared we were not going to make our scheduled train.

However, the head of our Indianapolis committee was with us, and she went ahead to the correct track and started yelling loudly in Italian at the conductor. "We've got the mayor of Indianapolis; hold the train, hold the train." My security guard and I were hurrying as fast as we could, and when we got to the packed train, which did hold for us, everyone was looking at us, wondering, "Who is this mayor of Indianapolis?" I can still see our committee head holding that train up.

As a sister city, Piran seems an odd choice. It has a population of fewer than four thousand and is a tiny, beautiful resort town on the Adriatic Sea. I do not know the rationale for the relationship, as our two cities have little similarity. That said, we enjoyed every minute of our trip to Piran. The mayor, of Ghanian descent and a doctor who specializes in pediatric addictions, was more than gracious to us, taking us to lunch or dinner three times and engaging us in wide-ranging conversations. We stayed in the Hotel Piran, fewer than ten steps from the Adriatic Sea, which is a stunning blue color. Everyone treated us exceptionally well. This was a special trip for our last visit to a sister city.

Keeping the Bags Packed

I was also able to travel to Europe with the US Conference of Mayors. As I became more prominent in the USCM, I was asked to participate in various events. Tom Cochran, the legendary executive director of the USCM (for more than forty years) asked me if I wanted to travel to Florence, Italy, with four other mayors for an exchange with local Italian mayors surrounding sports tourism. My political team asked me not to go; they felt that I was traveling too much already.

I listened but acted otherwise. Turning down an all-expenses-paid trip to Florence for Winnie and me made no sense to me. We had visited Florence for a few hours on a trip through Italy while I was stationed in Stuttgart in the Marines, but on this trip, we would be spending multiple days in Florence, talking to fellow mayors and seeing the beautiful countryside.

There is no city in the world like Florence. Art is everywhere; it permeates the physical environment. And the topography is stunning. When we visited the Florence mayor's office, the walls were painted with beautiful medieval scenery. The cathedral is beautiful, but there is a smaller church, Santa Croce, that is the final resting place for Michelangelo, Galileo, Machiavelli, and the composer Rossini, among others. The mayor gave us a replica of the actual keys to the city of Florence when it was a walled city. There is a reason that numerous American universities use Florence as an overseas campus for their students. It is a magnificent city.

I made the right call to go.

Another trip was to Berlin, Prague, and Budapest on the twenty-fifth anniversary of the Berlin Wall coming down. I was trying to figure out how to do such a trip from Indianapolis when I casually mentioned to Tom Cochran at USCM that I'd like to be there for that anniversary in 2014. Tom found some money from another trip that was canceled, and four mayors had a meaningful trip to Europe.

I really wanted to talk to the mayors of Berlin, Prague, and Budapest, primarily to see what the changes were in their country when the wall came down. We did not talk to the Berlin mayor, but we were able to talk to the Prague mayor and several deputy mayors in Budapest. I was particularly interested in how the military adjusted from working for the Soviet Union one day to their own independent country the next day. It was fascinating.

The attitude of the Prague mayor versus the Budapest deputy mayors was also very interesting. The young Prague mayor was proud of the openness of his city and how it was becoming a beacon of modernism within the European community, while still embracing its past. In contrast, the deputy mayors in Budapest were coy with information. Hungary appears to be sliding toward authoritarianism, which would be tragic considering its Communist past. The deputy mayors told us the mayor was in another country, looking out for "Hungarian interests." Something did not feel right.

Both these countries remember Ronald Reagan fondly. ("Mr. Gorbachev, tear down this wall.") The US embassy in Prague is on Ronald Reagan Boulevard, and there is an eight-foot Ronald Reagan statue in the square next to the Hungarian parliament.

The train rides between the cities were also a highlight. We were a small group (four mayors, two wives, and some USCM staff), and Tom regaled us during the hours-long train rides with anecdotes about mayors from decades ago. We were laughing so hard. Just a terrific memory of camaraderie among fellow mayors.

One of the most memorable and hilarious moments of my entire time as mayor occurred in Berlin during this trip. We wanted to be part of the twenty-fifth anniversary celebration as much as we could, and we were in the middle of the thousands who participated in the outdoor festivities. However, before that, the four mayors and Tom were able to secure tickets to the main event in a Berlin concert hall that included former German chancellor Angela Merkel; the last leader of the Soviet Union, Mikhail Gorbachev; and former Polish president and winner of the Nobel Peace Prize, Lech Walesa.

President Obama had not sent a delegation to the event from the United States, so we informally designated ourselves as the "American delegation." Of course, no one else there knew who we were. However, we sat in the seventh or eighth row, close to the front. The hall was divided by a walkway down the middle; we were on the right side with the main dignitaries on the left side. When the event was finished, attendees were told to head toward the reception on their side of the hall.

When we got to our reception on the right side, we were not satisfied. Being in the same hall as Gorbachev and Walesa but not being able to talk to them did not sit well with us. We took the matter into our own hands. We walked around the back of the building and found our way to where the other, main reception was occurring. Approaching one of the entrances to the reception, one of us politely informed the security guard at the door that we were from the United States. That seemed to matter not at all, and he would not let us in.

This is when Don Plusquellic, then the seven-term mayor of Akron, Ohio, said something like "I'll get us in. Follow me." Don is a highly distinguished-looking gentleman with silver hair and an aristocratic demeanor, the kind of man who could gain entrance to almost any event in the world if he wanted. We went to the next door down, and he brushed aside the security guard and said in a strong, authoritative voice, "We're the American delegation," and we walked right in. It was hilarious. We talked to Gorbachev and Walesa and took pictures with both.

International Events

We created a Mayor's Latino Soccer Cup in Indianapolis in 2009. The first year we held it, we were able to field eight teams with young kids. Very few parents showed.

We knew why. The city was putting it on, and many parents who may have been wary of the government in their native countries were reluctant to attend. Those fears went away in the ensuing years. The Cup grew into about two hundred teams as we accepted more age groups. Medals and trophies were given. Carlos May from our administration and Tom Geisse, a local soccer advocate, were instrumental in the growth of this fun event.

We also created the Latino Expo, an event that, much like our bicycling and robotics efforts, was immediately successful thanks to pent-up demand. It was an important, well-attended event from the very first year. Again, food and dancing were part of the festivities, but we also brought in consular help from the Latin and South American countries, something that a few people were skittish about, but I thought it was important. If anyone at the state level was worried about it, that fear was negated quickly, as the governor and other state officials showed up because of the tremendous success of the Expo. Finding sponsors for the Expo was never a problem; commercial organizations wanted to tap into the still-burgeoning Latino presence in the city.

This was also an exercise in ensuring that appropriate credit be given. Something mayors and others must deal with is the old but accurate saying "Success has a thousand fathers; failure is an orphan." Carlos had worked with dozens if not hundreds of individuals and organizations to plan and execute the initial Latino Expo. It took months to pull it together. Yet one prominent individual in that community, who had not wanted the Expo to happen, then tried to take credit for it. It was bizarre. I was able to fend off this gentleman's attempt to take credit and publicly gave Carlos full credit for the vast amount of work leading up to the first Expo. Carlos received a well-deserved standing ovation at the initial breakfast.

In my last year in office in 2015, we conducted a futsal tournament based on the World Cup model. Futsal is soccer on a smaller field with fewer players and a slightly heavier ball. It is very fast paced and exciting to watch. We outlined several fields in downtown's Pan Am Plaza so that multiple matches would be going on simultaneously. We had teams representing different countries; to be eligible to play on a country's team, a player had to have some proof of ethnicity or ancestry. This made it more fun. A few days before the tournament, we held a blind drawing for the pairings at a local brewery. I drew the first country, which just happened to be the USA. It was a funny moment.

The day of the tournament, the International Center brought over the flags of the participating teams and countries, and we held a meaningful ceremony beforehand. It was a special moment for me; all these Indianapolis-area citizens were representing their ancestry. It is how I envision America: immigrants from around the world working and playing together. I got choked up. It was happening in my city, while I was the mayor.

I attended every international event I could in the city and particularly enjoyed the international representation marching in the Indianapolis 500 parade, the third-largest parade in the country. Before the parade began each year, I would seek out those who were marching and representing their native countries to say hi and take pictures. It was always a wonderful moment for Winnie and me.

Embracing immigrants and an international agenda can be dangerous for politicians. However, we are in a global economy. I feel it is important for mayors and governors to pursue relations and business with foreign countries. The downside is obvious: criticism that you are not spending your efforts on your city and state, and that the trips are nothing but junkets, a free vacation. Neither criticism is valid, but such rhetoric can play well in a political campaign. Of course, Infosys picked Indianapolis as its national headquarters, and the prestigious Brookings Institution recognized Indianapolis for its global outreach efforts and wanted to help the city even more. That should tell everyone that these efforts matter.

I continued my global approach throughout all eight years. All the international groups wanted me to run for a third term. I appreciated their sentiments. But it was time for me to move on.

One Last Thought: Peter from Prague

As mentioned earlier in this chapter, Winnie and I visited Europe with three other mayors during the twenty-fifth anniversary of the Berlin Wall coming down. Our tour guide in Prague called himself "Peter from Prague." He was well known in the capital of the Czech Republic and was excellent—very funny and informative. He spoke perfect English, of course, and seemed to know every nuance about America. Surely he had spent many years in America.

He had not spent one day in America. He told us he had learned everything about America from watching the TV show *The Simpsons*. It was an eye-opening and hilarious comment.

If you ever complain about America, remember this story: Peter's grandmother lived in nine different countries. *Nine.* Yet she never moved. She lived in the same house she grew up in until she died.

Nine countries. One house.

18

SUSTAINABILITY

As mayor, I never used the word "green" while speaking of the environment. By the time I was in office, the word was nearly a pejorative in the Republican Party. I frequently joke that people must learn how to speak "Republican" and speak "Democrat," as they are two separate languages. Words matter. "Green" was a Democratic word at the time. "Sustainable" was a better word for a Republican mayor in a Democratic city.

"Climate change" was another phrase I never used. At the time, if you mentioned that phrase to Republicans, you could see their eyes glaze over and brains turn off. They were not listening to any words that followed that phrase. That is not so today. I've seen multiple polls that confirm that most Republicans now recognize climate change as a concern. That seems not to be true for most Republicans in office, but I suspect that has to do with polling that suggests these issues are not top-of-mind for the party. What to do about climate change is still a question for Republicans, but there is no question that the Republican tide is shifting on this topic.

David Sherman, my great public-works director, knew how I thought about environmental sustainability. I felt that Indianapolis was behind in its approach compared to other cities. The actions that we took seemed aggressive to some, but I thought we were just catching up to what other cities were already doing. I also knew that a civic environmental conscience was important to attracting talent.

A New Office

In 2008, we created the Office of Sustainability, Indianapolis's first department ever to address environmental actions, led by Kären Haley. It was not lost on the citizenry that it was a Republican mayor doing this, but to me, it seemed the right thing to do. We needed a central point where these issues could be addressed, with our own collection of experts in-house.

Although this effort did not have a pent-up-demand response like bicycling, robotics, or the Latino Expo, it did not meet much resistance either. Many Republicans were wondering what I was doing just by talking about these things, let alone taking action. Normal Democrats were happy I was addressing these issues, but the elected Democrats, I sensed, were seething that I was being aggressive on sustainability. I was on their turf. However, just a year before we opened the Office of Sustainability, the Democrats controlled the mayor's office and the council. They had done little.

In the fall of 2008, while I was gathering information and support for our efforts, I addressed the Tree Board in Indianapolis. This organization was made up of mostly environmentally conscious Democrats. I assumed they might be skeptical toward me, maybe even hostile. I walked into an auditorium type of room; the board (twelve to fifteen people, as I recall) was sitting in one long row in front of me with the chairman in the center of the row. I thought the setup was odd. Most organizations would have placed the tables in a rectangular fashion for a meeting. I said a few words to the board about what we wanted to do, and then said, "Just so you know, we have a bias for action."

The chairman looked as if he wanted to say something. He turned his head, looking at the members on one side, and then he did the same for the other side, saying, "Does anyone here have a problem with a bias for action?" Instantly, I sensed their frustration with what had gone on before. I knew that this group, and probably many others in the city, would welcome a "bias for action" regarding environmental initiatives.

Actions

The Green Document was one of our first actions. (This was an internal document, so the "green" word was not out in public.) It was more of a guidance handbook than a regulatory mandate, but it told developers and city administrators that certain sustainability guidelines were to be considered with new buildings. We also upgraded the energy and water posture of sixty-one city-owned facilities, including the City-County Building, which was then almost fifty years old.

The energy and water upgrades, including the LED lighting that is common today but not so much a few years ago, earned the building the EPA's Energy Star certification and saved the taxpayers several hundred thousand dollars per year. Both energy and water consumption decreased by more than 30 percent. These are the sort of commonsense sustainability efforts that Republicans should focus on. In so many cases, the taxpayer wins when sustainability is considered.

The sewer repair mentioned previously was the largest environmental action ever taken by the city. Sewer overflows into the White River during rainstorms will be reduced to only twice per year on average, versus the dozens of times annually in the past. The massive piping being used for both storage and conveyance was critical to this effort. Again, our reengineering of this project saved nearly a billion dollars for the ratepayers.

As mentioned above, bicycling became a prominent feature in the city, with Indianapolis becoming a Bronze Level Bicycle Friendly City as designated by the League of American Cyclists. I also won a leadership award from the league. I was a featured speaker at the 2013 National Bike Summit, with the city hosting a breakout session at the summit for other cities whose leaders wondered how we had moved so far so fast. My address, very well received at the summit, is still on YouTube.

I have mentioned the expansion of the Great Indy Cleanup in coordination with Keep Indianapolis Beautiful. This effort kept much more trash out of our waterways and out of our neighborhoods than before the expansion. It also engaged hundreds more people in ensuring the environment near their homes was much cleaner year round.

We emphasized urban gardens for neighborhoods. In addition to being a great educational experience for children, urban gardens can provide fresh vegetables for poorer areas of the city. We partnered with Purdue University and the Marion County Health Department to provide guidelines for people who wanted to grow these gardens. Urban gardens are also a great use for unkempt, empty lots as long as the soil is tested. In 2011, I established a goal for establishing fifty urban gardens in the city; it was easily met. When I left office, there were well over a hundred urban gardens in the city. More importantly, there was a sense that growing healthy, fresh food in an urban area such as Indianapolis was possible and welcome.

Recycling

I never thought the recycling advocates would be against more and easier recycling. But they were.

We tried hard to increase recycling efforts in the city. When I took office, only 3 percent of the citizens were recycling. Citizens who chose to recycle put their material in a different bin, separate from their trash. We tried to increase the rate of recycling through outreach. We did triple it, but that meant only 9 or 10 percent of the citizens were recycling—hardly a victory.

In my second term, a company approached my staff to market a new technology that promised to allow citizens to combine their trash and recycling material into one trash can. Before I even knew of this effort, someone prominent in the nonprofit state recycling efforts approached me and asked me to not go in this direction, saying, "They're just going to burn all of it." I had no idea what she was talking about.

I went back to my staff, who explained the technology. Although all the material would come from only one pickup from home, there were sensors along a conveyor belt that could separate the recyclable material from trash. It would give us a 100 percent recycling rate and would be easier for the citizens. We decided to pursue it.

We would have gone from one of the worst recycling communities to the best, almost overnight. Additionally, the city guarantees a certain amount of waste to our contractor because they burn that waste to create steam. The year before we began this process, the city had missed the total waste requirement and had to pay a $600,000 penalty for not generating enough trash for them to burn to create steam. We knew that if we started pulling recyclables off the front end, we would miss that commitment on the back end and pay even more penalties. We negotiated with the company so that we would not have to pay those penalties. We also had them take all the risk. They would build the facility at their expense and take the market risk of recycling the material.

The nonprofit recycling advocates came straight for us. I thought they would be thrilled with this new technology, but that "They'll only burn it" comment should have been a warning to me. The recycling advocates pleaded with us to not use this new technology, even though the amount of recyclable material collected in the city would increase by multiples. They said they would soon have a better solution, one as economical as ours. Of course, that never materialized (and still hasn't).

There were some who told me that the recycling community wanted to make people physically separate the material at home so that people would remain conscientious about the need to recycle. However, I believe the Indiana Recycling Coalition was worried about its funding; much of its donor base was made up of the companies that received the recyclable material from the current system. If the new system went into effect, then funding for the nonprofit could diminish.

The nonprofit advocates ensured that there was court action against the city, trying to stop our implementation of the new recycling technology. Their arguments were flimsy; we won in district court but lost on appeal. We believe we would have prevailed if we had taken the case further. I was nearing the end of my term, and the courts are rarely a speedy process. They ran out the clock on us; my successor did not pursue the case. The new process faded away.

A Bold Move

In December 2012, I gave a speech to the Greater Indianapolis Progress Committee (GIPC), a unique organization of influential people who work for the betterment of the city. Over the years, the mayor has addressed this organization to present new ideas and sometimes to gather support. I did so when we needed a new public hospital (Eskenazi), along with other initiatives. This time, I presented that the city was going to move toward electrification of the city fleet, adding hybrids, plug-in hybrids, and all-electric vehicles where feasible.

I couched this speech in terms of national security, because our nation spends about $80 billion annually to protect the oil supply for the entire world, using US troops. Most people do not know that the primary reason our troops are in the Middle East is to protect oil. Also, most of the defense effort over the last fifty years, both wars and smaller conflicts, have revolved around the Middle East. I was in the Persian Gulf War in 1990–91, a war that was only about oil. Over the last several decades, ensuring that oil continues to flow throughout the world has cost the United States more than seven thousand lives and $7 trillion.

Most people do not know that terrorism against the West, including the United States, is primarily funded by the very sale of that oil that we protect. Eighty percent of the oil reserves in the world are in the hands of authoritarian nations, most of whom are not friendly to us and cause most of the strategic unrest in the world. Since 70 percent of the oil in the world is used for transportation, moving away from gasoline and diesel as transportation fuels makes a lot of sense for international security reasons. I eventually wrote a book, *Less Oil or More Caskets: The National Security Argument for Moving Away from Oil,* published by Indiana University Press, on this topic of oil and national security. When Indianapolis moved in the direction of converting the city fleet toward electrification, we were the first city in the nation to do so. It is common now.

I received a standing ovation after that speech, the only time that happened at GIPC. I had my communications team work to get an article in the *Wall Street Journal* about why I was moving in this direction and did not give an interview ahead of time to our local newspaper, the *Indianapolis Star.* The *WSJ* did a good job with the article, but when the *Star* published their article, the headline read "Going Green."

That was why I did not want the *Star* to have the lead on the story. In my speech, I did not mention anything about the sustainability aspects of the fleet conversion, but that was still their default headline. I knew the positive sustainability effects of this fleet conversion, but I wanted to bring along other people to realize the need for moving our transportation away from oil.

Most of the early effort was simply in buying hybrids. We bought ninety-three Toyota Camry hybrids for the Office of Public Safety very early on in the fleet conversion. These were well received by those who used them; none were for patrol cars in the police department. My security team used them also.

Previously, all the police used Ford Crown Victorias that got about eight to ten miles per gallon. The hybrid Camrys got fifty miles to the gallon. Frequently, my security team, because of my extensive travel throughout the city, filled up the Crown Victorias every day. With the Camrys, they were filling up every week. With a $5 million annual bill for gasoline, the more hybrids and other more electrified cars we could use would save the city significant money.

As a result of my announcement and its coverage in the *Wall Street Journal*, people started to call me, wanting to meet. I got invited to several transportation conferences and spoke to different groups around the country. The Electrification Coalition, based in Washington, DC, held its annual convention in Indianapolis one year—the first time it was held outside of the nation's capital. I was asked to speak at the Washington, DC, car show along with the secretary of energy and was also asked to attend the prestigious Detroit Auto Show. The secretary of transportation asked me to attend a conference with the CEO of Ford about the future of transportation. I was asked to attend a conference in Delhi, India, where ministers of transportation and energy of more than a dozen countries presented on their movements toward electrification; I was the only mayor in the world in attendance. I received an international award in Barcelona, Spain.

At one of these events, a Ford engineer, knowing what I was doing in Indianapolis and realizing we were ahead of all other cities in this regard, took me aside to show me the replacement for the gas-guzzling Crown Victorias. He was pleased to highlight that their new patrol car would get thirteen miles per gallon instead of ten miles per gallon, a 30 percent improvement. I do not think he expected my response. Trying to keep my cool, I told him that we did not need a 30 percent improvement. We needed a 500 percent improvement. I wanted fifty miles to the gallon, not thirteen.

I also told him we would not be buying his car. I appreciated his understanding, and I maintained a good relationship with the Ford engineers throughout the remainder of my time in office. At least they were moving in the right direction; others were not at that time.

We bought some plug-in hybrids (part electric and part gasoline engines) along with a couple of all-electric Nissan Leafs. There was some pushback from the users of these cars, and some worry from the maintenance section; they initially did not understand the maintenance required (very minimal and much cheaper for all-electric cars). Sometimes I see the future a little earlier than others, but if I thought we could save money or break even, I wanted to move the fleet in this direction. That other cities started to move in this direction just a few years later validated our initiative.

Blue Indy

One of the companies that wanted to talk to me was Bollore, based in France. They were the founders of AutoLib, an all-electric car sharing service in Paris. Knowing about my move toward fleet conversion, they wanted to talk to me about bringing an all-electric car sharing service to Indianapolis. This sounded terrific to me, but I wanted to ensure that it was a good deal for the city. It took me three separate meetings with the US-based Bollore representative to agree to explore this possibility. We used the expertise of Energy Systems Network, a small statewide group of energy experts for analysis.

Bollore believed that two hundred sites with four or five charging outlets each would be enough scale to make the system work. Bollore is a huge European conglomerate run by billionaire Vincent Bollore. The company was founded in 1822 as a paper manufacturer. When Vince took over the company in 1981, he transformed it into one of the five hundred largest companies in the world. They have interests in music, media, communications, paper, transport and logistics, and several other areas. Many of the machines used in airports around the world are manufactured by Bollore, and they also own a significant portion of the media company Vivendi.

Bollore invested about $30 million to found Blue Indy, and all they asked for was for the city to pay for the electrical connections between the electrical system in place underground and the charging outlets on the street. Since these connections could be used in the near future anyway for the eventual electric vehicle conversion from internal combustion engines, we agreed to this. The amount was estimated to be about $6 million.

Bollore created a special car for Indianapolis at its own expense, different from the AutoLib cars in Paris. Bollore had several other sustainability initiatives throughout the world, including modular housing with small and local clean water systems attached, for use in remote villages in Africa. This massive European conglomerate was all in on sustainability and Indianapolis. They were determined to make this system work because it could provide a model for other cities. They also had a Hoosier industrial manufacturer interested in using the cars for travel between their campuses in Indiana.

When we announced Blue Indy in 2013, there was great excitement within some circles of the city. The Democratic president of the city-county council attended the press conference, and the leader of the Central Indiana Community Foundation was there, very excited for what was occurring. He thought Blue Indy would change Indianapolis. I thought it sent a strong signal that would attract talent to the area, the paradigm for almost everything we did while in office.

Vince Bollore wanted to come to Indianapolis to let the city know how important this effort was to his company. We held another press conference in Indianapolis in 2014 for Vince's visit that was the most extensive press conference I was ever involved in. They hired a local event management firm to coordinate all the details for the occasion. The events management firm asked Bollore what the budget would be for the event (a routine question) and was told that there was no budget. In other words, money would not matter. The owner of the events management firm told me that in the decades she had run her company, no one had ever given her an unlimited budget. It was quite the event, and one of my staff said that the event had four million Twitter hits. Such was the reach of Bollore.

Several national articles were written about Indianapolis after the 2014 press conference with Vince Bollore. The tone of these articles was "How is this happening in Indianapolis? This should be happening in Los Angeles, San Francisco, or New York." Blue Indy was on the cutting edge of both technology and business practice, and Indianapolis was leading the nation in the conversion to electric vehicles. Other cities were now talking about us.

I announced that I was not running for a third term later in 2014, and the Democratic council started pushing back on several initiatives, one being Blue Indy. I was still a popular mayor (with favorability ratings in the high seventies in a majority Democratic city) but because I was not going to be around within a few months, some of my influence was waning. I thought my announcement to not run again would allow the Democrats to help finish up some of the ongoing projects without controversy, but that proved to not be true. Even issues all Democrats believed in, like clean transportation, were attacked because it was I who initiated the project. Politics was again trumping the actual issues. As a former advisor once told me, "They just can't help themselves."

When they started to push back against Blue Indy, despite the council president's endorsement at the first press conference in 2013, I would go on TV and say as often as I could, "I have the only Democrats in the entire nation that are against clean transportation." I heard that they were not fond of me saying that as publicly as I was, but I did not care. They believed in the program; they were upset that Blue Indy was an initiative of our administration.

We held our final press conference on Blue Indy in the fall of 2015, just a few months before I left office. We had almost one hundred charging sites up and running, and we wanted to let the city know we were proceeding.

There were some hiccups. When Indianapolis Power and Light and Bollore started installing the charging stations, they did not talk to the neighbors or stores in the area; they just started installing them. This was an obvious oversight that someone should have realized before it happened, but the first ten or twelve sites that were installed caused some controversy because of the way they were handled. Also, when we went to spend the agreed-upon $6 million for the electrical connections, the Democrats caused some controversy and tried to block the transaction. Here we had a huge European conglomerate investing more than $30 million in our city, and my opposition was trying to hold up something that would be needed in the future anyway. That is not the way to have companies gain confidence and invest in your city.

Before I left office, there were about one hundred charging sites completed, but the remainder of the agreed-upon number of two hundred sites was never realized. I do not know why the rest of the Blue Indy sites were not developed as per contract with the city. Whatever the friction was, Bollore eventually pulled out. It is sad because this was a project that gave us enormous positive national attention. Of course, the private Indiana manufacturer now did not want to use Blue Indy because there was some controversy surrounding the city's deal with Bollore. (Private companies never want to be on the wrong side of a current administration). I understand that a grocery chain wanted to use Blue Indy also, but after I left office, I was told the zoning officials would not let that happen.

People—especially those with families—who used Blue Indy loved the service. Some families sold one of their cars; some single individuals sold their only car and used a combination of Blue Indy and the developing bike infrastructure to get around. We might have been a few years ahead of what people could conceive at the time, but the loss of Blue Indy seems like a missed opportunity to me.

What I also worry about is how Indianapolis will be perceived now by other multinational conglomerates who are considering investment in cities. Bollore was hoping to make a difference in our city, but I suspect they and other European businesses will be looking elsewhere in the future.

Awards

One of the ironies concerning the commonsense sustainability efforts of our administration was that we kept winning awards, both in the state and with the US Conference of Mayors. Early in our administration, I told a member of our staff that we could not win the Climate Protection awards from the US Conference of Mayors because I did not use the term "climate" at all. We wound up winning at least three Climate Protection awards because of the breadth of our initiatives. We never highlighted our winning of these awards because, as I said at the beginning of this chapter, such words as "climate" turned off Republican voters at the time. I suspect it is a bit different today.

We also won the Indiana Association of Cities and Towns Green Community Award in 2012 and the Governor's Award for Environmental Excellence in 2013. This latter award was a little awkward as Indiana is not a state known for its environmental efforts. In any case, it was nice the city was recognized for its efforts.

I still find it funny that I, the Republican, am known as the sustainability mayor in Indianapolis.

19

INDY'S SUPER BOWL XLVI

The Gold Standard

DURING THE RUN-UP TO SUPER BOWL XLVI IN 2012, I told many groups that this game was not the culmination of anything; it was just further evidence that Indianapolis was continuing to do those things to enhance its reputation as the premier sports-event city in the nation. Indy really is the turnkey city for big sporting events. The physical and human infrastructure is in place to host these events with great efficiency and effectiveness. The very real Hoosier hospitality is the icing on top. That said, it is difficult to overstate just how meaningful the Super Bowl was for the citizens of Indianapolis.

How did this happen? Here is an article I wrote for Rick Horrow's book *The Sports Business Handbook* that summarizes the ascension of Indianapolis to its current position.

> "How Indy Used Sports to Build Civic Pride"
>
> Before big sporting events became big sporting events, Indianapolis' reputation was mainly basketball. Our once legendary high school state championship produced not only Oscar Robertson, but also state legend Bobby Plump, who still runs a restaurant in Indy named Plump's Last Shot. Bobby, now 80 years old and as feisty as ever, hit the actual last-second shot memorialized in the movie *Hoosiers*. Also, the Pacers were the dominant ABA franchise, and Bobby Knight was soon to follow. Other states had similar unique reputations, but in most cases, national interest was secondary to regional followings.
>
> The ability of Indianapolis to host the biggest events with such precision didn't happen by accident. It was by design. Now, all those in the industry marvel at the relationship Indianapolis has with sports and the biggest events. The times in which this civic transformation occurred were much different from today. It happened mainly due to a civic sense of mission by so many who wanted to propel Indianapolis past the India-no-place and Naptown reputations. Businesses, nonprofits, foundations, and individuals would work together for the greater good. Some history helps.

In the 1960s and 70s, what we now know as March Madness was just another national championship. The Super Bowl was a nice ending to the NFL season but Roman numerals weren't used at the beginning, and the game wasn't originally known as the Super Bowl. It was Joe Namath's lifestyle, pregame prediction and subsequent win in Super Bowl III that got people more interested in the game. The Olympics caught our attention every four years, but the Olympic Trials held no interest for the general sports population. The Big Ten and the SEC had great football teams but nobody cared outside of the Midwest and Southeast. The NBA Finals were on tape-delay late at night. Baseball was still the game for most but it was local interest that mattered. For Indy, the Cubs, despite their foibles, held sway for many thanks to the reach of WGN. Nobody played soccer. ESPN did not exist.

Then in 1979, the Indiana Sports Corporation was formed, the first commission of its kind in the nation. The Sports Corp, as we call it, was one part of the broad civic mission by so many who wanted to propel Indianapolis into the national consciousness. The mission of the Sports Corp is "to create positive impact by hosting world-class sporting events that enhance vibrancy in the community, build civic pride, drive economic impact and media exposure, and encourage opportunities for youth." For most cities or states, they would focus on the words about hosting the events and driving economic growth, but in Indianapolis, what we take very seriously are the words about building civic pride and enhancing vibrancy in the community. As the former mayor of Indianapolis, I can personally attest that hosting a world-class sporting event is seen as an opportunity to enhance the city and its citizens. The phrase "It must be about more than the game" is the common sentiment. Super Bowl XLVI was but one example. Indianapolis involved breast cancer research, planting trees, helping the less fortunate, and so much more, all as part of the Super Bowl activity. There's a reason we had 13,000 people applying for the 8,000 volunteer spots.

Coincidentally and fortunately, ESPN was founded in the same year as the Sports Corp. As the nation was figuring out ESPN and the oncoming proliferation of sports programming, Indianapolis began in earnest its quest to raise the presence of the city into the national spotlight, with sports as a catalyst. Indianapolis hosted the National Sports Festival in 1982 and then the Pan Am Games in 1987. It is accurate to say that with the success of the high-profile Pan Am Games, the people of Indianapolis realized that they could successfully compete with any city in the nation in hosting events. It gave the city confidence. Final Fours came, Olympic Trials happened (particularly Swimming/Diving and Track and Field), national governing bodies were courted to Indy, the Colts arrived, and the NCAA moved to Indianapolis.

The nation tuned in. FloJo showed her stuff in Indy. Every major swimmer for the past few decades passed through. Coach K won his national championships routinely in Indy. Gymnasts won championships and wowed the crowds. The Colts would draft a Tennessee quarterback who owned the city and the country with his artistry and humor, which led to the most fan-friendly, best-organized Super Bowl ever. The sought-after national reputation was achieved. The plan worked due to the foresight and selflessness of so many.

> We capitalized on our greatest strength: smart, friendly, hard-working, civic-minded people who worked for the greater good. That's why we were successful. People. It's a good lesson for all.

This article does not mention the Indianapolis 500, the largest one-day sporting event in the world for decades. Or the massive risk the city took in building a football stadium without a pro football team. Or the purposeful development of the downtown to ensure that future sporting events and conventions would be walkable and customer friendly.

It took a bipartisan political effort at both the city and state levels along with significant buy-in from the corporate and philanthropic sectors. It took a populace that trusted its civic leaders that the sports strategy would position Indianapolis differently. It took an incredible volunteer effort, a spirit that caught fire for these events. Local sportswriter Bill Benner said in an article, "They not only wanted to witness a Carl Lewis long jump—they wanted to rake the sand pit too."

All these elements came together and were working before most cities in the nation even conceived of sports as a civic and economic driver. For Indy, it resulted in billions of dollars of economic activity, a much bigger convention business, tremendous sports infrastructure, and an estimated sixty thousand to seventy thousand hospitality jobs in Central Indiana.

All this *before* Super Bowl XLVI.

In 2007, my predecessor, along with the Colts and the business community, submitted a bid for the 2011 Super Bowl. By all accounts, this was a superior bid that was well received by the NFL staff and most importantly, the thirty-two NFL owners, the true voting bloc. A new football stadium, Lucas Oil Stadium, was in the works, as was a new airport. There was talk of a new one-thousand-room hotel, which eventually became the JW Marriott. The already great infrastructure in place was getting better.

Additionally, both individuals and the corporate community contributed the required organizational money up front (about $25 million). Most other cities try to raise this money after a bid is secured; in typical Indy fashion, we showed the NFL owners that we had the money already pledged, that the city was serious and ready to go.

As strong as the Indy bid was, the Dallas Cowboys, wanting to show off their new stadium, upped the ante by promising the owners far more money than they were originally expecting. Dallas won the bid, barely—but anyone attending the 2011 Super Bowl would tell you that karma came back to haunt them. This "warm weather city" had a terrible ice storm just before the Super Bowl. Indianapolis could have handled this storm (and the storm was so widespread that it actually reached Indy), but Dallas did not have the knowledge or equipment to handle it. They did not know what to do. They could not clear the roads. Many volunteers did not show. The stadium staff was clearing ice the morning of the Super Bowl. They also had seating problems that left some fans without seats. To its credit, the stadium had a massive screen above the middle of the field. It was so big and so clear that I found myself looking at the screen instead of the game right in front of me.

I am quite certain that Jim Irsay, the owner of the Indianapolis Colts, was not expecting the January 2008 call from the new mayor whom he had never met. Although I was in the Marine Corps while Indianapolis was in the early stages of executing its sports strategy, I knew how the city was building itself up. I had also learned of the bid for the 2011 Super Bowl. My sense was that "the iron was hot" and that we should resubmit. He agreed to do so.

I then called Mark Miles, whom I had met once during the campaign. At that time, he was president and chief executive officer of the Central Indiana Corporate Partnership, a regional nonprofit alliance of corporate CEOs and university presidents focused on long-term growth and economic development throughout central Indiana. Prior to holding that position, he was the CEO of the Association of Tennis Professionals (ATP), the men's professional tennis tour, for fifteen years. He had also very successfully run the Indianapolis ATP tournament in the late 1980s on a volunteer basis and was the president of the organizing body for the 1987 Pan Am games, which meant so much to the city. He knew sports at the highest levels. I asked him to run the effort for the 2012 Super Bowl bid, and he agreed to do so.

Mark became the chair of this latest bid. He kept key members of the previous effort, such as Jack Swarbrick, a well-respected attorney and a previous chairman of the Indiana Sports Corp. (he is now the athletic director at Notre Dame), and Allison Melangton, then a senior vice president with the Indiana Sports Corp.

Since we were going to bid, we attended the 2008 Phoenix Super Bowl between the then-undefeated New England Patriots and the New York Giants. Ironically, these were the same two teams who would play in our Super Bowl in 2012 with the same result. Phoenix was the first Super Bowl my wife and I had ever attended, and it was a terrific experience. I got to know more people who were working the sports strategy in Indy along with members of the Colts organization.

Incidentally, the 2008 Super Bowl game is still considered by many as the best ever. The Patriots were undefeated going into this game and were leading with less than three minutes to go. The Giants drove for the winning touchdown; the drive included the famous "helmet catch" by David Tyree. Our contingent was happy because this was during the Tom Brady-Peyton Manning rivalry between the Patriots and the Colts, and Peyton's brother, Eli, was the Giants' quarterback. Most Indy fans wanted the Patriots to lose.

What I fondly remember was that Phoenix was another "warm weather city" that was not so warm. I believe the game time temperature was in the forties, and the retractable roof was closed for the game. When its turn came, Indianapolis had much warmer weather for its game.

Our bid package was once again put together in a superb fashion. The organizing money from individuals and corporate entities was again secured up front. There were some subtle differences in this bid, but there were two major differences as well. Jack Swarbrick had the idea to ask thirty-two eighth graders to deliver the packages to the thirty-two NFL owners. This was a home-run idea and became a huge press event for the city. I went to the airport on the day that the students boarded their planes. I remember thinking that I could not imagine being an eighth grader and being asked to participate in such an important event for the city. The students were beyond ecstatic, and it was wonderful to see. The project was well received by the owners. Four years later, those same students, then seniors in high school, attended our Super Bowl.

The other new idea was to incorporate the Near Eastside Legacy Project, a bold attempt to help a struggling area of the city. There is always some sort of legacy project as part of a Super Bowl, but this one was much more ambitious in its scope. More on this in a moment.

The physical bid packages are in depth, so the actual presentations to the owners take only fifteen minutes. (The bid presentation to the NFL owners does not allow politicians to be present. Knowing so many politicians, I believe this is a good idea.) Mark went over the details of the package. Then the superintendent of the Indianapolis Public Schools, Eugene White, spoke about the importance of the Near Eastside Legacy Project and its long-lasting impact for tens of thousands of residents.

Frank Supovits, a wonderful man and the NFL's senior vice president of events, said, "The scale and scope of that project was unlike any ever seen with the Super Bowl, because the number of people that it would impact was enormous. That was something that became immediately apparent." Shortly thereafter, in my office, I received a text from Mark.

"Got it." It was an answer I expected.

Although he does not talk about it, Jim Irsay was the secret weapon. He is well respected by the other NFL owners for his willingness to work on difficult league issues, and his opinions matter to them. He also runs a highly regarded professional sports franchise. People rarely leave the Colts organization, a sign that almost everything is in good order. Before I was the mayor, I had a friend who was friends with Jim's former wife, and she described him as "an old hippie with a big heart." I still think of him this way, though he does not know that. He is extremely generous in quiet ways that most people do not know about (as is Pacers owner Herb Simon).

Now was the time to get to work making this event "more than the game." The first order of business was to get the host committee organized. Mark was gracious enough to chair the effort for the four years. He asked me if I was OK with Allison Melangton as the president and CEO of the Super Bowl Host Committee. I knew Allison a bit from the Phoenix Super Bowl but not well. However, she was well known and well respected within the sports circles of Indianapolis. According to a Kate Fagan espnW article in 2012, "Melangton's résumé is more epic novel than haiku: she's directed 100 national and international competitions for USA Gymnastics, directed Olympic trials, World Championships, Big Ten tournaments, and the NCAA Division I Women's Basketball Championships. She's also worked seven Olympics, including the past four, and won four Emmys for her work with NBC."

I knew some of this but not all of it.

Of course, I said yes to Mark's request. According to Fagan, the conversation asking Allison to be the president and CEO went like this: "We don't want to have a selection process; we just want to know if you'll do it." This occurred two days before she left for the 2008 Beijing Olympics. Allison was already a superstar within the sports community, but she soon was to become a well-known, valued treasure in the city of Indianapolis. To this day, I still tell people that Allison is the best in the country at what she does, organizing major events with integrity and efficiency but with a hospitable touch. In the final year before our Super Bowl, the entire nation got to know her a bit.

Allison and Mark named eight board members, and five were women. To some people, this was a big deal, especially in this male-dominated sport. Until some recent research, I had no idea of this because I usually do not think of such things. I just knew these people were competent at what they did and that Indianapolis was lucky to have them. The Indianapolis Super Bowl was in good hands. I did my part by staying out of the way unless asked.

A major part of the secret sauce of Indianapolis hosting these events is the volunteer base. The Super Bowl Host Committee estimated that they needed eight thousand volunteers for the entire Super Bowl effort. However, thirteen thousand people applied. A major difference between Indy and other cities is that our volunteer base is willing to undergo training and *always shows up*. This goes back to the 1987 Pan Am games, where the volunteers had such a great experience that the culture of volunteering for sporting events has been passed on through the years. During our Super Bowl, all the volunteers (and the hospitality workers) were famous for saying to everyone who crossed their path, "Have a Super Day." This may sound corny to some, but in Indianapolis, it worked beyond expectations because of the sincerity of the approach.

There were about sixty committees formed for the Super Bowl, but the host committee had only thirty-four paid staff. Volunteers handled an incredible number of details along with numerous separate but substantial programs associated with the Super Bowl effort. Indianapolis has highly influential people in the prime of their careers volunteering—along with the retired grandma who wants to help in any way she can. It is a magic recipe for success.

At the previous four Super Bowls and with ours, I worked with Chris Gahl of Visit Indy to get interviews on sports radio shows from throughout the country, from Honolulu to New York. This took place in a designated area called Radio Row and was usually a great time. Most sportscasters are just looking to have a good time with their broadcast, and they like to have political figures on their shows discussing the importance of sports. I had a blast, and so did Chris as my front man.

Prior to our Super Bowl, I would tell all of them that Indy was going to have great weather for the big game. We are what NFL officials call a "cold weather city." Over those few years, this was a bit of a running joke as the same sportscasters would have me on their show every year. It was funny that we actually had great weather, with temperatures in the sixties, for our Super Bowl week.

One sportscaster in particular whom I remember fondly was Nestor Aparicio from Baltimore. The first time he interviewed me on live radio, he began with something like this: "I've only seen my dad cry twice in his life, and one of those times was when the Colts left Baltimore for Indianapolis." On live radio!

I was taken aback a bit at first. The Colts' move in 1984, with the pictures of the Mayflower moving vans relocating the team during the night, had never left his mind. In the few years leading up to our Super Bowl, Nestor said that he was coming to terms with the move. He eventually wrote a glowing article about the Indianapolis Super Bowl and the city. It was a great experience talking to him every year.

We did put on a great Super Bowl, one that most people still consider the best ever. A large reason for that was the groundbreaking concept of the Super Bowl Village. Before that, however, we had to create the infrastructure for the village. Again, Indy's folks working together made it happen.

Georgia Street

In downtown Indianapolis, Georgia Street was a dark, unremarkable, three-block stretch that connected Bankers Life Fieldhouse (where the Pacers play) to the convention center. It had a few restaurants on it and some other businesses, but it was not at all special.

Bill Brown, a local architect, had the idea that this space would be good for Super Bowl activities and wanted to remake it into something similar to Las Ramblas in Barcelona, Spain. (Two years later, I visited Barcelona to receive an international award and had the opportunity to walk along Las Ramblas myself.) He also envisioned it as a place that could be a gathering spot beyond the Super Bowl activities. He connected with Mark Miles, who ran with it, working with state and federal officials along with our public-works people. In all, the revamp cost around $12 million, with the city putting in $2 million of that total.

It is the most environmentally sound three-block stretch in the city, with a self-draining infrastructure and walkability beyond a normal street. It has lighting, heaters, and sound. It also has a bronze of legendary UCLA basketball coach John Wooden (a Hoosier high school and college player who attended Purdue University), and ten markers highlighting prominent Hoosiers. We formed a commission to determine thirty prominent Hoosiers, with the Super Bowl Committee agreeing to foot the bill for the first ten markers. Somewhere there is a list for the next twenty prominent Hoosiers to be so honored if funding is found.[1]

The village was set up along the three-block stretch of Georgia Street with the perpendicular streets of Pennsylvania, Meridian, Illinois, and Capitol also part of the village—especially Capitol, in front of the convention center, featuring the famous zipline that was used all day and night for the ten days. There were fireworks every night. There were two stages that alternated bands throughout the day and night. There were some very famous names on stage, including Darius Rucker, En Vogue, LMFAO, the Village People, Morris Day and the Time, and Patti Labelle—along with other famous groups that my kids knew but I did not. There were also some local, high-profile entertainers like Jenny DeVoe and the Hunter Smith band. The music was continuous.

A few of us wanted to rename Georgia Street before the Super Bowl. We were making it into something special and wanted a name that would signify that—something like Legacy Boulevard or Championship Avenue. The businesses seemed OK with it, but some who took a preservationist view were having none of it. Like a lot of cities, many of our streets are named after states. We have Illinois, Pennsylvania, Delaware, Alabama, and so on, so changing this one three-block stretch seemed innocuous to me. The preservationists started to put up a fight. I knew that if we were going to change the name, we would have to do it before the Super Bowl; afterward, there would be no chance of changing the name. However, it became such a messaging fiasco that it was taking away from the buildup to the Super Bowl, so I just let it go. It was not worth it. I still think the name should be changed. I would also like to see the other twenty markers installed.

We were the first Super Bowl ever to have a Super Bowl Village. So many Indianapolis citizens, during the ten days leading to the Super Bowl, remarked, "I can't believe this is my city." The village was the physical representation of this sentiment.

Unless things have changed in the last few years, this concept is now a requirement for Super Bowls. The idea came from Allison's experience with the Olympics, and it was an unqualified success. Over a million people traveled through the village over the ten-day period. I can personally attest that the evenings were packed beyond anyone's imagination. The overall mood was of joy and celebration.

A few weeks after the Super Bowl, a reporter asked me if Georgia Street was a failure because no one else was using it. I replied no, as organizations had just seen its utility during the Super Bowl, and they would eventually use it. It is now used virtually year round for dozens if not hundreds of events. It can be used as a one-block, two-block, or three-block package and is the site of food festivals, ethnic celebrations, tailgating parties for sporting events, and so many other activities.

Each day in the village had a different theme and activities surrounding the theme. The themes were:

Friday, January 27	Super Kick Off
Saturday, January 28	Indy's Super Cure
Sunday, January 29	Super Families
Monday, January 30	Super Community
Tuesday, January 31	Super Sports
Wednesday, February 1	Super Biz Bowl
Thursday, February 2	Super Heroes (Military, Public Safety)
Friday, February 3	Super Fans
Saturday, February 4	America's Super Game
Sunday, February 5	Super Bowl Sunday

Within the village, open alcohol containers were allowed (mostly beer cans in this case), yet there were almost no incidents of crime or disturbance and no violence at all. People just got along and were happy. There seemed to be three distinct phases of visitors to the village, although some of the types of visitors overlapped. The first few days, it seemed it was mostly Indianapolis folks and the surrounding suburbs. Then as the word spread, people from the rest of Indiana and surrounding states like Ohio, Illinois, and Kentucky were coming over to check out the buzz about the Super Bowl. Then the last three or four days were the visitors who came in for the game.

It was packed every night, but it was not a standstill situation for the ordinary visitor. Although in a still photo it might look like everyone was just milling about, actually people were moving just fine and getting to different parts of the village. However, this was something I could not do myself past Wednesday. I stopped going onto Georgia Street directly after Wednesday because, although everyone else was moving, I could not.

When I was in the village, hundreds of people wanted a picture with me (also with the governor). They did not want a picture because I was the mayor; they wanted a picture because they were so happy to see their city putting on such a magnificent, joyous event. I was a symbol of the success that Mark, Allison, and others had worked so hard to produce.

On that Wednesday night, I was at Meridian and Georgia streets and hungry in the early evening. I wanted to go one block east to Pennsylvania and Georgia to put some food in my belly—a cinnamon roll. I had an hour to perform this one-block task before I had to appear somewhere else. One half hour into my quest for the cinnamon roll, I had moved one half block, and it was clear that I was going to fail in my attempt. Everyone else was moving, but I was not, because so many people wanted a picture. I was not going to say no to their request; they were just so happy to be a part of the Super Bowl celebration. Any future in the village for me was restricted to the outskirts and not the heart of the village.

Our public-safety team set up a command center a mile or two away from the village. I can remember clearly watching the end of the LMFAO concert (on the second Friday night, I believe) and the excitement of the crowd. It looked like people were being forcibly squeezed closer and closer to the stage as the band kept playing encores. We were screaming at the computer screens (essentially to ourselves) for them to stop playing encores as we were getting scared that many people could get hurt. After what I believe was their fourth encore, they moved offstage, and everyone was fine. Typical Indy. Great fun but doing it the right way.

There were ice sculping events by a famous duo from the Food Network, but they had trouble with the warm weather in our "cold weather city." Next to the village was the NFL Experience (football-themed interactive events) in the convention center that 265,000 people attended—an NFL record. It was quite the scene every night.

Other Super Programs

The Legacy Project

As mentioned, every Super Bowl must have a legacy project; the city hosting the game needs to improve the city in some way. The legacy project in the bid for the 2011 Super Bowl was the athletic center that would be given to Indianapolis Public Schools after the game. This had to be built anyway as part of the bid, as both the AFC and NFC champions must have similar practice accommodations (the AFC team would use the Colts facility, but another facility had to be built for the NFC champion). For the 2012 bid, Mark Miles wanted something that had more of a "Wow" factor, along with the general feeling in Indianapolis that it must be about more than the game.[2]

Some background helps. In the early 2000s, the Near Eastside, like many neighborhoods in the city, were banding together to help themselves in any way they could. When neighborhood groups would ask me how to get help from the city or other entities, I always told them that they (1) must be organized, (2) must know what they want, and (3) must be ready to receive the help. The Near Eastside, well before I became mayor, already fulfilled all three of these requirements.

The group was led by a quiet bulldog, James Taylor, the head of the local John H. Boner Community Center. My predecessor had begun a program called the Great Indy Neighborhoods Initiatives (which I continued), encouraging neighborhoods to write their own quality-of-life plans. Again, the Near Eastside was ahead of most everybody on this. Additionally, in most cities, there is a local chapter of the national nonprofit Local Initiatives Support Group (LISC), which helps communities with their development. Our local director was Bill Taft.

Mark Miles had remembered a presentation by the former NBA star and Sacramento mayor Kevin Johnson about neighborhood redevelopment.[3] Around the same time frame that the Super Bowl Host Committee was rethinking the legacy project, Bill Taft of LISC called Mark Miles to inquire whether the committee could help a neighborhood. Quite the coincidence. People who work with cities and neighborhoods know that there can never be some outside entity swooping in and saying, "We know what's best for you, and here it is." The change must be organic, home grown. It needs buy-in from the neighborhood itself. People in Indy already knew this.

The NFL loved the idea, the bid was ours, and the Near Eastside suddenly had many partners wanting to help. They were already organized, knew what they wanted, and were ready to receive the help. Millions in federal grants came, the Lilly Endowment contributed over $5 million, and United Way and the NFL added a million each. Businesses and foundations chipped in, as did individual donors. The host committee produced just under a million dollars to pay the salaries of three staff members, each with deep roots in the neighborhoods, to oversee the legacy project and to support a growing contingent of neighborhood-based organizations.

Over $150 million was invested in the area, changing it for the better to this day. Housing was upgraded both by rehabbing properties and building new affordable housing. Infrastructure like streets and sidewalks were upgraded. The Chase Legacy Center (as in JP Morgan Chase) was built—a 27,000-square-foot multipurpose center with a multimedia lab, a wellness facility, and the NFL Youth Education Town, among other components. Also included in the legacy center was programming from Big Brothers/Big Sisters, the YMCA, the Indianapolis Symphony Orchestra, and others. An NFL-quality artificial turf was installed at a nearby local high school, and its track was renovated.

In true Indianapolis fashion, our legacy project was complete before the game, unlike other legacy projects that usually start after the Super Bowl is played. I watched how this project developed over the years leading up to our Super Bowl. It was remarkable how enthusiastic everybody was on the Near Eastside. To see a change truly happening, not just window dressing, was fulfilling.

Best of all is a different feeling in the neighborhood. It is not an area managing decline. New relationships have been built; there is more of a supportive, neighborly atmosphere; and the area looks like a place where one would want to live. All endure to this day.

In an article by Bill Benner, Taylor remarked, "You can always judge the character of a man by how he treats those who can do nothing for him. Likewise, you can judge the Super Bowl Host Committee by this same standard. They had nothing to gain by partnering with us, yet chose to take a major risk in an ambitious endeavor that honestly could have failed. Once again, it's what separates us from other communities."

I agree.

Super Cure

Many people make connections in their minds, putting ideas together but then letting it end there. A select few have the initiative and tenacity to act. Allison Melangton is one of those people.

The Susan G. Komen for the Cure Tissue Bank (KTB) at the Indiana University Simon Cancer Center (as in the Indiana Pacers' owner Herb Simon) began collecting healthy breast tissue in 2007 and sharing those samples with researchers around the world. A Hoosier breast cancer advocate named Connie Rufenbarger had attended conferences where researchers discussed the lack of healthy breast tissue, surmising that healthy women would not donate to such an effort. Ms. Rufenbaeger disagreed. Connecting with Dr. Anna Maria Storniolo and Dr. Susan Clare, and with a $1 million grant from the Susan G. Komen for the Cure Research Grants and Awards program, they established the tissue bank in 2007.

As a result of this tissue bank, an incredible story developed. Kate Fagan, then working for espnW, wrote in 2012:

> Melangton's best friend, Traci Runge, was diagnosed with breast cancer in 2010. Upon learning her diagnosis, Runge immediately called the Komen for the Cure Tissue Bank (KTB) at the Indiana University Simon Cancer Center. She'd donated a healthy sample of breast tissue in 2007 after watching the mother of a girl she coached battle the disease for three years. After receiving her own ominous news, Runge felt compelled to donate a cancerous sample before receiving any treatment that might taint the tissue's clinical value. . . . "As I was laying on the table, they asked me if I had any idea of the impact of what I was doing that day," Runge said. "That's when they shared with me that I was the first person in the world, ever, to donate a healthy and then cancerous tissue."
>
> Runge couldn't believe it. When she shared the news with Melangton, her friend responded by saying, "We have to let the world know what we have here. It can make a difference around the world, not just in Indiana. . . . There are still people that don't know about this place."
>
> Many people don't know that KTB is the only repository in the world for normal breast tissue. And it's not just everyday people who don't know, but researchers around the world, people who could analyze this tissue and effect change.

Allison immediately brought KTB into the Super Bowl's powerful orbit. The local publicity for Super Cure was overwhelming, and the efforts of Super Cure added more than two thousand donations of healthy breast tissue. Super Cure stressed the need for tissue from a variety of different races and nationalities, and it worked, with a 46 percent minority donation rate, including that of my wife, Winnie, who is of Asian descent. "That's probably the single biggest degree of participation in a clinical trial by a minority population in this country," said Dr. Storniolo. The Super Bowl effort also raised well over a million dollars for the tissue bank. On one weekend alone, over seven hundred women donated tissue, which provided the center more samples than they normally collect in a year.

When people again questioned if women would donate healthy breast tissue, Dr. George Sledge, a researcher at the IU Simon Cancer Center, laughed. "They don't know Hoosier women," he said. "Every time we do this, we have to turn away women. . . . They don't want their daughters to get this disease."

Three other women have provided before-and-after samples since Runge did in 2010, and more are expected. Storniolo explained the breakthrough provided by Runge's dual samples—and future ones like it: "Between samples from two different people, there are differences—like height and hair color—that are just bystanders. There's noise that needs to be subtracted out . . . When you have one person's before and after, the noise cancels out and you're left with the true differences: What makes those two samples different? What happened to make normal go abnormal?"

This may be a key part of unlocking the mystery of breast cancer. Dr. Storniolo went on to say that if this proves true, then "it was the women of Indy who helped end breast cancer." That would be quite the legacy.

Allison and the rest of the people involved hope that Super Bowl XLVI will have played a role in the eventual cure for breast cancer.[4]

Super Scarves

Allison got the idea for Super Scarves from a friend who saw a similar idea at the Special Olympics in Idaho. The host committee knew that not everyone could attend the game, and Super Scarves was an idea to get more of the community involved. Again, there were some skeptics. After all, who would want to make scarves for complete strangers?

It was wildly successful. The host committee originally invested about $25,000 to buy enough yarn for some four thousand scarves. All the scarves were different, but all were done in blue and white, and the Indianapolis Super Bowl logo patch was knitted onto every scarf. Lessons were offered at local libraries for people who had not done this sort of thing before but wanted to learn. The committee was hoping to get enough scarves for the eight thousand volunteers—but it went well past that.

Each kit included a postcard for the creator of the scarf to include a note about themselves. One scarf maker wrote that the time knitting the scarf helped her keep calm while she sat next to her husband in the hospital. Another knitted a scarf during her kidney dialysis. There was one great-grandmother from Michigan City, Indiana, who knitted more than 250 scarves.

People who joined in went well past the stereotypical grandmother sitting in her rocking chair. Many people who had never knitted before took up the hobby, including prisoners. It caught on well beyond Indianapolis. Remarkably, volunteer knitters came from forty-five states and four foreign countries (England, Canada, South Africa, and Belgium).

In total, more than thirteen thousand scarves were made. Every volunteer received one, as did the first-line hospitality workers. Visitors from out of town, particularly media, tried to buy them from volunteers, but no one was selling. My wife and I still have ours, and I suspect almost everyone else still has theirs in a safe place.

It was one more item that united the city in the Super Bowl effort. The irony was that scarves are a cold-weather clothing item. The temperature for almost every day of the ten-day village run was in the sixties, but the volunteers and hospitality workers still wore them. It was a prized possession.[5]

Forty-Six Murals for XLVI

I have always loved murals in cities. I believe they add a nice touch to a city's culture. I have envied other cities that had prominent murals in high-profile locations. Indianapolis had a few, but I always wanted many more. I still do.

Like other organizations in the city, the arts community was attempting to figure out how they could provide impact for the Super Bowl. After my election night in 2007 when the arts community was upset at me through no fault of my own, I had worked hard to build their trust. I did have a minor lingering issue with the Arts Council, which always wanted more money for future projects. I tried to explain that most people fund specific projects, rather than just give money away in hopes that something will happen. In most cases, there must be an idea, something tangible, before people donate their hard-earned money.

My former deputy mayor for economic development, Michael Huber, a musician and singer himself, worked with the Arts Council on this. I knew they wanted to have some impact, and my love of large, visible murals was no secret to them.

One day Michael texted me something like "How about murals?" It did not take long for me to respond. The idea of commissioning forty-six murals for Super Bowl XLVI was born.

The Arts Council executed the program flawlessly. There were over one hundred submissions from all over the country, and forty-six were chosen from among thirty-four artists. The murals were placed throughout Indianapolis. Several were placed in the heart of downtown, including a now-famed mural of noted Indianapolis author Kurt Vonnegut.

It is always about more than the game, and the arts community stepped up big time.

There were many more programs associated with our Super Bowl. I will quickly summarize a few of the others.

Super Baskets of Hope—During Super Bowl weekend, baskets of goodies (toys, books, games, etc.), packaged by over nine hundred Indy volunteers at Bankers Life Fieldhouse (home of the NBA's Indiana Pacers), were delivered by NFL players and others to seven thousand hospitalized children in the thirty-two NFL cities. Tony Dungy—former Indianapolis Colts head coach and one of the finest men I have ever met—and the Riley Children's Foundation were involved. The Baskets of Hope program existed before, but the Indianapolis Super Bowl was the first time the Super Bowl was involved. The Super Baskets of Hope continues today.

Super Cars—Another example of the Indianapolis community coming together. The Indianapolis Motor Speedway put together thirty-three cars (the number of cars that compete each year in the Indianapolis 500) that represented the thirty-two NFL teams and the Indianapolis Super Bowl. These cars were displayed just off Monument Circle in the middle of downtown Indianapolis and near the Super Bowl Village. Visitors from out of town were mesmerized by this display.

First and Green—An environmental effort that included tree plantings, recycling programs, environmental education, and clean-up projects along with other efforts. Of note was an electronics recycling drive by Recycle Force (who hires only ex-offenders) and Second Helpings, a local nonprofit that recovered prepared foods from the Super Bowl week events.

Emerging Business—The NFL and the host committee helped minority- and women-owned businesses land contracts for the Super Bowl activities. If needed, they helped the businesses get certified by local and state government and coached them on presentation. Other organizations, including the NCAA and Visit Indy (the convention sales organization), were made aware of these businesses.

University of Indianapolis—This is a great private university on the south side of Indianapolis, where I became a visiting fellow after I left office. UIndy was the lucky recipient of the indoor practice facility that was built for the NFC champion (the AFC champion used the Colts' facility). As mentioned, the practice facilities had to be of similar quality, so this facility was built from scratch. It is being well used by the university.

There were so many additional activities that surrounded the Super Bowl that I cannot list them all here. There were the typical NFL events like the NFL Experience, the Hall of Fame Luncheon, and the owners' dinner. However, the Indianapolis host committee went way beyond what cities normally do. Besides those listed above, here a just a few additional highlights:

- First Super Bowl Social Media Center ever.
- Jimmy Fallon, for the first time ever, moved his show from New York. He is immensely talented and was great to the city. He had me on his show the last night and gave me a "Mayor" sash, reminiscent of the sash worn by the mayor on the TV show *The Simpsons*.
- More than fifteen thousand people were trained in "Super Service."
- Several thousand students across Indiana participated in community programs surrounding the Super Bowl.
- More than thirty-six thousand Super Welcome cards were placed in hotels to greet our guests. They were personal, handwritten notes from young schoolchildren, from every county in the state, telling the guests what they liked most about Indiana.
- Some 3,800 people attended the Health Fair.
- There were more than five thousand credentialed media.
- ESPN broadcast 110 hours from the Pan Am Plaza in downtown Indianapolis.
- The Super Bowl website received in excess of 4.5 million unique visits.
- The ease of entry into our Super Bowl was the best ever. Long lines of two hours or more are common at Super Bowls. In Indianapolis, it was about fifteen to thirty minutes.

There were two aspects to the Super Bowl that received no mention as far as I could tell. First, even though people were in the village until 2:00 or 3:00 a.m. on some nights—and most nights had about one hundred thousand people in the village—by 7:00 a.m. the next day Georgia Street was spotless. Clean as a whistle. David Sherman, our public-works director, ensured this every day. I was there near 7:00 a.m. most days, checking out if anything had happened in the village, and I was in awe of the job the public-works people did in keeping the village in such pristine condition day after day.

Another noteworthy item that never got mentioned: there were zero homicides in the city during the ten days of the Super Bowl celebration. Indianapolis is like any other major city, with violence issues that can happen at any time. However, Indy is lucky in having Reverend Charles Harrison leading the Indianapolis Ten Point Coalition, a group of ex-offenders who patrol many streets at night and convince the bad guys on those streets to do less harm to themselves and the city they live in. We worked with Ten Point closely throughout my administration; they have close ties on the street and can talk straight to the mostly young men who commit the violence in the city. Reverend Harrison put out the word that he would like to see no violence during the ten days of the Super Bowl celebration. We did not have one homicide during this time frame.

Thanks to the success of our Super Bowl, the NFL staff asked us to resubmit for the 2018 Super Bowl. We were not expecting that, but the NFL thinking of returning to the same cold-weather city so soon shows just how impressed everyone in the football world was with our efforts. We submitted another excellent bid, with an even more robust fan experience, but it was not to be. I believe we came in third on the bid, which was won by Minneapolis. This is when our organizing team knew for sure what many suspected: there is an unstated policy in the NFL to bring Super Bowls to cities that have new publicly financed stadiums. Minneapolis did not even have a shovel in the ground yet for their new stadium, but they won the bid. We were OK with the decision, proud that the NFL recognized our efforts.

Was It Worth It?

I was told before the Super Bowl to not expect any long-term economic benefit to the city. There would be immediate economic benefit, as detailed below, but cities usually see no long-term effect.

That was not true for Indianapolis. Visit Indy, our convention organization, has been strong for decades, and with over $3 billion in annual convention business, Indy already was known as a terrific convention city. The area has more than seventy thousand hospitality workers and many great downtown hotels (the Conrad, Marriott, Sheraton, etc.) and restaurants. Our downtown has always been rated highly in the nation. We knew what we were doing before the Super Bowl.

However, after our Super Bowl, the convention folks told me that they had 1,100 more leads on conventions than before the big event. That is a huge number. The combination of the overwhelmingly favorable image of the city as portrayed in regular and social media, along with the addition of the large JW Marriott hotel, helped in this. Indianapolis benefited from hosting the Super Bowl even after the game.

However, there was also great economic impact during the event. The Super Bowl Host Committee hired Rockport Analytics to do an economic impact study for the Indianapolis Metropolitan Area for Super Bowl XLVI.

There were about 116,000 visitors who came to Indianapolis for the game and related activities. Hotel occupancy for the four days leading to the Super Bowl was 99 percent for downtown hotels and 93 percent for the area.

Total gross spending for Super Bowl XLVI was $384 million, with $342 million of that amount coming from people and businesses living outside the Indianapolis area. When the displacement numbers (normal tourism spending, based on the previous four years' average, that would have occurred without the Super Bowl being in town) are calculated, these numbers become $337 million net spending, with $295 million coming from outside the Indianapolis area.

These are conservative numbers, as events such as the NFL Experience and the Super Bowl Village activities were not included. Rockport also did not calculate the financial impact of the capital spending and community outreach on related activities, such as the Georgia Street renovations and its continued impact on downtown, the human impact of Super Cure, or the $150 million impact of the Legacy Project, along with other projects.

Total tax receipts, using the displacement formula, were over $36 million in federal tax receipts, almost $22 million in state tax receipts, and over $18 million in local tax receipts. There was overtime paid to public-works and public-safety personnel, but not anywhere close to these numbers. State and local government revenue was positive.

Rockport and a third-party vendor, Vocus, calculated the media exposure for Indianapolis to be worth $8.4 million. That is a big number. Vocus also found that of the 2,100 media exposures, 99.9 percent were positive. Only three were scored as neutral, and *there were no negative mentions.* These numbers are incredible. They also mentioned that, at the time, Super Bowl XLVI was the most-watched television event in history, with almost 167 million viewers; 71 percent of the TVs turned on at the time in the country were watching the game.

Rockport calculated the future convention economic impact or the "halo effect." They mentioned the incredible number of possible future leads and room nights. For one fiscal quarter alone, they estimated the impact would be between $81 million and $169 million.

What was most heartwarming about all this increased economic activity was that the hospitality workers, from what they told me, received three or four months' worth of rent and mortgage payments in this ten-day period. Of course, businesses profited well above average also, ensuring increased employment for their workers. When you add in the increased potential for future convention revenue, the effect of Super Bowl XLVI was tremendous for the hospitality workers in the Indianapolis area.

I went to the airport the day after the Super Bowl to see some fans off, though no one in particular. I went up to them and asked if they had a good time. They could not believe the mayor was there asking how they were doing and if they had a good time. It solidified in their mind that Indianapolis did things differently from other cities. It was a magical time for the city and the state.

However, so much of the goodwill and public relations gains that Indianapolis received during this period were about to be undone by a misguided, harmful piece of legislation at the statehouse just a few years later.

Notes

1. From that additional list, I would like to see Ryan White's marker go up someday. Ryan, from Kokomo, contracted AIDS in 1984 at the age of thirteen after a blood transfusion. This was in the early stages of AIDS when the world was just learning about this then-fatal disease. Ryan's quest just to attend school with his friends became a national story. He died in 1990 at the age of eighteen, but not before the country and the world learned much more about AIDS because of him. Just after his death, Congress, in August 1990, passed legislation bearing his name: the Ryan White Comprehensive AIDS Resources Emergency (CARE) Act.

2. Much of the narrative here came from a Bill Benner article in the Host Committee's postgame publication *More Than a Game*.

3. Kevin, while contemplating his run for mayor of Sacramento, visited me in my first month in office to ask how I had won. It was fascinating that someone like him would come to get advice from someone like me, who was nobody just six months prior. Both of us were interested in the education of urban children, and when he won his race, we became friends. He eventually became president of the US Conference of Mayors.

4. Much of this narrative came from an article by Lori Roberts in the Host Committee's postgame publication *More Than a Game*.

5. Much of this section also came from a Lori Roberts article in the Host Committee's postgame publication *More Than a Game*.

20

RFRA

The Religious Freedom Law That Was Not about Religious Freedom

LATE IN 2014, I ANNOUNCED that I was not running again for mayor. I made it clear to everyone I could that I was physically and mentally exhausted, and that I would not make a good third-term mayor. My energy level would not be where it needed to be. Citizens deserve a mayor who is "all in," and I was afraid I could not be that kind of mayor anymore.

I knew no one in my administration was going to coast that last year, but I did not anticipate that the state legislature would pass a bill (and that the governor would sign) that would position Indiana nationally as a bigoted state. It made for the most difficult ten days of my tenure in office as I had to publicly spar with people I considered friends.

Some (maybe much) of that friction continues to this day. However, as the saying goes, "I had to do what I had to do." Even now, there are still those who claim nothing bad happened, but they are wrong. There are still some effects today, but what could have happened, if not for the very robust public and private pushback to this bill, would have been much, much worse.

Part of the tragedy of the Religious Freedom Restoration Act (RFRA) was that there was no precipitating event. There was not a religious freedom incident. There was not a restaurant that made the news for its treatment of the LGBT community (which would be unusual in Indianapolis). The LGBT community was not in an uproar about any particular subject. Indianapolis was doing its usual magnificent work with conventions. The Final Four was around the corner. All was calm. But for some reason, the legislature desired to please their religious supporters with a deceptive bill.

Background

I believe that most people who enter public service through elected office do so for the right reasons. Some are led astray by perks of the office and by people treating them deferentially, but I liked almost everyone I worked with in the Indiana legislature and believed they meant well. There are parts of legislative action that I do not like but seem common and accepted. I am probably too straightforward in my approach to serve in a legislative capacity.

Over the previous few years, some members of the state legislature had kept trying to add an anti–gay marriage amendment into the Indiana constitution. There were three religious groups that pushed this effort. We knew that these groups were close to many of the legislators, but now, unfortunately, they also had the ear of the governor, Mike Pence.

Although this may seem odd to some, Mike Pence is the nicest person I ever met in politics. He is true to himself and his beliefs. You could disagree with his beliefs and policies, but he would still ask how you and your family are and mean it sincerely.

To pass an amendment to the Indiana constitution requires that the amendment must pass using the exact same language by two separately elected legislatures. This means that there must be an election between the two votes so that two different legislatures vote on it, somewhat assuring that the amendment has firm support throughout the state over a period of time.

The first vote for the amendment passed in 2011 with overwhelming Republican support. This helped to solidify the Republican religious right base but had no practical effect. The next vote with the new legislature came in 2014. However, the language was slightly modified, narrowing its focus, but also starting the clock over to place an anti–gay marriage amendment into the Indiana constitution. Both these votes were uncomfortable to many urban Republicans, as the average citizen was starting to openly question why gays could not marry. People's views on this issue across the nation were rapidly changing.

The second vote with the slightly modified language in 2014 was a maneuver that allowed Republicans to once again say to their religious right base that they had voted to prevent gays from marrying, but the practical effect backfired on them. The religious right advocates were now frustrated that the Indiana legislature seemed not to be serious, and certainly not in a hurry to put an anti–gay marriage amendment into the constitution. The legislature had kicked the can down the road and might do so again if necessary.[1]

As happens in most every state, if groups cannot get their legislation passed one way, a new angle is tried. These religious groups and their supportive legislators wanted to please their base constituency. Since the gay marriage prohibition was clearly not going to become an amendment to the Indiana constitution soon, something else inhibiting freedom for gays was needed for these groups. It was just part of their agenda. Thus, the Religious Freedom Restoration Act was devised.

Ryan Vaughn, my former chief of staff and the former president of the city-county council, was now the head of the Indiana Sports Corp., an organization that would be negatively affected by this legislation. He put it to me in a way that has made the most sense to me ever since. He said to me, "Why would the party that believes in limited government want to regulate the primary personal relationship of anyone?"

Republicans must answer this question for themselves. Is it individual liberty and limited government you believe in, or is it more important to control the personal lives of people you do not even know? Is personal, private behavior a matter for God or for the government?

In fairness, I do not believe I have ever witnessed in my lifetime a political or social issue that turned as quickly in people's minds as gay marriage and the public acceptance of gays in the military. When I joined the Marines in 1978, LGBT individuals were not officially allowed in the military, but everyone knew they were in the services and had been for decades. Most everyone accepted that fact and them individually. They were hiding their orientation, but the attitude in the services was "Do your job, and you're fine." Also, gay marriage was not the norm even when I retired from the Marines in 2001. Some states were still passing anti–gay marriage laws, such as Nevada in 2002. At the federal level, as usual, it was the courts, not Congress, that would determine the direction of this social issue.

To understand how RFRA happened, one must understand how most legislatures work. I am frequently asked about legislative actions and particular legislators. I have always been kind to them because they are criticized often by constituents who expect them to be well versed in dozens if not hundreds of issues, when in reality they are usually well versed in only two or three issues. They rely on the advice of fellow legislators who are expert in other areas to give them guidance on how to vote. Even before a vote is taken in committee and then on the floor, the leaders of the legislative bodies (the House and the Senate) look to guidance from these experts to help determine the ultimate direction of a particular bill.

For instance, there was one wonderful, respected long-term senator, a former nurse, from the south side of Indianapolis who knew the medical field inside and out. If she said, "This bill is good to go," then that bill got passed. If she did not like a particular bill, it usually did not make it out of committee. This reality of legislatures played a part in the passage of the horrible RFRA.

Ten Difficult Days

I rarely took long vacations. I believe that a mayor is always on duty. The Marines taught me this. A commanding officer is responsible for everything his people do or fail to do and is always responsible for the organization, even on vacation. In March 2015, my wife and I took what was only our second week-long vacation out of Indiana (other than Christmastime). Just before I left, I was hearing rumors that the legislature was again attempting to pass a discriminatory bill, but most of the people around me did not think it would pass. This one was called the Religious Freedom Restoration Act, but many knew the bill to be discriminatory (when combined with other Indiana code) and not about religious freedom. Surely the legislature would understand this.

Not long after Winnie and I were in Florida, my staff became worried that this bill might pass. If I recall the timeline correctly, it passed both houses by Tuesday. On Wednesday, my communications director, Jen Ensley, called me and told me something that was hard to believe. If I, as the mayor of Indianapolis, did not put out a press release *that day*, repudiating the Religious Freedom Restoration Act, then Gen Con, a tabletop gaming organization and our largest convention at the time (sixty thousand to seventy thousand attendees then), would pull out of Indianapolis.

Gen Con had been in Indianapolis since 2003, and its attendees, sponsors, and everyone else associated with the convention loved coming to Indianapolis. We loved having them, as it was a fun convention for everybody and provided a nice economic boost to the city and state. I loved going to it just to see everyone have a good time in our city. However, their sponsors and attendees were furious with the passage of RFRA. They were pulling out. Immediately.

This was serious. Indianapolis had been rated the best convention city in America in 2014 by *USA Today.* Indy had a sterling reputation in the convention industry; it was not only the connected infrastructure downtown but also the wonderful way that we treated visitors, as highlighted in the Super Bowl chapter above. We did not have the largest facilities in the country, but they were large enough to have a significant economic impact on the city and the state. Hospitality was a more than a $3 billion industry annually, not the largest industry in central Indiana but still a sizeable piece of the local economy. More than seventy thousand people in the area were employed by the hospitality industry.

This was all now in jeopardy. If our largest convention was pulling out even before the bill became law (with the governor's signature), what were all the other organizers of future conventions and sports events thinking?

My main thought through this ten-day period was this: "This city has been built up over the last forty years to a point that almost no one could have believed, and it's all going away in a matter of weeks." It was not just the national media that was pressing down hard on us, but most large conventions from out of state were calling to say they were pulling out. The NCAA was threatening to pull all their future sporting events (which was a lot of events) other than the Final Four, which was the next weekend, and I was receiving phone calls from my fellow mayors around the country who were saying something like, "I love you, Greg, but I must tell you that I am not allowing anyone on city business to visit Indiana. Sorry, that's just the way it is."

Several governors also forbade any travel to Indiana. The well-earned reputation for hospitality would be gone, tens of thousands of jobs would be gone, our status for being the city that was best at hosting the most prestigious sports events, gone. I felt the weight on my shoulders of all that the previous mayors had accomplished, all the way back to Richard Lugar in the 1960s. All that those former mayors and their corporate and nonprofit partners had done to raise the image and economy of the city over the last forty years was in jeopardy. Some did not believe that—almost no one in the statehouse did—but it was happening, and it was happening fast.

If you read the bill by itself, it seems harmless. However, when combined with language already in Indiana law, the bill could be interpreted as discriminatory against the LGBT community. Lots of people knew this, and legislators were told this before the vote, but somehow the legislators who voted for this bill were convinced that was not the case. As I mentioned earlier, if a trusted colleague says about a bill, "It is good to go," then they vote that way. Any suggestion of this bill being discriminatory was characterized as a left-wing political hit job or liberal media hype.

The legislators believed the bill was about religious freedom only. Even the governor publicly stated that this bill was the same bill that President Clinton signed at the federal level. But the people initiating the bill knew otherwise, and they got this bill through committees, onto the House and Senate floors, and onto the governor's desk. There's a saying about the Indiana legislature (and probably others) that it takes a few years to pass a good bill, but it takes only one year to pass a bad bill. RFRA was the latter.

The governor signed the bill on Thursday. By that time, I had cut my vacation short and was driving back from the south of Florida, leaving early Thursday morning and arriving home at 2:00 a.m. on Friday. At ten o'clock Friday morning, I was in the governor's office, not with the governor but with two of his closest advisors, both friends of mine and steadfast, high-character men. It was clear they thought no harm was done.

I asked them about a picture on social media. Their response was, "What about the picture?" They really did not know. As I was driving back, my wife was scrolling through Twitter and found a picture that seemed like a *Saturday Night Live* skit. My wife did not grow up in America and sometimes does not understand much of American nuance, but she showed the picture to me, and even she asked me if this was from a *Saturday Night Live* skit. I found out later that even legislators in the statehouse thought it looked as such.

The picture is of the bill being signed with the governor sitting at his desk, pen in hand, with about twenty religious leaders, including nuns in habit, surrounding him. It was not a public bill signing; the press was not there because the bill had become too much of a very public, very negative story. A supporter of the bill posted the photo on Facebook, and it found its way to Twitter. Considering how many people were feeling about this bill and the uproar around the country, the picture was completely tone deaf. One of my friends called it "jarring."

The reaction to the bill being signed was swift and overwhelming:

- Nine CEOs from major companies in the state—Angie's List, Salesforce Marketing Cloud, Anthem Inc., Eli Lilly and Company, Cummins, Emmis Communications, Roche Diagnostics, Indiana University Health, and Dow AgroSciences—called on the Republican leadership at the statehouse to enact legislation to prevent discrimination based upon sexual orientation or gender identity. Angie's List was now openly questioning the $40 million expansion of its Indianapolis-based headquarters because of concerns over the law. Also, there was massive local pushback to RFRA by individuals and groups led by Freedom Indiana, the LGBT advocacy organization, that was funded by the most prominent companies in Indiana.
- National CEOs joined in. Marc Benioff, CEO of Salesforce, a prominent employer in Indianapolis, described the bill as an "outrage" and announced that the company would cancel all programs that require customers or employees to travel to Indiana. (Both the governor and I were talking to Benioff throughout these ten days; what I was hearing from the governor speaking publicly about Salesforce was different from my conversations with Benioff.) Tim Cook, CEO of Apple, said he was "deeply disappointed" in the law. Yelp CEO Jeremy Stoppelman stated, it "is unconscionable to imagine that Yelp would create, maintain, or expand a significant business presence in any state that encouraged discrimination by businesses against our employees, or consumers at large." PayPal cofounder Max Levchin told CNN that opposing the law is "a basic human decency issue," and said, "I'm asking my fellow CEOs to look at how they're thinking about their relationship with the state and evaluate it in terms of the legislation that's getting signed into law." Warren Buffett stated that if the law "could in any way be prejudicial to gays or lesbians, I'd be opposed to that."
- Virtually every business I talked to, particularly our national and global businesses, both during this time frame and months later, was greatly worried that they would not be able to attract talent to the state and Indianapolis in particular. I heard many times of individual cases where a company wanted to hire someone or transfer them in, but the employee or spouse did not want to move to Indiana.
- Our universities chimed in. Mitch Daniels, the former Republican governor of Indiana and former president of Purdue University, stated that his university was opposed to any governmental measure that interferes with their antidiscrimination policy. James Danko, the president of Butler University, called the bill

"ill-conceived legislation at best" and commented, "No matter your opinion of the law, it is hard to argue with the fact it has done significant damage to our state." Michael McRobbie, president of Indiana University, called on the government to "reconsider this unnecessary legislation" and added, "the damage already done to Indiana's reputation is such that all public officials and public institutions in our state need to reaffirm our absolute commitment to the Hoosier values of fair treatment and non-discrimination." I know that many universities lost incoming students (and their tuition) because of this bill.

- The sports community chimed in. The NBA, the WNBA, the Indiana Pacers, and the Indiana Fever collectively put out a joint statement that read: "We will continue to ensure that all fans, players, and employees feel welcome at all NBA and WNBA events in Indiana and elsewhere." USA Track & Field stated they were "deeply concerned" by the bill. Mark Emmert, president of the NCAA, which is headquartered in Indianapolis, issued a statement that expressed concern at how student-athletes, employees, and visitors would be treated and said they "intend to closely examine the implications of this bill and how it might affect future events as well as our workforce." Arn Tellem stated that the bill "codifies hatred under the smoke screen of freedom and jeopardizes all that has been recently accomplished" and called for sports organizers to reevaluate their short- and long-term plans in the state. The four head coaches of the teams coming to the Final Four—Bo Ryan, John Calipari, Tom Izzo, and Mike Krzyzewski—released a statement though the National Association of Basketball Coaches that stated that "discrimination of any kind should not be tolerated." Charles Barkley described the bill as "unacceptable." NASCAR stated, "We will not embrace nor participate in exclusion or intolerance."

Indy is a turnkey city in America for sports, with both the physical and human infrastructure in place to hold almost any event. We are the only city that routinely hosts Final Fours. We earned the designation of hosting the most fan-friendly, best organized, and most innovative Super Bowl ever. National championships in many sports and Olympic trials are common. National governing bodies and the NCAA are in Indianapolis. We were the first city in the nation with a sports commission, the Indiana Sports Corp. Sports matter to us. All this was now in jeopardy with the passage of RFRA.

The local newspaper, the *Indianapolis Star*, used almost all of page one to say "Fix This Now" in bold white letters against a black background. This is very unusual for any newspaper in the country but demonstrates just how dire most saw this situation.

All the living former mayors in Indianapolis (three of the four being Republican) and I, in a combined statement, called on the legislature to repeal the law. I put out a separate statement calling on the legislature to repeal the law or to add in protections for sexual orientation and gender identity, and to allow those cities that had local human rights ordinances (Indianapolis being one of them) to be exempt from this law.

A few conventions canceled, but thankfully the majority took a wait-and-see approach. It was important that I, as the Republican mayor of the capital city, was out front nationally saying, "This is not who we are." If the bill stood as written, the convention business would have been devastated.

Later the same Friday that I returned from Florida, the governor called a meeting for 4:00 p.m. to discuss the situation. The local and national media were now overwhelming in their condemnation. In addition, almost all the sectors of our economy were making their voices heard. I was at the meeting, both the state and local chambers of commerce were there, the convention people were there, and so was the Sports Corp. Of note, no legislator was present, but the House and Senate each sent an attorney to this meeting. There were a few others, but I cannot recall who they were.

Since I was the mayor of the capital city, I started the meeting by saying that I and others were worried about the effect of this bill on our reputation and economy. Other attendees said similar things, but with such details as what conventions were saying to Visit Indy, the effect on future sports events, what the businesses around the state were hearing, etc. It was clear that the governor thought all this was media hype and that the bill was sound.

Then, one attendee mentioned that the website of one of the three religious groups had words to the effect of "We won. We don't have to serve gays anymore." The already low-key, respectful meeting fell into an awkward silence. It was a devastating comment that exposed the real truth behind the bill.

During the meeting, the same question was asked four times in slightly different ways. "If a gay couple goes out to eat in Indianapolis, can they be denied service?" The refusal to answer, particularly from the lawyers representing the House and Senate, spoke volumes. The governor never answered that question either. Did they know, or not know, the answer to that question?

The governor closed the meeting by telling all of us that "If we just stay silent on this subject over the weekend, this will all blow over. It will go away." He still did not understand what was happening. His closed bubble of advisors was leading him astray.

The governor did not take his own advice. He went on a national news show on Sunday morning, where he was interviewed by George Stephanopoulos. During that interview, Stephanopoulos respectfully asked him that same question six more times in some fashion or another, yet the governor refused to answer. He just kept saying the bill was not about discrimination. Did he not know? I know that he had been briefed over the weekend that the main subject of the interview would be discrimination against gays, but he ignored that, trusting other advice and believing he could turn the interview to the religious freedom aspect.

Very soon after the Stephanopoulos interview, I texted one of my most trusted political friends saying, "That was a disaster." He concurred. Everyone in Indiana concurred. The next week, which included the Final Four, was going to be very difficult.

After this text exchange with my friend, I called a senior member of the House with whom I had a good relationship. I told him that if the legislature does not solve this on Monday morning, then "it won't be your enemies coming after you; it will be your friends."

His response stunned me. His family is associated with a wonderful, impactful charity in Indianapolis, but his chairwoman had resigned within the last two days, just before a major fundraiser for the charity on Saturday night, the night before I called him. She resigned because of RFRA. He was upset. However, he then accused me of being involved with her resignation. I told him, "I do not even know who your chairwoman is."

Stunned, I did not know what to think. Then it hit me suddenly. The Republicans in the statehouse thought that I had been part of orchestrating the outrage over RFRA.

Where did that come from? Before I went on vacation, I did not think the bill would get passed; it was not on my mind very much at all. It got through the legislature while I was in Florida, and I was on my way back from Florida when it was signed. When could I have generated any outrage? I did put out the press release the previous Wednesday to save Gen Con but did nothing else publicly. Plus, almost everyone who knows me understands that my generating outrage would be out of character. I certainly was trying to mitigate the damage already caused by RFRA because the central Indiana economy was in danger, but at this point I certainly was not leading the charge, hyping up the media and other people.

That was soon to change.

After the governor's interview on Sunday, the House leadership contacted prominent business leaders in central Indiana to help solve the problem. Legislative leadership now realized they screwed up, were panicking, and knew they had to make this go away. This was also when the legislative leadership took complete charge, no longer paying attention to the governor or anyone from his office. Such was the effect of the Stephanopoulos interview.

The business leaders formed an ad hoc group and had a war room at the Indy chamber office. For days, they met for long hours and sometimes into the evening, helping to devise an acceptable solution. Discussions ranged from just getting Indiana out of the national news to crafting a state policy that would address all the concerns of the LGBT community. This group proved important to an eventual solution.

On that Monday morning, on the advice of my staff, I canceled a planned trip to northern Indiana. They felt that I would be needed that day and that I should stay close to home. They were right. In Indiana, I was the most prominent Republican who opposed the passage of RFRA. Since there is only one major city in Indiana, the mayor of the capital city has outsized importance in the state. People listen to what the Indianapolis mayor has to say.

The legislature did nothing tangible to correct the situation on Monday. I knew that the Republicans who had helped build the city over the last forty years were not happy and were doing all they could behind closed doors to undo what the legislature and governor had done. My team and I decided to hold a press conference at 2:00 p.m., to call on the legislature and the governor to fix this dire situation. The convention business and the sports business were already in panic mode; the organizers of future events scheduled for Indianapolis were making their feelings clear about the passage of RFRA. They were going to pull their events if nothing was done, meaning millions of dollars lost for the city and the state along with the thousands of workers who would not be able to work those events. Most in the legislature still thought it was all a façade, empty rhetoric, but it was not. As mentioned, I also had my fellow mayors from around the country calling me telling me they had forbidden travel to the state.

My career in the Marines helped greatly during this time. "What is the right thing to do?" is always paramount in my mind. The right thing in this case was clear, but so many of my fellow Republicans could not see it. Also, there are certain things that a leader must do himself; delegating is not an option. No one else in the state of Indiana could have held a live press conference, publicly standing up to the legislature and the governor, that would have had major effect. I had to do it. And I did.

Within the hour before I held the press conference, I received phone calls from both the House and the Senate leadership (again, people I considered friends) asking me to not hold the press conference. They had found out I was doing it and did not want the additional pressure from the mayor of the capital city. I told both that I would lighten up on some phrases, and I did. But anyone who watches that press conference on YouTube today would not think I lightened up.

Standing behind me at the press conference was as diverse a collection of political persuasions as one could find. Ryan Vaughn, former Republican president of the Indianapolis City-County Council, my former chief of staff, and then head of the Sports Corp; Bill Oesterle, a prominent Republican donor and business owner; Jane Henegar, the executive director of the American Civil Liberties Union of Indiana; Tony Mason, the head of the Indianapolis Urban League; and many others stood behind me as I delivered my short but very direct remarks. It was carried live by every TV station in Indianapolis and was also carried live on a national outlet (CNN, I believe).

I talked about how Indianapolis had worked for the past forty years to be an open, welcoming, and inclusive city, and that RFRA "threatens what thousands of people have spent decades building." I told all those attending the Final Four that weekend that they would be extended the Hoosier hospitality that visitors to Indianapolis have come to expect. I talked about talent recruitment and added that I had issued an executive order affirming that "any entity receiving public funds from the city of Indianapolis must agree to abide by the terms of our city's human rights ordinance." The executive order also urged the legislature and the governor to add "sexual orientation and gender identity as protected classes in state law."

I said, "Discrimination is wrong, and I hope that message is being heard loud and clear at our statehouse." I am quite sure that the members of the statehouse were furious at that statement, but I did not care. They had yet to concede that they passed a discriminatory law, still believing the lie that the bill was about religious freedom. I called on Governor Pence and the legislature to "fix this law" and to "do so immediately." I used the phrase "Indy welcomes all," which became the rallying cry and was soon emblazoned on a sticker displayed by almost every retail business in Indianapolis within days.

The leaders in the statehouse were not happy at being called out so directly; again, I did not care as my city and others were being ravaged by this discriminatory law. It was bringing national shame to our state, and the hospitality workers in central Indiana and other areas around the state were feeling the effect.

I spent the rest of the week on national TV and radio explaining my (and most of my citizens') position while members of the governor's staff were doing the same on their position. It really did not matter what the governor's folks were saying; the legislature and I both knew by this time that the law would not stand for long, as both the local and national outcry became deafening. The governor's people were in an untenable position, yet they held on, still believing it was media hype.

My very visible national interviews proved important. Many conventions that were considering pulling out did not do so because Visit Indy (our convention organization) was calling them, essentially saying, "Look at what the Indianapolis mayor is saying. This law is not who we are." Also, while I was doing the national interviews, those business leaders and other longtime prominent Republicans, those who really had built up the city in the last forty years, were spending time behind closed doors in the statehouse, essentially saying to the House and Senate leadership and the rank and file, "What the hell are you guys doing?"

I suspect this had enormous influence on the legislature, as these longtime Republicans were the very people who set the table and raised the money for all those legislators to hold office.

One meeting that I heard about was the head of the local Salesforce team (Indy has the second-largest Salesforce organization in the country, behind only San Francisco), talking to the speaker and the senate president pro tem and telling them that "tech is gay." I have been told "their jaws dropped." Of course, one cannot take that phrase literally, but it did tell the legislative leadership that the tech community is behind gay rights and was not taking this law well. I knew that personally because of my talks with Marc Benioff, the CEO of Salesforce, throughout the week.

Benioff was unhappy with what was happening. It reflected poorly on his company to be in a state with a law such as RFRA. I know he was also talking to the governor, but again, what I was hearing directly from Benioff differed from the governor's public interpretations of his conversations with Benioff. Benioff offered to host a discussion on the subject, which I thought was a good idea, but that quickly morphed into holding a concert with a huge name the Thursday before the Final Four. (I cannot remember exactly who, but I believe it was Bono.) He was willing to put this together on very little notice, literally two to three days. One must wonder how anyone could do this, but Benioff has those sorts of connections, money, and power. I did not doubt for an instant that he could and would do this. However, the NCAA was not happy with the idea of a concert, as it would take the focus away from their premier annual event, the Final Four. For a few hours, I was in an awkward position, but fortunately, Chris Gahl, one of the senior leaders for Visit Indy who knew what I was doing all week and sensed my awkward position said, "I'll take care of it." And he did. We did not have the concert, but that would have been something to see.

On Tuesday, the governor, finally sensing the damage that was occurring, held a press conference demanding a solution by Friday, but as mentioned, the legislative leadership was ignoring the governor at this point. He was out of the solution loop.

The legislature did not rescind the law but passed another law saying that any local ordinance could override the state law. That way the law could stand but be of little effect; this was a typical political solution for those who wanted to maintain their ideological position. Indianapolis and other cities already had ordinances in place that could override the new law and several more cities passed similar ordinances within weeks. The irony of this is that the Indiana legislature is famous for passing state laws that squelch local laws the legislature does not like. Here they did exactly the opposite to salvage some dignity.

The legislative leaders held a press conference on Friday to announce "the fix." I was obviously not invited. I watched it from my office and found some of the speakers to be too casual with national cameras in their face, not realizing just how serious a matter this was. The bill was sent to the governor's office for signature and—unbelievably to me and others—the governor sat on it for hours. There was much speculation as to why this occurred, but I cannot contemplate what he was thinking.

In the early evening that Friday, I was at an event with the Final Four coaches and sports commentator Jim Nantz. (Because of the uproar, I had personally welcomed the coaches and their teams upon their arrival to Indianapolis a few days prior.) Now I was wondering if the governor was going to sign the fix. Some thought he would not sign it in hopes of protecting his future political ambitions. Not signing it would have been disastrous for Indiana. He did sign it in midevening, then quietly boarded a plane to Europe for a family vacation.

During this entire ten-day episode, phone calls about RFRA kept coming into the office. Like in most major cities, sometimes issues crop up that draw attention well past local interest. For this one, the organized religious right across the nation flooded our phone lines. We had two ladies who routinely took such calls and emails, usually from constituents. America has benefited from the religious nature of its people, but the barrage of calls from the religious right had one of those ladies in tears for days as they spewed their venom.

We had heard their viciousness before on a more minor issue, but this time it was horrible beyond belief. "Damning you to the fires of hell" was a benign comment compared to most of what they said. It was hardly Christian-like. Of all the groups who called in to constituent services over the eight years of my administration, the organized religious right was easily the worst, most contemptible group of calls that we received.

Aftermath

My relationship with the legislators and the governor remained cordial but distant; it has never been the same. What bothers me most about this is that my actions had given them time and cover to fix the problem. My national visibility that second week was holding off the cancellations of conventions and sporting events while the business community and prominent Republicans worked with the legislature to solve the problem.

It does not matter at this point. I had to do what was right to save my city, and in this case, also the state, since central Indiana accounts for a full third of economic activity in the state. My visibility in saying, "Indy welcomes all" was important, but lots of prominent people helped.

Some feelings remain raw to this day. A couple of years after I left office, a brilliant former member of my administration interviewed for a position with the state senate. The first question was "Weren't you a member of the Ballard administration during RFRA?" He did not get the job—but he is making a lot more money doing other things now. Indianapolis did lose tens of millions of dollars in convention business, but this was a small amount compared to what could have happened.

I was asked to be the grand marshal of the Gay Pride Parade in Indianapolis shortly after the RFRA debacle. I could not have imagined being asked to do this just a few months before. In fact, no mayor, Republican or Democrat, had ever been the grand marshal before, and here I was, a Republican, being asked to do so. I graciously accepted. I had been to the Gay Pride Festival (which follows the parade) in past years, which has well over fifty thousand attendees every year. I had been treated mostly cordially, but sometimes I was the subject of vitriol because I was a Republican. That said, many Republicans participate in the parade and attend the festival annually. The county party also had a presence while I was the mayor. Urban Republicans understand this; other Republicans do not. It was important for people to realize that the real intent of RFRA did not represent Indianapolis.

As mayor, you represent everyone in the city, not just those who voted for you.

The Lesson

Many Republicans today say they believe in the notions of individual liberty and limited government—true conservative principles. However, RFRA was a textbook example of Republicans going against conservative principles; instead, they wanted to tell people how to live their lives, something they criticize the Democrats of doing routinely. The religious right's influence on the party seems to drive much of this.

The chilling effect on our LGBT community is also one example of many Republicans failing to understand talent attraction. As I have said previously, unlike when I grew up, the talent now moves to where they want to live based on the quality of life of the area. This is basic to understanding economic development. LGBT rights are part of that quality of life that talent seeks. Legislation like RFRA hampers a city's ability to attract talent, thereby hampering the expansion of a city's tax base. Too many Republicans believe that tax breaks are the only thing that matters for businesses and do not realize that without a talented workforce available, no business is moving to a city or state, no matter what tax breaks are available. Businesses move to or expand to where the talent is. That's the baseline, not tax breaks.

Note

1. The US Supreme Court ruled in June 2015 that gay marriage was legal across the nation, rendering the Indiana amendment moot.

21

NEXT STEPS

At noon on January 1, 2016, my eight years as mayor were over. By 9:00 a.m., Winnie and I were driving west to Santa Barbara, California, for rest and relaxation. Our son lives in Los Angeles (one and a half hours south of Santa Barbara), and weirdly we spent only a couple of days with him. Such was my state of mind; I wanted to be alone as much as possible.

It was a typical introvert's recharging period, only on a much deeper level. The feeling was similar to a military change of command, where you are in charge of everything for a period of time; then, when the guidon is handed to the new commander, all responsibility and accountability is passed on. Only this time, I did not feel like it had left me at all. In fact, it took about four months before I felt like the mayor's office was in different hands—that the responsibility was not on me anymore. I was all in for eight years, putting in enormous hours and mental effort, and it had worn on me. I needed to rest and then get on with whatever my future would be, but physical and mental rest were what I needed at this moment.

After just over a week in California, we came back home to Indianapolis for a few days and then drove to our small condo in Myrtle Beach, South Carolina. We bought this place in 1991, soon after I returned from the Persian Gulf War. I went to the war from Camp Lejeune, North Carolina, which is about two and a half hours north of Myrtle Beach. We kept spending weekends in Myrtle Beach, and when I returned safely from the war, we decided to buy a piece of property for the first time. It was not big enough to live in comfortably but was just fine for vacationers.

We spent another week there. We must have driven seven thousand miles in total in early 2016 and spent time on the Pacific and Atlantic

Oceans. Long-distance driving is relaxing to me, and doing so during this time frame was a big help in clearing my head. We came back to Indianapolis not knowing what lay in store.

Since I had announced my intent not to run again about fourteen months before a new mayor would take over, several organizations were talking to me about my future while I was still in office. That made me feel confident that there would be some sort of opportunity after I left office, something I was not quite sure of when I made the call to step down. Before my election in 2007, I was an unknown quantity in Indianapolis and Indiana, not at all familiar with the major influencers, those who made the city and state run. Consequently, I was not sure that there would be impactful opportunities for me once I left office.

The earliest overture came while I was still in office in 2015: an offer to become the president of a Catholic high school, my alma mater. It is still a high-performing school that produces intelligent, college-bound students. I talked to the school over a few months but ultimately felt that I was not ready to be all in again, something the president's job would have required. I also believe that I was not quite ready to decide on my future just yet. They ultimately found a great president.

In late 2015, a member of the Ivy Tech Board of Trustees contacted me to ask if I would be interested in taking over as president in mid-2016. Ivy Tech is one of the largest community colleges in the country, serving more than 150,000 Indiana students in class, online, and as dual credit for high schoolers. I knew from being the mayor that important gaps in the future workforce were going to be in the two-year degree and certification occupations, and that Ivy Tech could be even more of a major player in this space.

Although I did not want to be all in again for a while, this was something I had to look at seriously, and I did. I was quietly pursuing this opportunity before the public knew that the terrific then-president was retiring. The board member with whom I was in contact assured me that I had much support on the board of trustees, who would make the choice of the new president. There would be a national search, which I understood, but it soon came with a twist.

For some reason in 2016, the lieutenant governor of Indiana, Sue Ellspermann, a top-notch public servant and someone I admire greatly, resigned her office heading into the 2016 reelection campaign with Governor Pence. I never asked why, and frankly I do not know if this was the governor's request or Sue's desire. It was after the RFRA controversy, and many speculated that played a part, but I do not know that to be true. However, when the governor announced that she was leaving, he very publicly said that Sue Ellspermann would be his choice to lead Ivy Tech.

This was really odd. Here was a well-regarded lieutenant governor with a PhD in industrial engineering leaving her post, not for another job but for the opportunity to interview for another job—but with the governor's very public endorsement. I did not know what to make of the situation. I was reassured that the board of trustees would make an objective decision.

However, the entire board of trustees is appointed by the governor. I had just been in an executive government position and appointed dozens of people to various boards and commissions. My team and I generally let those boards and commissions make their own call, but again I was different from most officeholders. Occasionally, we would make our desires known, but it was rare. In this case, however, I did not seriously think that the governor was going to let the board make its own decision after his very public pronouncement.

The board was sensitive to being seen as a puppet board for the governor, and I was asked to stay in the race. There were many candidates for the position, but there were three who drew the most attention: me, Sue, and a highly qualified gentleman from Tennessee. As the initial interviews were approaching, my name and the others became publicly known as candidates for the position. I understood the board's sensitive position and told the board member with whom I was working that I would interview through the first round and then withdraw. I did just that.

The board made the right choice. They chose Dr. Ellspermann, and she has done a remarkable job. Even if I had stayed in the race, they still should have chosen her. A significant part of the job entails dealing with the legislature, and my relations with them were still frayed as a result of the RFRA controversy from the year before. I have the utmost respect for her.

Two international water companies made overtures to me while I was still in office. They did this because of my tenure as the chair of the Water Council for the US Conference of Mayors. Both companies were sponsors of the council. I was not sure I would have been a good fit for either of them, but I certainly wanted to hear what they had to say. Unfortunately, at both companies the national leadership changed and moved in a different direction, and I was out.

Four universities contacted me, and three of them made significant offers, of which I was very appreciative. Again, I was looking for something where I would not have to be all in but could relax a bit. The University of Indianapolis, also the first college to contact me, made me such an offer. The president, Rob Manuel, a highly respected administrator with a dry intellectual wit, had recently come from Georgetown University in Washington, DC, where former elected officials were given "a soft place to land" after their term ended on their way to other endeavors. He wanted to provide me such an opportunity.

UIndy stores the mayoral archives for the city of Indianapolis. As such, I became a visiting fellow of the Institute for Civic Leadership and Mayoral Archives. Rob offered me the opportunity to teach, but I declined, wanting to concentrate on writing and studying new areas while also interacting with students and the university community. Outside of UIndy, I had dozens of requests for speaking and writing articles, and I became a member of several boards; the university graciously accommodated all of this.

One of the first things I wanted to do was conduct video interviews of all the living former mayors. The archives had not done these previously, and along with Ted Frantz, a superior professor of history and head of the archives, we set about arranging such interviews. Ted and I came up with a standard set of questions, and Ted masterfully conducted the interviews, improvising when required.

The timing was fortuitous as both Richard Lugar and Bill Hudnut died soon after the interviews. We also arranged to have a video interview of the architects of Unigov, the unique governing arrangement that made Indianapolis famous across the nation as it combined the city and county boundaries into one area and consolidated several government functions. Unigov was a master stroke of political compromise, and getting the details on video was important. We also wanted to get more details about mayoral governing and interviewed my chiefs of staff to get such detail. Hopefully, that will continue with future mayors.

At UIndy, I also conducted an internship, having students with a variety of majors from both UIndy and IUPUI (Indiana University-Purdue University at Indianapolis) write an energy plan for the state of Indiana. We brought in speakers from all different points of view, which was interesting to the students, but these students had their own robust views also.

It was a tremendous effort on their part, which culminated with a public presentation at the university. I also sent a copy of the plan to the governor and to every legislator in the House and Senate. I wanted them to know how this generation of students felt about the energy we use. I was proud of their efforts. Indiana has no energy plan or even direction, which is embarrassing to me. I once had a utilities chair in the legislature tell me, "We will do anything the utilities tell us to do." The people at the statehouse are still moving too slowly for my liking, but at least legislators are now starting to talk about the energy future. I like to think these students had some impact on this.

I also held a Great Decisions seminar, bringing in a few students, faculty, and alumni to discuss global topics. Each year, the Foreign Policy Association out of Washington, DC, publishes a magazine outlining eight global topics that are important for the future. The idea is to convene a conference group where the members read the material and then discuss the subject. I participated in this one year as an additional learning experience at Quantico when I was there for Command and Staff College. It is available to anyone nationally who is willing to put a conference group together, and I had a wonderful time with the group at UIndy.

With the help of Lara Mann, UIndy conducted a Ballard Summit every spring, targeting talented high school sophomores from around the state, with the ongoing theme of Embracing the Future. I gave a keynote address largely about how the world is getting much better on several levels, despite some media reports. I sometimes addressed topical issues, like I did at the 2020 summit, where I told the students that the presidential campaign they would soon witness will seem disgusting but that previous presidential campaigns were much more so, yet the country survived.

We then held breakout sessions on individual subjects, bringing in experts to talk to these bright high school students. The most popular session was always the Fail Fest where local IT entrepreneur John Wechsler brought in people who have failed at certain parts of their lives but found a way to ultimately succeed. I believe this was an important session, as young students today seem to be bombarded with messages about how they must succeed at everything, when history says just the opposite. It was a powerful session. With the president of UIndy and Lara having moved on, the Ballard Summit no longer takes place. I loved doing it.

About the same time that I was starting to work with UIndy, I helped to found a nonprofit, Indy Women in Tech (IWIT). I was most fortunate to have a mutual friend introduce me to Dan Towriss, the CEO of Guggenheim Life and Annuity based in Carmel, Indiana. Guggenheim Life (now Group 1001) is a stellar fifty-state company that few people in central Indiana then seemed to know about. Dan was giving back with some charity events and donations but wanted to make more of an impact, and he thought I could help him.

Once I settled back in Indianapolis in April 2016, we started talking in earnest about what we could do together. It was clear that he was very serious about making an impact. I asked him to give me a few weeks to think through the possibilities. I thought about issues with hunger, with veterans, and in other areas but settled on the idea of helping to train women for tech fields.

IT has been primarily a male domain. Additionally, from my work as mayor, I knew that there were going to be over a million unfilled jobs in tech nationally in the near future. The outreach to women in Indy and the nation was poor. I thought there was a rather obvious solution, which was to provide visibility and enhance the opportunities for women to fill those tech jobs. It was not only an equity issue within the tech field but also simply a workforce issue; we need more people working to fill the tech jobs of the future. Relatively few women were moving in that direction, but many more continue to be needed. IWIT helps with this.

Part of the reason women do not gravitate to tech is cultural. Women have been encouraged to go into more traditional roles such as teaching or nursing by both teachers and parents, sometimes under the assumption that girls are not good in math or science. Thankfully those notions are moving aside, but they are still present.

Just a few years back, I was in a meeting at my former high school talking about a new science/innovation center, discussing the subject of girls studying math and science. A math teacher mentioned that she had one brilliant female student that had aced all her Advanced Placement math and science tests, yet her parents thought she was more suited for English and social studies subjects and urged her to pursue such careers.

IWIT helps to change this dynamic. Working with some wonderful women at Group 1001, and ensuring we had strong partners throughout the city, IWIT worked with a coding academy and Ivy Tech. We provided scholarships to the coding academy but also, importantly, helped remove barriers such as transportation and childcare along with providing needed mentoring. IWIT also works with Dress for Success, a local nonprofit that provides donated professional work clothing for women who cannot afford such clothing.

At Ivy Tech, IWIT provided the initial funding to set up IvyWorks, a new IT curriculum, including initially paying for the director position.

They also provided scholarships to women in areas such as cybersecurity and website management, along with providing the same wraparound services available that we provided to those who attended the coding academy. Many of these women come from lower-paying service jobs, and getting such an education, with a dramatically improved income, changes their lives.

One of my favorite stories about this program is that a year or so into it, two women who graduated from the coding academy and two other women who graduated from Ivy Tech called their respective schools looking for advice; they thought they had been overpaid and did not know what to do about it. Of course, they were not overpaid; that was their now-normal paycheck.

IWIT also has an annual visit to a college campus for five hundred to six hundred middle school girls so that they can visualize what being at college looks like. It is a STEM Day where IWIT has many organizations set up interactive booths in science, technology, engineering, and math. IWIT has held this day at two different universities. The comments from these students make us realize just how important this day is to them. Indeed, for many of them, it changes the way they look at their future.

For three years, IWIT hosted a Ladies Professional Golf Association tournament at the Brickyard Golf Course at the Indianapolis Motor Speedway (IMS). It is a spectacular Pete Dye–designed course, and the women loved being able to play at such an iconic venue as IMS. This tournament made everyone in the tech arena in Indianapolis realize that IWIT was serious about emphasizing the need for more women in the tech field. It is important and heartwarming work, and I am proud to have been a cofounder. IWIT continues to make the Indianapolis area up its game in recruiting women into tech fields.

For a short while, I worked with Advanced Energy Economy, a national nonprofit designed to promote new ways to use clean, affordable energy. Graham Richard, the innovative former mayor of Fort Wayne, Indiana, headed up the organization. He recruited me because he knew of my strong interest in the area and because such organizations are always looking to balance their political affiliations, which means they need more prominent Republicans on their board. I was happy to help but worked with them only for about a year.

The most interesting prospect came from the White House. After President Trump was elected in 2016, I was asked to come to New York for an interview at Trump Tower. I was interested in serving my country one more time, and I also remembered what it was like to be a new officeholder looking for talent. I wanted to help.

I went expecting to talk about a position with Veterans Affairs, Transportation, maybe Energy. I was hoping for a cabinet slot, but I was in listening mode. This was just a few days before the inauguration and on the day when President-elect Trump held a controversial press conference.

After I flew in and made my way to Trump Tower, the Secret Service held me in an inside gazebo connected to the main building as the press conference was going on. I knew several people who were with the Trump/Pence team, and some had worked with me while I was the mayor. One of them sent Anthony Scaramucci down to tell me that I would be asked up after the press conference. It was a funny moment because Scaramucci was a known quantity by then and good friends with some of the people I knew.

When the press conference was over, I was escorted through the room where the press conference was held and up the famous elevators that were on every evening news program showing who was going up those elevators to be interviewed. I am quite sure that I made no national program, but it did make the local news. An Indianapolis businessman who happened to be on the same flight to New York with me asked if I would like to take his cab to Trump Tower. I accepted, and he tweeted about the cab ride and where I was headed. Another funny moment.

Once I was upstairs, there were many prominent faces on the same floor as me, but they were already working with the Trump administration. I sat in a lobby for a few minutes before I was called in to talk to two gentlemen whom I did not know. Jeannine Pirro, a former prosecutor, judge, and now a political commentator, was in the room, but it was clear the two gentlemen did not want her to stay, and she left the room. After fifteen to twenty minutes of being interviewed, something strange happened. K. T. McFarland, the national security expert and political commentator, interrupted the meeting. At that time, she was slated to become the deputy national security advisor and held that role for a few months after the inauguration.

She took me aside from the interviewers and asked if I would be interested in becoming the ambassador to either Panama or Kuwait. I realized immediately that she or somebody else had researched my background, because Panama and Kuwait were places I had been during my Marine Corps career. She dismissed the other positions I was talking about with the interviewers and said the Trump administration was creating a third type of ambassador with specific security backgrounds.

Ambassadorships are normally filled by senior State Department personnel, but about a third of them, the higher-profile ambassadorships, are filled by prominent donors of the incumbent administration. This third category that Ms. McFarland talked about was to be a small separate group of ambassadors with specific backgrounds. I was thrilled to be considered, especially since she was so specific, essentially asking me to pick which one. Within two days of the interview, I emailed back that I would prefer Panama, as my wife much preferred that assignment also. Most of the people that I knew who understood the requirements for such a position thought I would make a fine ambassador.

A former member of my political team who was now in Washington told me that I would be nominated as the ambassador to Panama in June 2017. That did not happen, but I understood there could always be delays. I was told later during that summer that Reince Priebus, then President Trump's chief of staff, was readying the announcements, but he was gone from the White House a week later. It dragged on a bit, but Winnie and I were still mentally preparing for a move. I was trying to not be a pest, inquiring only occasionally about where the nomination stood.

I then heard that President Trump's first secretary of state would have to move on first, and at times it seemed as if I knew that Rex Tillerson would be removed before he did. He was unceremoniously removed in March 2018. Still no word on my nomination. After a few more months, I informed the people who were close to me and the presidential administration that I no longer wanted to be considered. I am not sure when that post was eventually filled, but I believe it was in 2019.

The United States went without an ambassador to Panama for over two years, as did many other nations. It did not reflect well on the administration. I still believe the world is a safer place when America leads with a robust and dependable foreign policy, and showing simple respect to our fellow nations by filling the ambassadorial positions is not very difficult. I wanted to represent America. I was fine, but the disrespect shown to other nations has stuck with me.

One other possibility was to become the president of Franklin College, a small, private college of just over one thousand students located twenty minutes south of downtown Indianapolis. A member of the Franklin Board of Trustees had asked me to consider the position in 2015 when I was still the mayor. I declined then, but when the position was to open again in 2020, the same gentleman asked me to consider it.

This time I was seriously interested. I knew of the opening before it became public and started making inquiries, doing research, and meeting with board members. It seemed a great fit for me, and the board members I talked to seemed enthusiastic, as did others. My ability to connect Franklin more closely with prominent individuals in Indianapolis, in addition to wanting to increase its international exposure, seemed to make sense to everyone I talked to. Yet because of some internal turmoil, the college extended the search for another year. I decided to move on.

Several other organizations talked to me, including a children's foundation. I was flattered by their interest, but at the time I did not think I would be a good fit for them. I was also asked to consider running for governor (something I still hear), US senator, and US representative. After some serious consideration of all of them, I have declined these opportunities. I am still not politically ambitious; I want only to serve.

I joined several nonprofit boards besides IWIT. I served three years on the Indianapolis Women's Fund board, and served on the Indiana War Memorials Foundation board, the Governor's Commission on Veterans Affairs, and the Purdue Policy Research Institute, and was the initial chair of the Indiana-India Business Council. I have amicably moved on from most of these boards, but I am still on the President's Advisory Council for Marian University because of my immense respect for Dan Elsener, who took a small college in danger of closing and within twenty years had turned it into a major Catholic university with a burgeoning enrollment and the second medical school in Indiana. It also has won several NAIA national championships in various sports.

I believe that all these opportunities came about because of my practical but forward-thinking outlook, and because people understood that I was trying to position the city and the citizens of Indianapolis to succeed without any thought of personal benefit. The irony of this is that there was some reputational and financial benefit after I was out of office. People continue to tell me that they would like to see me in office again in some capacity because of how I governed. The multiple job offers were humbling, and none of them conflicted with decisions that I made in office. I like to think I conducted myself with honor and integrity. Most people seem to agree.

I have been happy that I have been able to write. I have always wanted to do so, and although I am not as diligent as I should be, I am still writing. On the encouragement of my leadership book's publisher, I added a few pages to *The Ballard Rules: Small Unit Leadership* and republished it with a new cover. They and I were counting on my notoriety to sell more books, but I was not up to becoming a full-time marketer for the republished book. The irony was that I sold quite a few copies of the original version the first two quarters after I became mayor in 2007. People wanted to learn as much about me as possible, and I sold hundreds of the 2005 edition very quickly with no effort whatsoever.

As mentioned, I wrote a book about the intersection of oil and national security called *Less Oil or More Caskets: The National Security Argument for Moving Away from Oil*. I was fortunate that Indiana University Press chose to publish it, and I was able to do some marketing for the book. I am still known nationally in some circles on this subject, and I have presented on this subject dozens of times.

In addition to this book, I have a few others that I would like to write, including a sequel to the oil book, this time providing a wider perspective of the need for clean energy from several perspectives. I also am fascinated by the documents that ended World War I and how those documents led to another century of warfare that we endure to this day. There are two others I would like to research and write—one on sports leadership and another on the nations of the world and their relationships to America. I am also interested in writing a novel. I wonder if I will have the time to do all of these, but I would like to try.

Winnie and I moved to Myrtle Beach, South Carolina, in early 2021 for some relaxation, but we moved back to the Indianapolis area in 2023, ready to engage again. I am doing some consulting for municipalities in the state and joined the board of the International Center. It is good to be back home again in Indiana, helping where I can.

22

IS THERE A FUTURE FOR URBAN REPUBLICANS?

OVER THE PAST FEW YEARS, as major cities have dealt with protests, riots, and even the occupation of city blocks, Republican media and federal officeholders have lambasted the Democratic mayors who lead these cities. Headlines such as "US Protests: More Riots and Lawlessness in Cities Across Nation" were common. The implication was that these cities were led by bad mayors (because they are Democrats) who were not doing enough to quell the protests. It was often openly asked, "Why are these Democratic mayors not taking charge of their cities?"

That is the wrong question. The far more appropriate question for the Republican Party should be, "Why are there not more Republican mayors in these cities?"

As of this writing, of the top twenty-five cities in America by population, only two are run by Republicans. The large population centers in the country such as New York, Los Angeles, Chicago, Houston, Philadelphia, and others are in the hands of Democratic mayors. In most of the big cities in America, Republican candidates for mayor are either noncompetitive or nonexistent. We must ask ourselves why this is.

For several years while I was the mayor, Indianapolis was the largest city in America with a Republican mayor. As such, I had some status among mayors. I was invited to speak to a group of Republicans in Cleveland the morning after the first Republican presidential debate of the 2016 campaign. When they asked me to speak, I pushed back a bit and told them that they may not like what I have to say. That confirmed for them that they wanted me to speak as they were having the same difficulties I was having, overcoming the rhetoric of federal Republican officeholders and candidates.

I explained to them what we had been doing in Indianapolis. In some ways, I was a typical Republican executive, balancing the budget, bringing the debt down by two-thirds even during a recession, increasing public safety by bringing the murder rate to levels not seen in decades, initiating massive savings for taxpayers and utility ratepayers by innovative practices and policies, holding AAA bond ratings, and the like.

However, we also created the city's first-ever Office of Sustainability; embraced urban gardens; began the robust bicycle culture that exists today in Indianapolis by putting in bike lanes and trails and holding cycling events; increased recycling; introduced electric cars well before they became common; and so on.

With great partners, we created the Chinese Festival; the Indian Festival that celebrates India's independence from Great Britain; the Latino Expo; and the Latino soccer tournament. We held a futsal (a modified form of soccer) tournament based on the World Cup, complete with an opening ceremony that included national flags representing sixteen countries. We built cricket fields to attract South Asian talent and doubled the number of sister cities to include cities in China, India, Brazil, and the United Kingdom. I attended every international event I could.

We embraced and funded pre-K with a combination of city and private dollars even though education funding is a state responsibility. We stood up to discriminatory state laws. We worked with ex-offenders, changing people's opinions on how we should treat them. I talked with gang members to understand their mindset. We paved roads in poor neighborhoods that had not been repaved in decades. I was the only Republican mayor on President Obama's My Brother's Keeper advisory board.

These issues matter to urban residents. I won initially in a protest vote against increased taxes but was also reelected in my Democratic-majority city. Heading into a potential third term, which I declined, my personal favorability ratings were in the seventies, and my "Is the city heading in the right direction?" numbers were in the sixties. Those are overwhelmingly positive numbers.

I moved the electoral needle significantly in Indianapolis. One year after my initial election in 2007, President Obama won Indianapolis by 108,000 votes. Four years later and one year after my reelection, President

Obama won Indianapolis by 80,000 votes. Indianapolis is a Democratic city, but the people wanted me as their mayor.

Because of my status as a major-city Republican mayor, several people thought that the Republican National Committee would want to speak with me to see how we were winning in a majority-Democratic city. I would have been happy to help, but the RNC declined. That was disappointing. When the RNC briefed the Republican caucus at the US Conference of Mayors on Mitt Romney's losing presidential bid in 2012, the common sentiment among the Republican mayors was anger. The mayors could not believe how out of touch the RNC was with cities, particularly the minority populations.

A couple of years after I had completed my two terms as mayor, a representative of the RNC came to Indianapolis to talk to me, telling me it was the initial discussion for the RNC to finally get up to speed on urban populations. About six months later, I was told she had moved on from the RNC. I never heard from them again.

I could have told the RNC that urban Republicans desire to live in a welcoming community, one that embraces the immigrants who want to live in our country. Immigrants come to our country not to undermine it but to participate in it. We should know that. With the density of city life, urban Republicans are more urgent in their concerns for the environment. They view urban violence as both a societal issue and an individual act of aggression, but not as the end of our culture. Urban Republicans value individual liberty but also understand that we live in a society that must embrace all viewpoints without retribution, as our Founding Fathers intended. The dismissive term RINO (Republican in Name Only) is used frequently to describe those who do not vow strict obedience to whatever is the issue of the day, but urban Republicans are more original in their notion of conservatism, of natural rights, particularly of individual liberty, than other parts of the Republican Party.

American cities today hold concentrated populations of numerous ethnicities. These groups are almost unfailingly patriotic and beyond grateful that they now reside in the United States. While most are proud of their heritage, they want to assimilate into our country because of its promise of freedom and equality of opportunity. Any mention by Republicans that dampen these notions of freedom and equality of opportunity, that make immigrants feel unwelcome, provide a window of opportunity for Democrats to sway an entire voting bloc. Why do we give them this opportunity? Too many times it proves effective, particularly at the city level.

Not for an instant do I believe that most Republicans, including those running for office, are prejudiced or discriminatory. However, when our president makes comments mentioning the Proud Boys affirmatively during a presidential debate and wanting to exclude all people of a particular religion from entering our country—a country that was founded on freedom of religion—we easily feed into the Democrats' portrayal of Republicans as racist. Such careless rhetoric by Republicans at the national level make it nearly impossible for urban Republicans to win elections in cities, whose populations hold far more minorities than suburban and rural communities.

Democrats help Republicans across the country when they talk about socialism or defunding the police, or portraying legitimate, hard-working business owners as greedy and corrupt whenever there is an economic crisis. Such notions are absolute gifts to Republican candidates at every level of political office. Conversely, Democratic politicos and their media partners like to portray Republican candidates and officeholders as racist and uneducated. That is the baseline for a Democratic political campaign at every level of government, a starting point unless proven otherwise.

When I was elected mayor, a commentator on a local radio show said something like, "Now the white hoods will be on the Circle in Indianapolis." For eight years, that radio show routinely brought on guests who portrayed me as racist and insensitive to minorities. When I was asked personally about this by others, I would usually respond with, "Have you seen my wife?" The racist take was a common theme that was hurtful to me personally and yet maintained by local Democratic operatives for my eight years in office. Republican candidates in urban areas must be prepared for this.

In a 2021 interview for *Politico* magazine, George Will discusses the intellectual underpinnings of conservatism in his book, *The Conservative Sensibility*. In essence, he asks "What do conservatives want to conserve?" According to Will,

> The answer is the American founding, which is basically three things. First, there is a constant human nature—we are not just creatures who acquire the impress of whatever culture we're situated in. Second, there are natural rights—that is, rights that are essential to the flourishing of creatures of our constant human nature. Third, governments are, as the declaration said, instituted to "secure"—the most important word in the declaration—those rights, which preexist government. And the structure of government must be such that, in our Madisonian way, government is strong enough to protect the rights, but not too strong to threaten our rights.[1]

In simpler terms,

1. There is a constant human nature.
2. There are natural rights that preexist government.
3. Governments should secure/protect those rights and not threaten those rights.

I doubt many Republicans today would characterize conservatism with those three thoughts.

The Republican Party claims conservatism as its own, but one could wonder if the original notion of conservatism has been hijacked. The word "conservative" today is a catchall phrase for things that Republicans are supposed to believe no matter what, especially if the issue has a cultural, Christian bent. If a Republican differs with the current beliefs of the day, then they will be pejoratively called a RINO.

Many of these beliefs have little in common with the original ideas of conservatism such as natural rights, individual liberty, and limited government. For instance, when Republican state legislators pass anti–gay marriage laws, are they protecting the natural rights of life, liberty, and the pursuit of happiness for that part of our population? Is the liberty of gay people enhanced or threatened when they cannot marry? Is the pursuit of happiness reserved for heterosexuals? Additionally, if a Republican were to ask Hindus about the state legislature using Jesus as justification for passing laws, they would be met with silence. Are we really a freedom-of-religion nation, or is that phrase just lip service as legislatures pass laws based on Christian tenets?

Urban Republicans see these issues differently than do other Republicans. In cities, they are living and working closely with people who may not think like them or look like them. They see up close the pain of Americans who are disillusioned by their own nation's history of denying them opportunities. They understand that our members of Congress refuse to solve the difficult issues of immigration, the national debt, and gay marriage, so that they can continue to use those issues to raise money for future campaigns. Urban Republicans see the anguish and fear of immigrants when our federal officeholders make hateful, negative comments about those wanting to assimilate into America's cities, who want to contribute to our country.

A merging of urban Republican thought with the rest of the party, resulting in a more widespread and electable notion of a conservative

America, would be powerful. If the Republican Party were more in line with the Founding Fathers' original intent but moved toward the inevitable and obvious future, I believe the party could be dominant for decades. As I write this, I am not hopeful this will occur soon, which means very few urban Republican mayors in the near future.

Note

1. Zack Stanton, "Does 'Conservatism' Actually Mean Anything Anymore?," *Politico*, September 17, 2021.

FOR INDIANA UNIVERSITY PRESS

Jesse Balzer *Journals Marketing and Exhibits Manager*

Tony Brewer *Artist and Book Designer*

Gary Dunham *Acquisitions Editor and Director*

Anna Francis *Assistant Acquisitions Editor*

Anna Garnai *Production Coordinator*

Katie Huggins *Production Manager*

Darja Malcolm-Clarke *Project Manager/Editor*

Dan Pyle *Online Publishing Manager*

Michael Regoli *Director of Publishing Operations*

Stephen Williams *Assistant Director of Marketing*

Jennifer Wilder *Senior Artist and Book Designer*